500 Questions
New Parents Ask

Gerber® Library

500 Questions New Parents Ask

Pediatricians Answer Your Questions
About the Care and Handling of Your Baby

A DELL/NORBACK/GERBER TRADE PAPERBACK

A DELL/NORBACK/GERBER TRADE PAPERBACK

Published by
DELL PUBLISHING CO., INC.
1 Dag Hammarskjold Plaza
New York, New York 10017

Dell ® TM 681510, Dell Publishing Co., Inc.

ISBN 0-440-52609-4

Printed in the United States of America
First printing—October 1982

Contents

Preface

In a familiar Newborn Nursery scene, a new mother excitedly greeted her pediatrician with the question, "Is my baby all right?" After receiving an affirmative reply, she exclaimed, "Oh, I have a thousand questions to ask you!" Undaunted, the doctor quickly responded, "Write them all down so you won't forget any, and I'll go over them with you next time I come in."

500 Questions New Parents Ask does not undertake to answer every single question a parent may have, but we have covered many of the areas of concern regarding the health, safety, and care of children up to the age of two years. We hope these answers will serve to inform you and reassure you, relieving some of the anxieties associated with child-rearing in this modern and confusing world.

As a new parent, you are constantly barraged with information from many sources, and it is difficult to sort it all out. There may be several different answers to any one question, and they may all be correct. While your own doctor is the best source of information and answers, it is important for you to become educated so that you will be able to decide how best to handle certain situations in the course of caring for your baby. A good doctor enjoys seeing parents grow in capability and responsibility just as he or she enjoys seeing children thrive and grow.

You should never be ashamed or embarrassed about the questions you ask your pediatrician, and you should never be afraid to ask. The questions in this book were all actually asked by new parents, and they reflect many common fears and uncertainties.

Most of the contributors to this book are practicing pediatricians. Each of them sees many patients, is asked many questions, and tries to come up with constructive answers. Their contributions to this volume represent many years of experience and much care and concern for the health and well-being of children . . . and the confidence and happiness of parents.

Merritt B. Low, M.D., F.A.A.P.

CHAPTER 1

Allergies

My infant just vomited the aspirin I gave him. Does that mean he is allergic to it?

The answer is no. Aspirin is irritating to the lining of the stomach, and it is not unusual for a child to throw up an aspirin tablet, especially when it is given on an empty stomach.

Allergy to aspirin is rare in young children. When such an allergy is present, it usually manifests itself as difficulty in breathing, as wheezing, or as a skin rash, which develops within minutes or hours following the ingestion of aspirin.

SOHAIL R. RANA, M.D.
Washington, D.C.

I have heard that many people are allergic to eggs. How can I introduce eggs to my infant's diet, and how can I recognize an allergy?

Many people are allergic to eggs, and one can become allergic to either the white or the yolk of the egg. However, allergy to egg white is much more common than is allergy to the yolk. The yolk of an egg is a very nutritious food, rich in protein and iron and highly beneficial in the diet of the infant. It can usually be safely introduced to an infant's diet after four to six months of age. It rarely will produce an allergy if it is kept entirely free of the egg white, which is highly allergenic and should be withheld from an infant's diet until the child is at least one year of age. Egg white and yolk can be totally

1

separated by a variety of means. The simplest method is to hard-boil the egg, removing the white from the yolk, then mash up the yolk and put it in with other foods, such as cereal. If the raw yolk and white can be completely separated, yolk can also be used in making custards and puddings, which are good for children after six to nine months of age. Allergy to eggs is no different from any other food allergy. It may cause diarrhea and, occasionally, vomiting. It can cause a variety of skin rashes and also respiratory problems. Egg allergy can be differentiated from other food allergies only by the process of elimination. The egg is removed from the diet. If the allergic symptoms then disappear, the egg should be reintroduced. If the symptoms recur with the reintroduction of the egg, then both the removal of the egg from the diet a second time and the disappearance of the symptoms will confirm that this was due to egg allergy.

RICHARD A. GUTHRIE, M.D.
Wichita, Kansas

My husband and I are both allergic to bee stings and need to carry bee sting kits. Should we assume that our infant is allergic, too? Should we take the same measures if he is stung?

People who have severe allergic reactions to bee stings experience massive swelling around the site of the sting and may have difficulty breathing or swallowing because of swelling in the throat. These reactions may be life-threatening and can be treated with injections of adrenaline immediately after the sting. This type of reaction is often hereditary and the new baby may well be allergic if the parents are. Treatment of an allergic infant after a bee sting involves injection of adrenaline, but the dosage is much smaller than that given for an adult. The exact dosage is based on the child's weight. The plan of treatment should be discussed with a physician before it is really needed. Even with the proper treatment, some highly allergic children will still have difficulty breathing or swallowing after a sting. If this happens, the physician should be consulted immediately.

ALAN R. RUSHTON, M.D., Ph.D.
Flemington, New Jersey

I'm allergic to penicillin. Will my baby have this allergy, too?

In most cases, children born to parents who are allergic to penicillin will not have problems with this antibiotic. It is usually possible to use an alternative drug if the child does need an antibiotic to treat an infection. Skin tests are now available to determine whether a child is, in fact, allergic to penicillin. If a child must receive penicillin for a specific infection, skin testing prior to utilization of the drug is a reasonable approach. Such testing is usually performed by an allergist.

ALAN R. RUSHTON, M.D., Ph.D.
Flemington, New Jersey

My infant sneezes a lot. Should I assume that he has an allergy if he does not have any other cold symptoms?

In this case, one should not assume that the infant has an allergic condition. It is not easy to establish a diagnosis of allergy in this age group. However, if either or both parents have definite allergic problems, and the child should continue to develop recurrent respiratory symptoms such as nasal congestion and profuse clear nasal discharge in addition to sneezing, one may then suspect the presence of nasal allergy.

REUBEN G. WAGELIE, M.D.
Tucson, Arizona

My infant is allergic to milk. Should I remove all milk products and any food prepared with milk from her diet?

If your infant is allergic to milk, it is best to go back to square one and take away *all* foods and products prepared with milk. Then you can experiment gradually, one step at a time, trying a new food every four or five days. Sometimes cooked, powdered, evaporated, fat-free, or otherwise changed milk products can be used if they are introduced gradually. There are plenty of nonmilk products available that can be used with your doctor's direction without compromising your child's nutritional status. Milk allergies in infants usually show up as intestinal-digestive upsets, runny noses of some duration, or skin rashes (eczema). In older children, asthma or chronic nasal irritation can result from milk allergies.

MERRITT B. LOW, M.D., F.A.A.P.
Ashfield, Massachusetts

We discovered through allergy testing that our infant is allergic to wheat. What can we substitute in her diet?

Wheat in any form should not be included in the diet. Labels on prepared food should be read carefully to make certain that wheat products have not been used during manufacture. Good nutrition is extremely important for normal growth and development of children, and this goal is certainly possible with a wheat-free diet. Bread, cereal, and crackers made from corn, rye, rice, soybean, or potato flour can be used. Cheese, yogurt, eggs, butter, and milk are all allowed. All kinds of fruits and vegetables are also permitted. Meat, fish, and poultry are acceptable unless wheat products have been used as a filler. A well-balanced, nutritious, and tasty diet for both children and adults can be prepared for the three meals and snacks each day without using wheat products.

ALAN R. RUSHTON, M.D., Ph.D.
Flemington, New Jersey

CHAPTER 2

Anemia and Blood

What causes anemia in newborns?

After birth, most newborns experience a decrease in red cell numbers and hemoglobin concentration, which has been called the physiologic anemia of the newborn. This is a normal and expected drop in red blood cell values that begins soon after birth and reaches its lowest point approximately ten to twelve weeks after delivery. Never does it result in severe anemia. Although there are a number of factors that contribute to this phenomenon, the most significant seems to be a decline in red cell production. Because of the way babies obtain oxygen from their mothers during pregnancy, they require a particularly large number of red cells to meet their oxygen needs and are born with a hemoglobin level that is high in comparison to that of older infants and children. Following birth, when oxygen is obtained more efficiently through the lungs, the number of red cells needed to provide adequate oxygen to the tissues is less, so the drive to produce red cells ceases. It is not until the low point in the anemia that red cell production begins again. Two other factors that may contribute to the anemia are an increasing blood volume as the baby grows and a shortened red cell life span due to immaturity within the newborn red cell of several systems that ordinarily protect it from everyday stresses.

In contrast to the above are the anemias that represent truly abnormal situations. These can be categorized into three major groups: blood loss, increased destruction of red cells (hemolysis), or decreased production of red cells.

In an otherwise well baby, an explanation for blood loss unique to the newborn is that of bleeding into the bloodstream of the mother or even a twin, either at the time of delivery or chronically during pregnancy. Significant anemia on this basis is readily recognized in the newborn nursery. Hemolysis may be caused by any number of defects in red cell enzymes, hemoglobin structure, or membrane structure. These disorders are usually hereditary and only rarely lead to problems in the newborn period. Destruction of infant red cells by a maternal antibody, which has developed because there is an incompatibility between the Rh or ABO red blood cell group of the mother and newborn, can result in both anemia and marked yellowing of the skin, which is called jaundice. Obstetricians and pediatricians routinely screen mothers and babies who are at risk for this problem before they are discharged from the hospital. Clearly, not all newborns who experience jaundice have Rh or ABO incompatibility. Finally, bone marrow failure as a reason for anemia in the newborn is rare but has been described as a chronic disorder known as pure red cell aplasia or Diamond-Blackfan syndrome. The cause of this syndrome is not presently known.

ROBERT P. CASTLEBERRY, M.D.
Birmingham, Alabama

Is anemia harmful to my baby? Is there anything that can prevent anemia?

Anemia is harmful to the physical as well as developmental growth of infants. Iron deficiency anemia is the most common type of anemia and is also the most prevalent nutritional disorder in the United States.

Physical symptoms of moderate to severe anemia may include paleness, fatigue, listlessness, constipation, and lack of appetite. The child may be overweight or underweight. Physical symptoms are directly related to the reduction of oxygen available to body cells. The cells need oxygen to perform their chemical roles, and iron plays a major role in the transport of oxygen from the blood to the cells.

The physical symptoms may interfere with the child's mastery of developmental milestones, and may cause irritableness and what some parents consider generally "obnoxious" behavior. There is evidence that iron deficiency anemia can cause problems with a child's attention span and with learning in young children.

Iron-fortified formula, breast milk from a mother practicing sound nutrition, or fortified infant cereals, along with regular medical checkups, can help prevent anemia in the first year of life. In the second year, adequate amounts of iron-rich foods such as cooked red meats, eggs, and iron-fortified cereals should be eaten. In addition, be aware that homogenized milk is not a good source of iron and may be a cause of anemia when large quantities of it are substituted for iron-rich, solid foods.

SHARON POHORECKI, R.N., C.P.N.P.
Toledo, Ohio

My newborn is very pale. Is this common in newborns?

Many normal newborns look pale, even if there isn't anything wrong with them. Racial characteristics, room temperature and lighting, and the baby's skin circulation may all influence the perception of a baby's skin color. Although many newborns look very ruddy shortly after birth because their red blood cell counts are high, skin color becomes highly variable after the first few days of life. Anemia sufficient to cause a pale appearance is quite rare in normal newborns, and your doctor would probably have noticed this and requested a blood count if significant anemia were suspected in your baby. This is a matter that you could discuss with your baby's doctor, and in all likelihood the doctor will be able to reassure you that the baby's blood count is normal. If a newborn infant does have significant anemia, further tests will determine its exact cause. Normal babies develop a slight anemia between six and twelve months of age, and at this time some are given additional iron, especially if they are growing very rapidly. Premature infants have lower iron stores and tend to develop an anemia that occurs earlier and is slightly more severe. For this reason, many pediatricians recommend early iron supplements for growing premature infants.

WILLIAM J. CASHORE, M.D.
Providence, Rhode Island

How can I tell if my baby is anemic?

Parents cannot easily detect the pallor of anemia or a low blood count, as the change is usually over a period of weeks or months, and the paleness is not easily seen. Blood is composed of white cells that fight infection, platelets that stop bleeding, and red cells that carry oxygen. Blood is colored red when oxygen binds to hemoglobin, the pigment of red cells. Pallor is obvious only when the condition is extremely serious. Mild anemia does not affect the heart rate or respiration, and the physician may not necessarily see the change in color in the nail beds or the vessels under the eyelids. The physician may suspect anemia if a child drinks more than 16 ozs. of milk daily or has lost large amounts of blood from nosebleeds, vomiting, or clots in the stool.

Occasionally there are hereditary predispositions. These can be suspected if individuals in the family have required a splenectomy (removal of the spleen), have had gallbladder disease early in life, or have required transfusions. If familial anemias are known, this problem should be mentioned to the physician before the baby is born so that the doctor can screen for problems in umbilical cord blood. Amniocentesis may be considered. If the condition is recessive—that is, contributed equally by both parents who themselves have no problem, such as in the case of sickle cell disease or thalassemia—the parents should seek the appropriate blood tests and counseling, preferably before the child is conceived.

If the physician suspects anemia, a blood test can be drawn from a vein in the arm or from a fingerprick. The technician counts the red cells and determines their size and hemoglobin content. In iron deficiency, the most common cause of anemia in children under the age of two years, doctors usually find a history of excessive intake of whole milk, irritability, a dislike for solid foods, and, in severe cases, swelling about the ankles and changes in the nails. The blood test shows small, poorly filled red cells. Other, more sophisticated tests may be necessary for less common conditions. All of these findings of iron deficiency can be rapidly and completely reversed by supplementing the diet with medications containing iron, and by altering the diet so that it contains less whole milk and more of a variety of other foods.

ROBERT R. CHILCOTE, M.D.
Chicago, Illinois

My son has been very pale and tired lately. What could cause that?

The sudden onset of pale color and tiredness in a child suggests the development of anemia, or low red blood cell count. The red blood cells carry oxygen which is necessary for the normal function of body organs. Well-oxygenated blood is bright red and imparts the healthy pink color to skin. When inadequate red blood cells are available, the amount of oxygen in the blood is decreased, and the symptoms of paleness and tiredness develop.

A child may become anemic when the bone marrow does not make normal numbers of red blood cells or when the red blood cells are made normally but are broken down in the blood vessels faster than new ones can be made or through blood loss (obvious or hidden). Deficiency of iron or vitamin B-12 and folic acid prevent normal production of red blood cells. Toxic materials such as lead, insecticides, or certain drugs may damage the marrow and produce anemia. The normal marrow may also be replaced by tumor cells as in leukemia, or other cancers.

Red blood cells may also be produced normally, but have a shortened life span in the circulation. A number of hereditary diseases produce red corpuscles which are unusually fragile (such as sickle cell disease). Bacterial or viral infections may damage the red blood cells. The child's body may also produce antibodies against his or her own red blood cells and destroy them as if they were foreign tissue.

Many causes for anemia have been discovered. Your child should be seen by the physician as soon as possible to determine whether anemia is present and, if so, to find the cause for the problem and prescribe appropriate therapy.

ALAN R. RUSHTON, M.D., Ph.D.
Flemington, New Jersey

My toddler takes iron medication for anemia. Is she more susceptible to viruses now?

Some research suggests that iron-deficient children may contract more infections. Treatment with iron to correct the deficiency should reduce this susceptibility. There is no real evidence that treatment with iron increases a child's susceptibility to viruses under ordinary circumstances.

AVRUM L. KATCHER, M.D., F.A.A.P.
Flemington, New Jersey

Would my baby have to take medication to prevent anemia from recurring?

If your doctor has made a specific diagnosis of anemia and has treated it adequately, no further treatment is generally needed. This is just a minor, temporary depletion of the body's iron stores. Whether medication will be needed in the future depends on the child's iron stores and whether he or she is taking adequate amounts of iron. If there is a question about the child's intake of iron, his or her eating ability, and whether he or she has enough iron, then the child could need further iron supplement to continue to keep the hemoglobin at a good count. Generally, this is not the case, but because each case is different and each child is different, this may need to be considered to prevent anemia from recurring. This is something that should be discussed directly with your doctor.

JEROME E. KWAKO, M.D.
Duluth, Minnesota

CHAPTER 3

Animals

My child ate one of the dog's vitamin pills. What should I do?

First, are you certain your infant *really* ate the vitamin pill? Many times a pill may be missing, only to be found later elsewhere, perhaps under a chair or sofa. If you think your child did eat the pill, call your pediatrician, or if you do not have one, call your poison control center. Have the vitamin pill box available so that you can read aloud the list of ingredients over the telephone.

Usually, the major ingredient to worry about is iron and not most of the vitamins in the pill. Many parents are unaware that iron can be toxic, even fatal, if a large amount is taken. One dog vitamin, however, is not likely to cause trouble, but, to be safe, call your doctor or poison control center for help.

WAYNE SNODGRASS, M.D., Ph.D.
Kansas City, Kansas

My dog was diagnosed as having hookworms. Can my toddler get them?

Yes, your toddler can be infected by the dog hookworm, but it's very unlikely and not at all serious. It causes an unpleasant but easily cured skin eruption in human beings.

The dog hookworm spends its mature life in the bowels of dogs and cats. There the female lays thousands of eggs, which are passed in the feces. If the dog's droppings are left in moist soil, the eggs develop into larvae, very tiny immature worms, which can survive in the soil for two to three weeks. These larvae can invade the skin of any animal with which they come in contact. The larvae do not penetrate human skin. In dogs and cats, they migrate by way of the bloodstream to the lungs and then to the intestines, where they mature and continue the cycle.

You can prevent your toddler from becoming infected by carefully disposing of your dog's droppings, keeping the dog out of the child's sandbox, and keeping the child out of dirt that the dog may have used. If your child does come into contact with dirt the dog has been in, a prompt bath and change of clothes will help eliminate the chance of infection. The eggs must spend some time in moist soil before they develop into larvae, so fresh dog feces are not infective.

The good hygiene that you practice as a matter of course will take care of this problem, and you shouldn't lose any sleep over it.

WILLIAM J. BALL, M.D., F.A.A.P.
Aurora, Illinois

My toddler just ate some of the dog's food. Is that all right?

Dog food is not harmful. Most brands contain common nutrients such as protein, fat, fiber, vitamins B, C, D, E, and also iron, zinc, calcium, magnesium, copper, and iodine.

JAMES R. MARKELLO, M.D.
Greenville, North Carolina

We spray our dog with flea powder, and our toddler has been playing with him. Is there any danger that the child might have some of the powder on his hands and that he might swallow some if he puts his fingers in his mouth?

There are all kinds of flea powders. What you describe seems harmless enough. If you have any doubt about your dog's flea powder, check the label and confer with your physician, pharmacist, or poison control center.

MERRITT B. LOW, M.D., F.A.A.P.
Ashfield, Massachusetts

My toddler and our dog play with each other's toys. Should I be concerned if my child puts the dog's toys in his mouth?

No. Although the newborn baby is relatively germ-free when born, the entire intestinal tract becomes populated with bacteria that become part of the normal bacteria of the gut within a few hours after birth. The child also gets bacteria from putting his hands in his mouth and from all other sources in his environment. Parents should try to keep the baby clean, but realize that we live in an imperfect, unclean world and try not to be overly concerned about it.

GRANT MASAOKA, M.D.
Anaheim, California

My toddler just ate one of our dog's heartworm pills. Is this anything to be concerned about?

There are several different kinds and sizes of heartworm pills, so you should check this particular pill with your veterinarian or physician to be sure. Also, look at the label on the bottle for further specific information. No heartworm pills are intended for human consumption.

The ingestion of only one pill is probably not of concern, but this kind of exploratory activity should prompt you to keep all potential poisons and dangerous edibles out of reach, preferably locked up. You should have syrup of ipecac on hand for when your child ingests such substances. This kind of behavior doesn't usually end with just one pill.

MERRITT B. LOW, M.D., F.A.A.P.
Ashfield, Massachusetts

My cat scratched my toddler on the legs. I washed the scratches well, but is there anything else I should do? Can my child get cat-scratch fever from these scratches?

Careful cleaning of scratches with soap and water is the correct thing to do. A child may develop cat-scratch fever, which is probably caused by a virus and is transmitted to children when they are scratched by kittens that carry the virus. About two weeks after the child is scratched, a small pustule may develop at the site of the original scratch. Several weeks later, lymph glands near the scratch may become swollen and tender. Mild fever and generalized aches may also develop. The symptoms usually clear up by themselves. No specific treatment is available and no serious consequences are known.

ALAN R. RUSHTON, M.D., Ph.D.
Flemington, New Jersey

My toddler just drank some water from our fishtank. Is there anything I should do?

Probably not. Just watch for fever or stomach or intestinal upsets. If you want to get a jump on the situation, you could have cultures of the fishtank water done. If salamanders or turtles, which often carry diarrhea-producing bacteria (salmonella), are present in the fishtank, your child may require treatment if he or she has symptoms of salmonella infection.

MERRITT B. LOW, M.D., F.A.A.P.
Ashfield, Massachusetts

Can my dog transmit its fleas to my child?

Yes. Children are frequently bitten by fleas from cats or dogs. The saliva that the flea deposits when it bites causes an itchy reaction, which might be a small pimple or a large, red, swollen, or even blistered hive. Young children are most likely to have severe reactions to a bite, particularly if they are from a family with a history of allergies. Flea bites are usually multiple, occurring in groups on exposed areas or where the clothing fits tightly.

Treatment of flea bites includes the eradication of the fleas from household pets and from floors or furniture where the fleas may hide.

JOAN ADLER, M.D.
Philadelphia, Pennsylvania

14

My cat has leukemia. Can my infant catch it?

Generally speaking, leukemia is felt to have a multifocal etiology; that is, it may be caused by factors in the environment, infections, or some cause as yet unknown. Leukemia in the cat is one form of leukemia in which the specific causative agent, a virus, is known. Leukemia in human beings may also be caused by a virus, but there is no concrete evidence to prove this assumption. Viruses are generally spread by a form of contact. However, experimenters have not been able to transfer the viral agent of cat leukemia to human volunteers. Consequently, there is no evidence to support the fear that leukemia in your cat can be carried over to your infant.

OSCAR A. NOVICK, M.D., F.A.A.P.
Park Ridge, Illinois

My baby was nipped by our puppy, which hasn't had any of its rabies shots. What should I do?

Puppy nips should usually not be a cause for concern. Unless your puppy has been out running free, there is no real need to worry. Watch the animal for signs of illness (rabies always declares itself within ten days to two weeks). Watch the nipped area for any signs of infection and call your physician if there is spreading redness, local streaking, or fever. Be sure your baby is up-to-date on regular shots. As your baby grows, be sure to teach him or her how to handle animals properly.

MERRITT B. LOW, M.D., F.A.A.P.
Ashfield, Massachusetts

CHAPTER 4

Bites and Wounds

How can I know if my toddler's scratching his mosquito bites will get them infected?

Because children generally carry organisms that cause superficial skin infections on their skin or in their noses, any opening in the skin, such as a mosquito bite or certainly a scratched mosquito bite which results in an open surface, will usually get infected. If the mosquito bite becomes infected, you will notice an increasing area of redness, with a weeping surface that may have some purulent material in it. Infected mosquito bites will very commonly look like impetigo.

BETTY A. LOWE, M.D.
Little Rock, Arkansas

Our infant was outside in the playpen and now he is scratching at what look like mosquito bites. What can we use on his sensitive skin?

Anything that is cooling to the skin will relieve the itching. Using something as simple as a cool, wet washcloth will help. Not only will the temperature of the washcloth help, but even further cooling will result from the evaporation of the moisture that will be left on the skin when the cloth is removed. For more sustained relief, try an unmedicated cold cream.

L. ROBERT RUBIN, M.D.
Danbury, Connecticut

My child was bitten by the neighbor's dog. I don't think she'll need stitches. It looks like a puncture wound. How should I care for this? Will she need rabies shots?

Immediate cleansing of a dog bite is an important step in the prevention of rabies. Cotton-tipped applicators should be used to swab the puncture wound carefully with soap and water. Clean water is then used to rinse the wound. The area is left open to the air and allowed to dry.

The dog bite episode must be reported to the police, who will then inform local health department officials. The dog's owner should determine whether the dog has recently received a rabies vaccination. The dog must be closely observed for two weeks. If any unusual behavior is noted, the health department will kill the animal and examine its brain for the presence of rabies virus. Canine rabies is unusual in most parts of the United States, but it has been reported frequently in the Southwest. If there is evidence that the animal involved did have rabies, the bitten child must receive a series of anti-rabies immunizations to prevent development of this potentially fatal disease.

The highest risk of rabies is related to bites or scratches from skunks, raccoons, foxes, bobcats, bats, and coyotes.

ALAN R. RUSHTON, M.D., Ph.D.
Flemington, New Jersey

My toddler just fell and hit his mouth. The little piece of skin connecting his upper lip to the gum is torn. Does this need to be stitched?

No. Two major reasons for stitches are to stop bleeding quickly, and to help bring the edges of the wound together to aid in healing. The piece of skin connecting the upper lip to the gum is composed of mucous membrane, as is the inside of the cheeks. This tissue has a generous blood supply, which helps any injury heal very quickly without stitches. Of course, it will bleed easily when injured, but the bleeding will stop relatively fast when the usual measures are employed: pressure on the wound and cold application. Crushed ice is sometimes placed directly in the wound, but this is impractical in the case of a toddler. The next most practical method would be to have the child eat crushed pieces of a Popsicle, which is flavored ice. As the wound heals, the injured tissue dies. This leaves an odor in the mouth. Drinks of water after eating to keep the area clean is of utmost importance to prevent secondary infection. In addition to this, rinsing the mouth with a solution of one part hydrogen peroxide and one part water is helpful in removing some of the dead tissue that accumulates in this corner of the mouth. A liquid diet would be advisable for two to three days, until the wound is no longer acutely painful.

EVELYN BAUGH, M.D.
Toledo, Ohio

What should I do if my child gets a small puncture wound?

A puncture wound is made by a pointed object that pierces the skin. Before a child begins to walk, these wounds are quite uncommon. Puncture wounds are different from scrapes or cuts because they often do not bleed freely (bleeding cleanses the wound) and because they are often much deeper than realized. The piercing object can introduce germs deep into the wound, where they can multiply and cause infection. Sometimes, the piercing object can be broken off in the wound. Because of the depth of the injury, it may be difficult to know that it has been left in the wound, and even when it is known that the object is retained, it may be difficult to remove it.

Most puncture wounds are seen in the feet, although they can occur on any part of the body; the treatment is essentially the same. A search should be made for the object that made the puncture wound. If it can be ascertained that the entire object has remained intact, one can be more confident that no foreign body has been retained in the wound. Many times, however, the object cannot be found. Puncture wounds bleed remarkably little but are often quite painful because of their depth. The area should be examined gently to see if there is a hard object within the wound. A very *gentle* squeezing pressure may be all that is necessary to remove an object near the surface. Do *not* probe the wound if a foreign body is found, for this may push it in farther. The child should be taken to the appropriate medical facility for removal of the object if it has been retained below the skin surface. Because the small amount of bleeding does not allow the wound to cleanse itself freely, puncture wounds are prone to infection. Soaking the affected area in warm water for fifteen minutes may help promote circulation and natural cleansing. You should make sure that the child's tetanus immunizations are up-to-date, since a deep wound, particularly one caused by a dirty object, may be more prone to the development of tetanus (lockjaw).

Puncture wounds in general, like most wounds, may be somewhat painful for twelve to twenty-four hours. Keep the wound clean with a Band-Aid. Signs of trouble include increasing redness or tenderness, pus draining from the wound, or simply a feeling that the injury is not getting better within twenty-four to forty-eight hours. In such instances, medical care should be sought since deep puncture wounds may cause an abscess and even involve the underlying bone or joint. Remember, these are special wounds that should be watched more carefully and medical attention should be sought more quickly if there is no rapid resolution within twenty-four to forty-eight hours.

ALAN A. ROZYCKI, M.D.
Hanover, New Hampshire

My toddler fell, and his front tooth went through his lip. What should I do?

This is a common occurrence as active infants and toddlers explore their homes and surroundings. Once the bleeding has been stopped with firm, direct pressure, three areas need to be examined to determine the extent of the injury. First of all, the teeth need to be inspected. Even though they are only the first teeth, loosened, displaced, or broken teeth need to be seen by a dentist—right away. This is the first priority. Next, the skin immediately around the lips needs to be examined. Cuts through the lip extending onto the surrounding skin generally tend to gape and heal poorly. Generally, they require careful suturing for a cosmetically pleasing result. Cuts involving the lip and adjacent skin need to be seen by a physician as they usually require sutures. Occasionally, the teeth (or tooth) will go through the inside of the lip and emerge through the skin just below the lip. This skin laceration also requires suturing in most instances. Finally, if the lip and *only* the lip is involved, sutures are not necessary. These lip injuries heal quickly without scarring or deformity. Gentle pressure and perhaps ice to reduce the swelling are all that is required.

WILLIAM E. BOYLE JR., M.D.
Hanover, New Hampshire

My toddler has scratched his mosquito bites until they are scabs. How can I stop him from scratching and getting the bites infected?

With continued scratching, the wounds will heal more slowly and the chance of infection will increase. Parents could try three possible approaches. First, put socks over your infant's hands, especially at night, when he may scratch at the bites. Second, apply calamine lotion or similar product to reduce the itching. Third, if the others fail, consider the use of systemic therapy (such as Atarax) to reduce the itching associated with these bites.

STEPHEN T. PELTON, M.D.
Boston, Massachusetts

How big must a cut be before stitches are needed?

It depends on how deep, not how long, the cut is and how much the cut "gapes" (that is, how far apart the cut skin edges are). Scratches and cuts that do not penetrate the entire depth of the skin's three layers heal after adequate cleansing with soap and water (or a mild antiseptic solution) and dry dressing to protect against further abrasion and bacterial contamination during the initial healing phase.

Lacerations, which involve all skin layers and reach into the fatty layer below them, should receive the attention of a person experienced in treating such wounds. Smaller deep wounds can be treated with special tapes that hold the edges in place for healing without the need for suturing. Longer cuts, or those in areas that are difficult to immobilize (joint surfaces, fingers, and hands), generally require suturing.

A final consideration is appearance. If the laceration is in an exposed area, where potential scarring or disfiguring might occur, attendance by an experienced surgeon will provide the best results. Until the healing process is complete, the area should remain covered with a dry dressing.

WILLIAM R. BROWN JR., M.D., M.P.H., F.A.A.P.
New York, New York

CHAPTER 5

Breast-Feeding

Is it important to try to regulate my newborn's feeding schedule?

Although the preferences of newborns vary a great deal regarding the frequency and regularity of feedings, most infants will accept daytime feedings every three to four hours. Breast-fed infants tend to demand a somewhat more frequent feeding schedule during at least part of the day for the first few weeks. These frequent feedings help stimulate the mother's milk supply.

The main advantage of developing some kind of a feeding schedule is that it helps the mother organize her day. Some babies, by their very nature, are quite cooperative, whereas others seem more demanding and unpredictable. A good approach is to adopt a flexible but not unreasonable schedule. This has been referred to as a modified demand schedule.

Offer your baby feedings with the approximate frequency with which he or she seems to demand them. Be prepared, however, for some variation from day to day, depending on the baby's mood and changing needs. Your schedule is also important, and it is not unjust to ask the baby for some compromise. If it is more convenient to feed your baby now rather than in a half-hour, you may awaken him or her and do so. If you are involved in another chore at feeding time, it will not hurt the baby to cry for a while until you are free.

Do not let your baby sleep for excessively long periods of time during the day without being fed. If babies are sleeping for more than five hours, they should be awakened to see if they are hungry. On the other hand, you need not awaken your baby at night; wait until he or she awakens you. In this way, babies learn to distinguish night and day.

MARK D. WIDOME, M.D.
Hershey, Pennsylvania

My newborn takes a supplement bottle of 4 to 5 ozs. of formula each time I nurse. Isn't she getting enough breast milk?

It is possible that your breast milk is insufficient. If you have enough breast milk, your breasts should be rather engorged prior to each feeding, with some tingling of the nipples or actual leakage of milk while you are preparing to nurse.

You may have plenty of quality breast milk, but if you offer a bottle at each feeding out of insecurity, your baby may find it easier to suck from the bottle than to get milk from the breast. Just remember, to breast-feed successfully, you must ensure proper rest for yourself, drink plenty of fluids, and take in an adequate supply of calories to help replenish your supply of milk.

ROBERT FOMALONT, M.D.
Princeton, New Jersey

A more supportive supplementation is to offer a small amount of infant cereal mixed with breast milk or apple juice if your baby seems hungry after feeding. This avoids the ease of sucking problem, does not introduce cow's milk to the diet and provides an assurance of satisfaction.

GERBER PRODUCTS COMPANY
Fremont, Michigan

I am having trouble with my milk. How can I supplement my infant son's diet?

Healthy, well-nourished mothers can usually supply as much breast milk as their infants need for growth for the first six months of life. So, before you start any supplement, check to see if your infant is growing in length and weight as he should. (Have this done at the doctor's office, clinic, or other health center.) If the infant is younger than six months of age and is growing at his normal rate, be reassured that your milk is sufficient for now. There is plenty of time for the gourmet menus. If your baby is close to six months of age, you can begin giving him foods that contain iron. Dry infant rice cereal mixed with water is a good first food. Continue to breast-feed as long as you and your baby enjoy this special time together. If you still have concerns about your milk or breast-feeding, talk to someone with experience who can give you accurate advice.

BETTY OSEID, M.D.
New Orleans, Louisiana

Can breast milk be bottled and even frozen and used later? What's a safe refrigeration time?

Yes, breast milk can be bottled and even frozen. The freezing of breast milk has been going on for several decades in medical centers and milk banks around the world. Frozen milk maintains almost all its active ingredients, except for some cellular components such as white blood cells, which are destroyed through the freezing process. It is possible to freeze breast milk for from three to twelve months, although we do not know its exact expiration date. Frozen breast milk should be reserved for special conditions, such as feeding sick infants or premature babies in hospitals. The freezing of breast milk for home use does not seem to serve any useful purpose.

Refrigeration of breast milk is possible, if done properly, and refrigerated milk can be given to a baby up to twenty-four hours after collection. Proper technique requires a sterile breast pump and pouring the milk into sterilized bottles. The sterilization of breast milk after bottling it makes enzymes ineffective and alters proteins, including protective substances and heat-sensitive vitamins, to such a degree that the benefits of breast milk are severely diminished. It would be easier and more advantageous to use a commercial, ready-made formula for the occasional time the nursing mother is forced to be away from home.

EDUARD JUNG, M.D.
Chicago, Illinois

My newborn has started spitting up after his feedings. Could this indicate an allergy to breast milk?

Spitting up after feedings is a very common complaint. Most children who spit up do not seem distressed by this nor do they seem ill. They continue to grow and develop normally. If your child fits this pattern, no reason for concern. If your child's growth and development are normal, a careful search should be undertaken for the cause of this problem. Food allergy is a possible cause. However, allergy to breast milk is highly unlikely. In fact, feeding only breast milk for the first six to nine months of life is recommended as the best diet for children in allergy-prone families to prevent or delay the development of allergies. Unlike cow's milk or soybean formulas, which consist of foreign proteins that can be highly allergenic, human milk contains proteins that are not allergenic to babies.

However, it has been noted that minute quantities of the foods that a breast-feeding woman eats can be found in her breast milk. Some physicians also advise that breast-feeding mothers ingest only small amounts of highly allergenic foods.

The frequency of sensitivity to breast milk is not as great as for other food sources. If your child is spitting up, other causes should be evaluated. Although sensitivity to breast milk is very rare, it should not be ruled out.

JAMES A. NICKELSEN, M.D.
Greenville, North Carolina

I'm taking an antibiotic. Could this give my nursing newborn diarrhea?

Yes, your baby will receive some of the antibiotic with your milk and may develop diarrhea. Your pediatrician will advise you, depending on the type and amount of antibiotic you are taking, about whether you should express and discard your milk and use formula for the baby for the time being. This is usually advisable.

M. E. SYMONDS, M.D.
Mountainside, New Jersey

I smoke. Can my baby get nicotine from my breast milk?

Smoking ten to twenty cigarettes a day results in the appearance of 0.4 mg to 0.5 mg of nicotine in each liter of milk. Nicotine suppresses the milk

j oxytocin and may inhibit lactation. Nicotine
.rs rapidly in breast milk. Anecdotal evidence
.s, vomiting, diarrhea, and rapid pulse rates in
.ed to maternal smoking.

DAVID S. SMITH, M.D.
Philadelphia, Pennsylvania

Are there any foods that I should avoid while I'm nursing?

Although many nursing mothers feel that foods such as garlic, chocolate, tomatoes, spices, or certain berries may cause poor feeding or gastric discomfort in their infants, there is no evidence to support these notions. Mothers may safely include any of these items in their diets. Another common misconception about maternal diet and nursing is that substances such as beer, oatmeal, and tea will somehow increase milk production; this belief, too, lacks scientific support.

The diet of a nursing mother should be thoroughly planned to include the additional calories, calcium, and fluid she will need, and above all it should be satisfying to her. If coffee, alcohol, or tobacco are important to the mother, they may all be safely taken in moderation.

GERALD B. HICKSON, M.D.
Nashville, Tennessee

Can I safely take medication for illness or pain while I am nursing?

Unfortunately, because of the consumer habits we practice today, we are constantly being urged by family, friends, and the media to eat, drink, rub on, or bathe in one thing or another to improve our overall well-being. Concurrent with becoming a "medicated" society, we have also developed an increasing awareness of the possible effects of "drug administration" to the baby by way of breast milk. Therefore, many drug companies, independent research laboratories, and universities have conducted studies to determine which substances the mother takes can be passed through the breast milk to the baby. This research determines whether each compound tested passes into breast milk, how much of the compound the mother has to take for it to be detected in breast milk, and what the potential effects are on the baby. The results of these investigations are contained in tables and lists in obstetric and pediatric textbooks and in medical journals. The mother's and the baby's doctors should have easy access to this information and will be glad to pass it along when asked.

A few examples are noteworthy. Diazepam (Valium) passes through breast milk, and large doses taken by the mother may sedate the baby. Because aspirin goes into breast milk in moderate quantities, its use by the nursing mother should be discouraged. Even alcohol will pass into breast milk in small quantities. Any medication taken by a nursing mother, whether prescription or over-the counter, and also alcohol and caffeine, should be investigated as to whether or not it can pass through breast milk to the baby.

RICHARD J. FLAKSMAN, M.D.
Akron, Ohio

Should I nurse my baby on only one side during each feeding, or on both?

The usual procedure is for a mother to nurse her baby on both breasts at each feeding, approximately ten minutes on the first breast and five minutes on the other breast. On the next feeding, she usually starts on the breast last used (and used for the shorter period of time). A vigorous, active nursing infant can essentially empty a breast in from five to eight minutes.

Usually a mother does what comes naturally to her. Even single-breast feedings can work well for many mothers, with both mothers and babies happy.

GEORGE J. KLOK, M.D.
Council Bluffs, Iowa

When is the best time to wean my infant from the breast to the bottle?

Weaning is really the process of changing the infant from total dependence on breast milk to other or additional sources of nourishment. At about six months of age, a baby's stores of iron become diminished, and it would then be appropriate to start him or her on some iron-fortified foods (usually cereals). Additional protein and bulk should be added to the infant's diet by about one year of age. Babies can continue to breast-feed during the time new foods are being introduced. A baby is usually able to learn to drink from a cup at six to seven months of age and some mothers will wean their babies from the breast directly to the cup or let the child both drink from a cup and nurse. A working mother is often able to partially wean her baby and continue morning and night breast-feeding for months or even into the baby's second year. There is probably no best time to wean an infant from the breast to the bottle. It will depend on many circumstances, such as the mother's work, demands from other children, and a personal desire to be free from breast-feeding. Any amount of time, whether it be six weeks or a year, that an infant breast-feeds is to its advantage. A mother's or child's illness may make weaning an emergency process, but normally it should be gradual in order to allow for adjustment by both the infant and the mother.

LINDA C. LONEY, M.D.
St. Louis, Missouri

Can I drink alcoholic beverages if I am nursing?

Nursing mothers should not drink alcoholic beverages. Alcoholic beverages are a cause of poisoning in infants and children. They may cause a low concentration of blood glucose, leading to convulsive seizures, along with other untoward reactions. Alcohol consumed by the nursing mother easily enters the breast milk. Absorption of alcohol by the stomach and small intestine may require from thirty minutes to six hours, depending upon the amount consumed, whether food is present in the stomach, and the rapidity with which alcohol is taken.

The time required to detoxify alcohol in the liver is fairly constant (it takes about one hour to detoxify about 10 ml., or about ⅓ oz., of 50 percent alcohol in a healthy adult). Less than one-tenth of the ingested alcohol is excreted in the urine. Alcohol blood levels of 80 to 150 mg per 100 cc of blood are considered to be at the intoxication level. Fifty to 150 mg of alcohol per deciliter of blood results in poor coordination and blurred vision; 150 to 300 mg of alcohol per deciliter of blood results in visual impairment, speech defects, and hypoglycemia. More than 300 mg per deciliter causes convulsions and, possibly, coma and death.

SABURO HARA, M.D.
Nashville, Tennessee

Can my baby get gassy from my breast milk if I have eaten something that usually causes me to have a gas problem?

Yes, foods eaten by a nursing mother are excreted in very small amounts through the breast milk. Therefore, some foods like garlic, onions, chocolate, turnips, beans, cabbage, broccoli, brussels sprouts, rhubarb, apricots, and prunes, when eaten by the breast-feeding mother, can occasionally cause gas problems, colic, or diarrhea in her baby. Most breast-fed babies, however, will have no problems after these foods are eaten by their mothers. If you question the effect of a food, you should avoid it or document its effect carefully by watching for gassiness in the twenty-four hours after ingestion. Therefore, you can continue to eat most of these foods, giving up only those which consistently bother your baby.

VERA A. LOENING-BAUCKE, M.D.
Iowa City, Iowa

I'm breast-feeding and have been drinking a lot of citrus juices. Could this be causing my baby's diaper rash?

It is possible, but unlikely, that the diaper rash is due to the citrus juices you drink. You can find out by not drinking fruit juice for five or six days and by noting if the rash improves. By and large, it is a good rule when nursing not to eat or drink exaggerated amounts of any one food, but to eat or drink moderate quantities of a wide variety of foods.

M. E. SYMONDS, M.D.
Mountainside, New Jersey

My newborn wants to nurse every two or three hours. Is this all right?

It is now a widely accepted practice to allow newborns to nurse every two to three hours. Surveys of breast-feeding mothers in the United States and in other countries have shown that this is very commonly done. This is especially true of mothers who do not give their infants supplementary feedings, but give them only breast milk. As the infant gets older, he or she will naturally lengthen the interval between feedings.

Some doctors encourage new mothers with first infants to feed on a rigid schedule, say every three hours for the first two weeks, until they feel more comfortable about feeding on demand. Suckling the infant at frequent, regular intervals encourages lactation (the production of breast milk). The only drawback may be an increased soreness of the nipples, but that is a common complaint among nursing mothers.

For infants four to six months of age, nursing more often than eight to ten times in twenty-four hours may indicate a need for supplemental feeding.

MICHAEL PARRINO, M.D.
Columbia, South Carolina

My first child was colicky from my breast milk. Will my new baby be likely to have the same problem?

The diagnosis of colic is a very difficult one to make. Your first child could have been more sensitive to the foods you ate or could have just been a more active, fussy baby. It is hard to say for sure whether a baby is colicky or not. Most newborns have a fussy period that occurs in the evening. Your new baby is not any more likely than any other baby to have colicky episodes from your breast milk. If this newborn is also sensitive to different foods that you may eat or is a sensitive, active, fussy baby, he or she is likely to have these periods of restlessness. Colic probably has very little to do with your breast milk unless the baby is sensitive to foods that you eat. You should watch for signs of this and avoid the foods that may be irritating your baby. It is not recommended that you stop breast-feeding. Breast milk is the best food for babies. If a baby is fussy on breast milk, it is likely that he or she will be fussy on commercially available formula preparations as well. Most

30

children grow out of this fussy, colicky stage and are completely well by three months of age. If this colicky period becomes a problem, you should contact your pediatrician to discuss the situation.

JEANNE M. EULBERG, M.D.
Kansas City, Kansas

What is breast-milk jaundice?

Jaundice related to breast-feeding may be more common than realized. Nevertheless, probably less than 1 percent of these cases are serious or need follow-up evaluation and treatment.

It is usual for babies and mothers to be discharged from the hospital on the second or third day after delivery. Breast-milk jaundice usually has its onset the fourth day after birth and may continue steadily for three to six days thereafter. It may actually overlap with the normal, physiologic jaundice of the first three days of life. It is not uncommon for a mother, especially with her first child, to have a temporary decrease in the volume of breast milk seven to ten days after delivery. This decrease may result, to some degree, in the baby's poor intake of fluid and in a falsely elevated bilirubin level. Plain water (without sugar) may be used to supplement breast milk at this time. Adequate rest and intake of fluids, a relaxed and pleasant breast-feeding experience, and support from an experienced mother will almost always guarantee success with breast-feeding.

Because of the timing of the two jaundices, parents should watch for yellowing of the skin at home. For non-Caucasian babies, yellowing of the whites of the eyes and the inside of the mouth are indications of jaundice. When jaundice is suspected, the child's physician should be notified and should decide whether a bilirubin level test or other lab work is needed.

If the baby has a high bilirubin level, the physician may temporarily ask the mother to alternate formula feeding with breast-feeding or even to discontinue the evening feeding. It is important, however, to keep the mother's breast milk pumped out to maintain good milk production.

Occasionally, babies may need to be hospitalized to receive photo-therapy (treatment by exposure to light rays) to help break down the bilirubin of the skin and the bilirubin excreted in the bowels or urine. Unfortunately, it is tempting to use phototherapy too liberally, when a modification of breast-milk feedings can often prevent the need for hospitalization.

Some breast milk may contain substances that decrease a newborn's liver activity, which helps remove the bilirubin naturally. Not all babies become jaundiced from such breast milk. The substance in the milk decreases in time, and the baby's liver slowly matures to diminish the jaundice sufficiently. Nevertheless, this type of jaundice may persist into the second month in healthy, growing babies. This is *not* infectious hepatitis. And, with the normal, lower levels of bilirubin, no residual neurologic damage results.

In summary, breast-milk jaundice may be relatively common, and in probably 99 percent of all cases, there are no problems. The physician should always be consulted if there is an increase in the yellowing of the skin, jaundice into the second week of life, family history of jaundice, or if a baby is ill or not growing. Breast-milk jaundice is diagnosed in normal, healthy babies, but that diagnosis is made only after excluding other diseases when the bilirubin level is high and of concern to the physician.

YOSHIO G. MIYAZAKI, M.D.
Omaha, Nebraska

Is it harmful if my baby doesn't burp after every feeding?

To answer in the simplest way: not always. The purpose behind trying to have a baby burp is to help the baby release the air that is swallowed along with the feeding, whether it is by bottle or by breast. In order to make this easier, it is important to position your baby during the feeding so that the head is upright and the air has a chance to rise. Of course, each feeding is a little bit different so the amount of gas will be unequal. Sometimes there will be very little gas to bring up. I would also suggest that the amounts of feeding taken be limited to only a few ounces at a time. You should then stop for a moment to burp the baby before resuming the feeding. It also helps to let the baby sit upright for a few minutes after the feeding is over to allow the stomach time to settle down. Many babies will simply overfill their stomachs during the feeding and naturally try to release the pressure by a little "spitting up" or, preferably, burping afterward.

ROBERT B. BAKER, M.D., F.A.A.P.
Margate, New Jersey

I am nursing my baby. How can I tell if he is getting enough milk?

Breast-fed children generally feed every two to four hours. They usually nurse on each breast from ten to twenty minutes at a time. Your child will nurse vigorously at the beginning of each feeding and probably will begin to fall asleep by the end of the feeding. You can tell if your baby is getting enough milk if he nurses on an average of every three hours when he is a newborn, if he is gaining around one-half ounce to one ounce a day, or if he seems satisfied and falls asleep after feeding. It is very rare for a baby not to get enough milk if he or she is a vigorous, normal newborn. You should not worry about your milk supply; your baby will get more than enough milk to grow and be a healthy baby.

JEANNE M. EULBERG, M.D.
Kansas City, Kansas

If I use a supplement while nursing, will my baby ever refuse to nurse?

An occasional formula supplement given to a thriving breast-fed infant will not alter his or her feeding program to any significant degree. Many breast-fed infants, however, will refuse *any* bottled substitute for the breast or may not take it from the mother. Other members of the family or a baby-sitter may have better luck with some infants. A supplement should not be introduced earlier than two to three weeks of age, or until the mother's milk supply is at its maximum and both mother and infant are comfortable with the feeding schedule. The best time of day for a formula supplement is usually late afternoon or early evening, when a mother may have other chores, may want to leave the infant for a short period of time, may want to include another family member in the feeding experience, or when her milk supply may be at its lowest as a result of frequent daytime feedings. There is, of course, no equal substitute for breast milk, but the use of a commercial formula supplement is certainly permissible. A baby will rarely refuse to nurse after trying or using a formula supplement if the mother's milk supply is adequate and has been satisfying him or her.

MICHAEL R. PAPCIAK, M.D.
Atlanta, Georgia

I have a breast infection. Should I stop nursing?

Depending upon the type of infection, there may be no need to stop breast-feeding. The breast infection can and should be treated promptly, and nursing probably will contribute to faster healing. The infected breast will be very tender from the infection, and the engorgement caused by the production of milk will add to the pain. Brief nursing on the infected breast will relieve the engorgement, and the infant can then finish the feeding on the noninfected side. The antibiotic treatment you take will not harm the nursing infant.

LOIS A. POUNDS, M.D.
Pittsburgh, Pennsylvania

Can I take either a laxative or medication for diarrhea while nursing?

Yes, both laxatives and medications for diarrhea can be taken by nursing mothers. Laxatives are frequently needed by nursing mothers, especially in the early postpartum days when soreness in the episiotomy area tends to result in some degree of constipation. There are many laxatives on the market that are not absorbed out of the intestinal tract and are perfectly acceptable for nursing mothers. Milk of magnesia and mineral oil are perhaps the safest, although slight amounts of magnesium may be absorbed from milk of magnesia. These do not cross into the breast milk in sufficient quantities to cause difficulty for the infant. Other laxatives, such as those which are predominantly stool softeners, are also generally not absorbed out of the intestinal tract and are not passed into the breast milk. Certain laxatives should be avoided, particularly those containing phenothalein, such as Ex-Lax and Phenomint. The phenothalein can be absorbed out of the intestinal tract, and small amounts may pass into the breast milk. This could cause diarrhea in the infant if large amounts are taken by the mother.

As for antidiarrhea medications, most of these can be taken by the mother without danger to the infant. Again, those which are not absorbed out of the intestinal tract, such as Kaopectate, are perfectly safe for nursing mothers. Antispasmodic drugs such as Donatol or Donnagel can be used if they are not given in very high doses. Some of their contents, particularly the atropine, will come through the breast milk in very small amounts, but not enough to cause injury to the baby if the dosages are kept small. One of the primary drugs used in treating diarrhea is Lomotil. This is an opiate derivative and is reasonably effective. Some of the opiate drugs do come through the breast milk in small amounts, and in general this drug should not be taken by a nursing mother. The breast is a reasonably effective screen, and levels of Lomotil in breast milk are only a fraction of those in the bloodstream. If dosages are low, there will be no danger to the infant. In conclusion, when used prudently, both laxatives and medications for diarrhea may be taken by breast-feeding mothers, but preferably under the direction of a physician.

RICHARD A. GUTHRIE, M.D.
Wichita, Kansas

After feeding, my baby cries a lot and draws his legs up. Is this the sign of a problem?

This is a common problem (often referred to as "colic") in the first three or four months of life and a frequent source of concern for parents. In the absence of other symptoms it seldom indicates a serious medical problem. Obviously the baby is unhappy, probably because of abdominal cramps related to digestion. This readily becomes the center of family disagreements as to what should be done, especially if some family tensions already exist.

To some extent, crying after feeding is seen in babies who have a tendency to be tense or high-strung. Tense parents may tend to have tense babies. Tension may be an inborn trait or it may be acquired by association. Either way, it is difficult for a distraught parent to calm an upset baby.

Despite the best efforts of your pediatrician, this symptom may persist until the baby is around three or four months old, at which time the problem (as well as many other problems related to feeding) may seem to improve. This change is attributed to maturation of the baby's digestive system.

You should try to reduce the family tension that frequently has developed. A mother should be free to deal with the problem as she sees best, without interference from well-meaning family and friends.

Your doctor may review your feeding techniques. Occasionally a baby seems to feed too fast or take too much. Babies may be like adults in that they don't really feel full until a while after they have finished eating, unless they eat very slowly. Most babies seem to know when to stop eating, but this may not always be true.

If the baby is on a regular formula (made from cow's milk), you might try a soy-base type formula, which frequently provides gratifying results. If the baby is breast-fed, your doctor may review your diet for foods, especially spiced foods or unusual amounts of any one food, that might affect the baby.

If none of the above helps, your doctor may reluctantly prescribe an antispasmodic medicine. This should be used with care because of side effects and possible overdosage. Finally, there are a few mothers to whom a doctor can only offer sympathy and a reasonable hope that the problem will not last indefinitely.

JOHN GRAVES, M.D.
Dubuque, Iowa

Is it all right to give my baby formula during times when I'm nursing?

If you cannot breast-feed your baby and cannot collect and properly store your milk (refrigerated or frozen) for a short time, formula feeding may be required. A properly prepared infant formula is an adequate substitution, but you should express milk to continue lactation.

GERBER PRODUCTS COMPANY
Fremont, Michigan

Can I transmit any illnesses to my baby through nursing?

Nursing is more likely to protect against the transmission of infection than to contribute to it. There are many protective factors in breast milk such as antibodies against viruses and bacteria, and interferons from cells such as lymphosytes, and enzymes which help to protect against infection. As a general rule, the nursing infant is better protected against infection than the infant who is not breast-fed. There are rare exceptions and these would require special discussion with one's pediatrician.

If a mother were known to be a carrier of hepatitis B virus, or if a mother were undergoing infection with cytomegalo virus, then she should consult first with her pediatrician about the advisability of breast-feeding. With those exceptions, one can answer the question quite positively, in a strong affirmation of the help of breast milk in preventing infection in infants, rather than being the cause of infection.

SAMUEL KATZ, M.D.
Durham, North Carolina

CHAPTER 6

Colds, Fever, and Swollen Glands

What temperature is considered a fever?

Normal, healthy children maintain a body temperature of anywhere between 97.2° and 100°, with a usual, or average, rectal temperature of 98.6°. Occasionally, a healthy child's temperature may even go as high as 101°. This is more likely to happen late in the day after a lot of activity. A "real fever," then, is any temperature greater than 101°, especially if it occurs in the morning.

JOHN HOWARD STRIMAS, M.D.
Johnson City, Tennessee

How high should I let my infant's or toddler's temperature get before becoming alarmed?

Fever is a fairly frequent occurrence in children and a cause of much anxiety to parents. A high fever may make a child uncomfortable, irritable, and may even cause convulsions. In some children, fever is accidentally detected when a temperature reading is taken during a routine physical examination. Children's reactions to fever vary. Some may feel and look sick with a low fever, whereas others may tolerate a much higher temperature without discomfort.

Body temperature is not constant and varies during the day; it is lower in the morning and higher in the late afternoon. Fever is usually defined as a rectal temperature of more than 99.8°. It is recommended that fever medicine (aspirin, Tylenol, Tempra, and so forth) be given when the rectal temperature rises above 101°. For a temperature of 101° or lower, only observation for other signs of illness is needed, with another temperature measurement taken within the next two hours to check for an increase in fever. Fever is only a symptom, and a parent should pay attention to changes in behavior and other signs of illness. It is helpful to remember that the rectal temperature is 1° higher than the oral temperature.

If your child has a fever for forty-eight hours or more or shows any other signs of illness, you should contact your doctor. In addition, all temperatures above normal in a newborn or a baby younger than two months of age should be reported to a pediatrician.

MIREILLE B. KANDA, M.D.
Washington, D.C.

I don't have any baby aspirin. Can I give my toddler half of an adult aspirin?

Yes, if he or she weighs as much as 28 or 30 pounds. For an average-sized child, a reasonable dose of aspirin is 1 grain per year of age every four hours. An adult aspirin is a 5-grain tablet, and a baby aspirin contains 1¼ grains. One-half of an adult aspirin is equivalent to two baby aspirins.

BEN B. CABELL, M.D.
Fort Smith, Arkansas

My toddler has a 104° rectal temperature and seems to have a stiff neck. Could this be meningitis? Are those the only symptoms?

You should be concerned, although your child may not have meningitis. Your first response should be to reduce the fever and immediately contact your pediatrician.

Evaluation of this problem begins with obtaining a thorough medical history. Symptoms of concern to your doctor, in addition to stiff neck, include poor feeding, vomiting, a weak cry, decreased muscle strength, unsteady gait, irritability, and marked lethargy in a child who is not in touch with his or her surroundings. This last symptom is extremely important, since the child may develop mental confusion and altered states of consciousness progressing to coma. A seizure is also of special concern and should be reported promptly. Symptoms of cough, sore throat, injury to the inside of the throat from a toy or a stick, a change in the sound of the voice as though the child is speaking with a hot potato in his or her mouth, or the presence of swelling at the side of the neck are also important as clues to other illnesses that may mimic some of the signs of meningitis.

Physical examination by your pediatrician will determine the presence or absence of stiff neck, bulging of the soft spot on the child's head, a purplish skin rash, and other signs of diagnostic importance.

After these findings are reviewed, a decision can be made as to what procedures and tests are necessary to confirm the presumptive diagnosis. A spinal tap will be necessary if meningitis is indeed a possibility. Examination of cerebrospinal fluid in the laboratory will allow your doctor to make a definitive diagnosis of meningitis if it is present.

ARTHUR B. DECHOVITZ, M.D.
Evanston, Illinois

My toddler is a mouth-breather and always seems to be congested. Could this be caused by swollen tonsils or adenoids?

Yes, it is possible. Remember, however, that mouth-breathing can be due to congestion and obstruction anywhere in the upper respiratory passage such as the nose, behind the nose (the nasopharynx area), and also the tonsils and adenoids. Recurrent colds and respiratory infections, as well as respiratory allergies in the nose and throat, can be the cause. These may sometimes lead to recurrent infections or collection of fluids in the middle ear, which may result in hearing or speech problems. Your physician would decide whether or not the removal of the tonsils and adenoids is necessary. Most of the time it is not. Your child's past medical history, a physical examination, and the result of medical treatment, perhaps along with an X ray and an ear-nose-throat consultation, will help in making a decision.

PARVIZ DANESH, M.D., F.A.A.P.
Chicago, Illinois

How can I tell if my toddler has a sore throat?

Infection in the mouth and throat makes swallowing food or drink very difficult, and infants and young children may refuse to eat. At times, the child may start feeding, but then stop after a while and start crying. Of course, children have more problems with solid foods than with milk and other liquids.

A sore throat can also cause coughing that may be brought on by feeding. Since infection is rarely confined to the throat alone, fever, irritability, vomiting, and a runny nose are also usually present. Enlargement of the glands in the neck and under the lower jaw is another indication of a sore throat.

At times a sore throat can cause pain inside the child's ears, even when there is no ear infection. You may notice that the child pulls on his or her ears or tries to push a finger into an ear. The child should be examined by a pediatrician to rule out the possibility of an ear infection. Your pediatrician will usually perform a throat culture, but the so-called strep throat is rare in children under two years of age.

SOHAIL R. RANA, M.D.
Washington, D.C.

My toddler has a cold. What can I do for his nasal congestion and watery eyes?

Nasal congestion can be relieved in some children by over-the-counter decongestant preparations. Because many children do not respond to these medications, however, some doctors recommend saltwater nose drops to clear thick mucus from the nose. The drops can be made at home by adding ¼ teaspoon salt to an 8-oz. glass of warm water. A rubber suction bulb, given to many families at the time of delivery, or bought in a drugstore, can be used to put a couple of drops into each nostril and then to suck out the drops and mucus. If the mucus becomes thick, causing nasal stuffiness at night, a cool vaporizer may help loosen secretions and let the child sleep more comfortably. There is no good treatment for watery eyes due to colds.

K. LYNN CATES, M.D.
Farmington, Connecticut

My newborn has a 102° rectal temperature. What should I do?

Fever in a newborn (a baby less than two months of age) is considered a more serious symptom than fever in an older child. The usual colds and viruses that frequently cause fever in children rarely cause fever in a newborn. Also, more serious bacterial infections, such as pneumonia or meningitis, may begin with fever as the only symptom. These serious infections require immediate diagnosis and immediate treatment. It is therefore important for a newborn with a 102° temperature to be seen as quickly as possible by a physician. The severity of the illness can be best assessed by examining the baby, and special tests may need to be done to make an early diagnosis. A newborn with fever is one of the few situations that require immediate attention.

H. GARRY GARDNER, M.D.
Darien, Illinois

What causes swollen lymph nodes (swollen glands)?

Lymph nodes are part of the natural defenses of the body against infections and toxins. They are located all over the body, but groups of them are found in the neck, armpits, groin, behind the knees, and in front of and behind the ears.

In children, the most common cause of enlarged lymph nodes is infection. The site of enlargement depends on the location of the infection. Throat and ear infections can lead to enlarged nodes at the neck. Bites by the black fly on the head make the nodes behind the ears swell up. An infected cat scratch on the hand or arm results in big nodes at the armpit. A wound on the foot from a nail enlarges the lymph nodes at the groin. Tuberculosis of the lungs results in a big lymph node inside the chest; this is easily seen by X ray.

The most frequent site of node enlargement in children is the neck. Mothers easily notice these enlargements and, naturally, they worry until their child is seen by the doctor. In most instances, the enlarged nodes are due to a throat infection, colds, tooth abscess, ear infection, or insect bite. However, if the node is at the middle front of the neck, or just above the collar bone, other causes besides infection, such as tumor, cyst, or a wandering thyroid gland, should be considered.

41

Most mothers think of cancer when they see a big lymph node in their child's neck. This is a natural reaction. It is true that cancer is one cause of enlarged nodes in children. However, infection is by far the most common cause. If a swollen lymph node is due to cancer, other physical findings, such as paleness, enlarged liver or spleen, or black and blue marks (purpura) on the skin will be seen.

If the doctor thinks that bacterial infection is the cause of the enlarged lymph nodes, an antibiotic will be given. However, if he or she is not sure of the cause, blood and urine tests, an X ray, skin tests, and biopsies might be necessary to confirm the diagnosis.

If your child has an enlarged lymph node, have it checked by a doctor. Don't worry too much; the chance is good that it is not serious.

L. LEO LEONIDAS, M.D., F.A.A.P.
Bangor, Maine

My eighteen-month-old has so much nasal mucus due to his cold that it is causing him to cough, gag, and vomit. What should I do?

The mucous membrane of the upper respiratory tract, which includes the nose, mouth, throat, and trachea, are endowed with such a large and good blood supply that any stimulant can create the production of excess mucus. Consequently, it is very important to try to reduce the number of causes of its production. One of the major problems is cigarette smoking in the home. Another is the use of spray cans, which produce substances that irritate the mucous membrane. Awareness and control of these certainly would help cut down on the stimulus of the production of mucus. Once this production is full blown, however, an eighteen-month-old child is not able to help himself by blowing his nose, so he swallows the mucus. This swallowed mucus will stimulate the cough reflex, and the child will cough frequently. As the child coughs, he may then also vomit the swallowed mucus.

If you can't stop the production of excess mucus by controlling the environment, you may have to seek other methods. Using a cold or warm air vaporizer, or pans of water near the source of heat to produce excess moisture in the air, seems to make a child more comfortable. Drinking extra fluids makes the mucus thinner and able to be coughed up more easily. Some other methods such as postural drainage seem to help eliminate the accumulation of mucus periodically. The method is simple and easy for any mother to handle. Give the child a bath in a steamy bathroom; then, after ten or fifteen minutes, dry the child off, put him in comfortable clothes, and turn him over on your lap, with his head hanging down slightly. Then pat his back from the waist to the shoulders, gently, with hands cupped; this encourages the child to expectorate some of the mucus he has swallowed. This is an excellent thing to do before the child goes to sleep. Certainly a child who is lying on his back will have more difficulty handling the excess mucus in the back of the throat; therefore, an inclined position is usually desirable for sleep.

EVELYN BAUGH, M.D.
Toledo, Ohio

Do continuous sore throats cause tonsillitis?

Sore throats do not *cause* tonsillitis. Tonsillitis is one kind of sore throat. With tonsillitis there is usually a sore throat; with a sore throat there may be tonsillitis. The tonsils are part of the throat, just as is the larynx.

MERRITT B. LOW, M.D., F.A.A.P.
Ashfield, Massachusetts

How often should I take my baby's temperature if he has a fever?

That depends mostly on how the child looks. The baby's temperature does not tell you how sick he is. It is more important to observe the child's alertness, irritability, general energy, fluid intake, and similar signs. If you know your baby has a fever, but he is acting normally, then it is not at all necessary to take his temperature frequently. Two or three times a day, when the child is awake, would be sufficient.

AVRUM L. KATCHER, M.D., F.A.A.P.
Flemington, New Jersey

My toddler has had a cold on and off for a month. Why doesn't the pediatrician order an antibiotic for him?

Antibiotics are basically used to kill germs. Unfortunately, colds are not caused by germ infections but, rather, by viral infections that go away only in time. The body will fight off a viral infection if the patient's resistance is normal. It is important to consider, however, the possibility of disorders other than viral colds that cause many of the same symptoms. For instance, sinusitis occurs in children and, in fact, even in young toddlers. Also, the possibility of nasal allergy should be considered in any child who has cold-like symptoms for a prolonged period of time.

DAVID J. TEPPER, M.D.
Chattanooga, Tennessee

What is the cause of meningitis? Is meningitis contagious?

Meningitis is an infection of the lining or covering of the brain and spinal cord. It may be caused by several different bacteria or by viruses. The most common causes of meningitis in infants and children are streptococcus, Hemophilus influenzae, pneumococcus, and meningococcus. There are also some viral causes of meningitis, including some of the more common respiratory and gastrointestinal viruses, and particularly the virus of measles. Because all cases of meningitis are caused by infectious agents, all are theoretically contagious. However, the extent to which a particular case of meningitis is contagious depends on the organism causing the disease and the extent of contact between the patient and other people, especially family members. The meningococcus is a particularly contagious organism. In many cases, however, the organism that produces meningitis in one patient produces only an upper-respiratory infection, or perhaps no infection at all in other family members. Because some organisms causing meningitis are more contagious than others, it is often appropriate for all members of the family to visit their physician after exposure to a case within the family, in school, or in a hospital. Once a case of bacterial meningitis is treated with effective antibiotics, it becomes noncontagious within twenty-four to forty-eight hours. If there is a case of meningitis in the family, or if one of your children is exposed to a child in school who later develops meningitis, you

44

and your physician should find out the exact cause and take appropriate preventive measures. Outside the immediate family or other situations involving close physical contact, most cases of meningitis are not as contagious as such common childhood diseases as measles and chicken pox.

WILLIAM J. CASHORE, M.D.
Providence, Rhode Island

Can I use decongestant nose drops with my toddler? How often should I use them?

It is not necessary to use nose drops at all. They provide little or no relief unless they are used too heavily. And the rebound from their use can be a problem in itself. But the problem with this "medicine," and in fact many "symptomatic medicines," is the fact that by using something for almost every symptom, the overusage of drugs and medicines is subtly encouraged. The universal trivial afflictions that beset all of us are best handled by our reasonable acceptance of them. It is difficult to be a parent and want to "do something," and then be told to be patient and do nothing. These very minor problems will handle themselves. In this case, there is no real justification for the use of nose drops.

THOMAS E. MORRISSEY, M.D., F.A.A.P.
Godfrey, Illinois

My toddler has a thick, foul-smelling drainage from one nostril. He does not have a cold. Could he have something in his nose?

From your description, the most likely cause of the discharge from your child's nostril would be some item that he stuck up his nose. Children of his age are beginning to explore all their bodily openings and frequently will insert an object in their noses or ears, just as earlier they were putting everything and anything in their mouths. In this situation, the object has to be removed by the doctor very carefully. If it is a pencil eraser or something similar, it can be removed in one piece without too much difficulty. However, if it is a peanut or a piece of food, it can easily be broken during the process of removal and this could lead to the child's inhaling pieces of the material, which can cause a chemical reaction in the lungs. Thus there is a need for extreme care in its removal by a physician only. A parent should certainly resist the temptation to use Q-tips or similar objects to get it out.

Incidentally, the foul smell of the discharge can be absorbed by the small blood vessels in the nose and in some cases can cause the child to have a foul body odor. Removal of the object from the nostril effectively cures the child of that odor.

THEODORE KUSHNICK, M.D.
Greenville, North Carolina

My child always gets bad colds. Should he have his tonsils removed?

There are few reasons for removing tonsils. Certainly, the only absolute reason is to treat cancer of the tonsil. There are, however, several times when a tonsillectomy is a good idea. Basically, these are when the infant or child has repeated episodes of strep throat (meaning more than four documented episodes of strep in one year). Occasionally, children who have very large adenoid tissue or recurring episodes of fluid in the middle ear may need their adenoids removed, and the doctor may take the tonsils out at the same time. Unfortunately, removing the tonsils and adenoids will not lessen the number or severity of colds that a child may get.

DAVID J. TEPPER, M.D.
Chattanooga, Tennessee

What temperature should my baby have before I give him aspirin?

In deciding whether or not to use a medicine for a fever, a physician usually takes into consideration how uncomfortable the baby is as well as how high the temperature is. The child may not need medicine if the temperature is 102° or less. If the temperature exceeds 102°, the child's doctor might prescribe an antifever drug, particularly if the child is irritable or crying excessively or seems otherwise distressed. Some children tolerate 103° and 104° temperatures well, and aspirin or acetaminophen may not be necessary. If the temperature goes above 104°, the child should be treated, regardless of how well he was tolerating his illness. Parents should contact a physician if the fever reaches this temperature.

J. MARTIN KAPLAN, M.D.
Philadelphia, Pennsylvania

Does my newborn have immunity to any diseases or viruses?

Infants who are born after a full, nine-month pregnancy will be immune to virtually all diseases to which their mothers are immune. The blood proteins (immunoglobulins) that protect the mother from infection are transferred across the placenta to the infant's bloodstream. This transfer of immunity occurs primarily in the last six weeks of pregnancy. Infants born before this time may have less protection than those born at full term. The duration of protection varies for different diseases. In general, however, these protective proteins are present for four to six months. By this time, immunization against several serious infectious diseases will already have begun and the infant will be building his or her own immune defenses.

However, newborn infants are not immune to chicken pox or whooping cough.

WILLIAM W. FRAYER, M.D.
New York, New York

CHAPTER 7

Constipation and Diarrhea

Can iron medication cause constipation in infants?

Infants who are fed formulas containing iron are receiving only the minimum daily requirement of iron. Iron is not really a medication, and in a recent study of infants fed formulas with and without iron, there was no difference in the babies' bowel patterns. An older infant who has been found to require iron medication two or three times a day for treatment of anemia is getting several times more iron than is provided in formulas. Some of these infants may have mild intestinal cramping, but constipation is unusual. Parents should remember that cow's milk, from which formulas are made, contains almost no iron, and all babies need iron for good health. If infants become constipated, it is usually because they need more fluid or fruit in their diets and not because of iron supplements.

LOIS A. POUNDS, M.D.
Pittsburgh, Pennsylvania

Is there anything I should do if my toddler is vomiting and also has diarrhea?

Because vomiting and diarrhea can quickly cause the child to become dehydrated due to loss of body fluids, it is necessary to replace those fluids. Although several illnesses may cause vomiting and diarrhea, most commonly they are due to viral infections of the intestinal tract and are treated symptomatically. Usually vomiting can be controlled by administering clear fluids containing carbohydrates (sugars) and minerals (electrolytes) frequently and in small amounts. Any regular diet should be discontinued for the first twenty-four hours of the illness, and only the liquids described above should be given. These fluids may include ginger ale or, preferably, one of the commercially available preparations such as Pedialyte or Lytren.

If the child improves with the clear liquid diet, *gradually* reintroduce other foods into the diet over the next few days. However, avoid whole milk until the stools have returned to normal. During that time you may use a formula that is not made from cow's milk, such as one of the soybean-based preparations. In this way the intestinal tract will be allowed to regenerate the cells that produce a substance (an enzyme) that digests the sugar (lactose) that is in the cow's milk. If the milk is introduced too soon, it could cause the diarrhea to return.

If the child does not improve, continues to pass loose stools and/or to vomit after a trial period of twenty-four hours on the above regimen, or if you note that he or she is becoming lethargic or unusually irritable, you should take the child to a qualified physician for further evaluation and treatment.

JOHN W. DOWNING JR., M.D.
Washington, D.C.

What would cause my infant's bowel movements to turn green?

Green stools are usually abnormal (unless they are caused by heavy ingestion of green vegetable foods, crayons, or paint), and are basically caused by the rapid passage of bile salts through the intestines. The rapid transit time does not allow the bile to mix appropriately with digestible foods. Green stools are usually associated with diarrhea. Fats are the hardest foods to digest and should be cut down or eliminated in the face of the problems usually present with green bowel movements. Poorly digested fats are converted by bacteria into fatty acids, and these fatty acids in themselves tend to have a cathartic effect. The whole condition needs treatment by diet restriction and sometimes medication as and when prescribed.

MERRITT B. LOW, M.D., F.A.A.P.
Ashfield, Massachusetts

What can I give my infant for constipation?

First ask yourself what you mean by constipation. Are you talking about hard movements, infrequent movements, painful movements, solid movements, difficult movements, or blood-tinged movements? Many parents give an unjustified label of "constipation" to their children's bowel movements. The best approach to constipation is to try to establish a regular time for bowel movements. Adding liquids and juices, fruits, and bulky vegetables can be helpful in loosening movements. Stool softeners are available, but they should probably be used only after consulting a physician.

MERRITT B. LOW, M.D., F.A.A.P.
Ashfield, Massachusetts

Is surgery necessary to correct prolapse of the rectum?

Rectal prolapse appears as a bright red, tube-like protrusion from the rectum. It may occur in children with altered muscle motion in the large intestine in cases of chronic constipation, ulcerative colitis, hypothyroidism, lower spinal cord damage, or cystic fibrosis. The prolapse often resolves spontaneously. The physician may need to gently push the intestine back into place. Surgery is not often indicated. Repeated episodes can be prevented by using stool softeners and taping the buttocks together until the child wishes to defecate. Occasionally, these measures are not effective and surgery is necessary in order to prevent permanent damage to the rectum.

ALAN R. RUSHTON, M.D., Ph.D.
Flemington, New Jersey

I've read that prolonged diarrhea or constipation can cause prolapse of the rectum. Is this true? When should I be concerned?

Rectal prolapse may develop in children with prolonged diarrhea or constipation, multiple rectal polyps, parasitic infestations, cystic fibrosis, or neurologic abnormalities such as a meningomyelocele. Approximately

20 percent of children with cystic fibrosis develop rectal prolapse; in nearly one-half of the patients, the prolapse precedes the establishment of diagnosis. Rectal prolapse is always a cause for concern, and prompt reduction is necessary to prevent injury to tissue. A measurement of sweat chloride concentration should be performed on any child with even a single episode of rectal prolapse.

DAVID S. SMITH, M.D.
Philadelphia, Pennsylvania

My toddler has to have a bowel movement but he is holding back and refusing to give in. What should I do?

If the child is holding back and trying to avoid stools, this is an indication that he is not ready for toilet training at this time. Do not push with efforts to train the child. At a later date, a behavior modification approach may be tried with good chance of success.

If the child is in pain, there may be a fissure that is causing involuntary withholding. In either case, it would be best to see the child's doctor.

AVRUM L. KATCHER, M.D., F.A.A.P.
Flemington, New Jersey

My baby is having "explosive" bowel movements. Is this serious?

The explosive nature of the bowel movement is not as important as the frequency and consistency of the stool. Babies frequently pass large amounts of gas, and this is of no consequence. Frequent, watery bowel movements should be reported to your physician, however, especially if they are associated with fever, vomiting, or blood in the bowel movement. During the first month of life, breast-fed babies are especially likely to have explosive bowel movements, often with each feeding, and this is quite normal.

STEPHEN E. WALLACE, M.D., F.A.A.P.
Springfield, Illinois

My toddler is taking an antibiotic and has diarrhea. Is this normal?

Knowing when your child first began having diarrhea while taking this antibiotic is probably the essential determinant of its cause. Many children who have ear infections and/or chest colds will also have diarrhea before, during, or after the acute phases of the illness. These illnesses are often treated with antibiotics. The diarrhea may appear after the antibiotic has been started. If this is not a life-threatening diarrhea—that is, if the child does not seem to be becoming dehydrated from it—and the illness is such that the antibiotic therapy needs to be continued, subsequent treatment of the diarrhea, whether or not it is from antibiotics, is essential. There are some antibiotics that cause diarrhea, but the diarrhea usually appears at least a week after the antibiotics have been started. There is one form of severe diarrhea, called pseudomembranous enterocolitis, which can occur occasionally, but this is unusual when a basically healthy child is taking antibiotics. If diarrhea is a concern, it must of course be treated by a physician.

EVELYN BAUGH, M.D.
Toledo, Ohio

My infant has had diarrhea for twenty-four hours. Could he dehydrate in that time? How can I tell?

An infant with severe diarrhea may become quite dehydrated in twenty-four hours. Whether or not this occurs depends on the imbalance between fluid intake and fluid loss.

One may recognize the development of dehydration by the following: the eyes may appear to be sunken; the lips may appear parched and possibly cracked; the mucous membranes of the mouth and the tongue may appear quite dry; if you pinch the skin of the abdomen and then release it, the skin smooths out much more slowly than it normally does. This is due to the loss of tissue fluids. There may be an acetone odor to the breath (somewhat sweet or fruity) and there is a marked decrease in the frequency and amount of urination.

BENJAMIN STEIN, M.D., F.A.A.P.
Bethesda, Maryland

Can I give my infant a suppository for constipation?

Occasionally, an infant may have difficulty passing a hard stool, becomes fussy, and cries while straining. If this occurs, it is all right to use an infant glycerin suppository, but do not administer these habitually. Or, you can use a Q-tip generously covered with petroleum jelly (Vaseline) to lubricate the anal opening, being very careful not to go in more than one-half inch.

JOHN HOWARD STRIMAS, M.D.
Johnson City, Tennessee

My infant's bowel movements have been black since she has been taking iron medication. Is this normal?

Children who are taking iron medication such as ferrous sulfate by mouth commonly have black stools. The reason for this is that there is an increase in the stool of iron sulfides, which are substances made by the bacteria of the gastrointestinal tract when iron sulfate is given to your child. The natural color of these iron sulfides is black. This is not dangerous to your child, and you need not worry.

You may have also noted that while your child is taking an oral, liquid iron preparation her teeth may have assumed a black stain. This complication can be reduced by brushing the teeth after your child has taken the iron medicine. Again, you need not worry about this complication. This does not harm your child's teeth and it will disappear after she no longer takes the iron medicine.

MICHAEL B. HARRIS, M.D.
New York, New York

Do all members of my family need medication for pinworms if only my child has the disease?

The majority of American children will acquire pinworms at some time during their lives. Pinworms are literally everywhere, and many infested individuals are relatively without symptoms. Symptoms consist of itching in the anal area, particularly at night. The itching is caused by the movement of the adult worms from the rectum onto the skin around the anus, where they lay their eggs. Scratching causes the eggs to be picked up by the fingernails or fingertips and then possibly swallowed and developed into adult worms. Eggs also may be shed in clothing or bedclothes. They are small enough to circulate in the air with dust particles and be inhaled. In warm, humid environments the eggs remain capable of infection for days. As an attempt to slow the rate of reinfestation, many doctors will test all the members of the family and treat those found to harbor the worms. Keeping the fingernails trimmed and insisting on good handwashing may also be helpful. However, regardless of precautions taken it is extremely likely that reinfestation will occur. It is reasonable, therefore, to treat only those who have symptoms.

KENNETH L. WIBLE, M.D.
Morgantown, West Virginia

I noticed tiny, threadlike worms in my toddler's stools. Are these pinworms? What should I do?

Yes, tiny, threadlike, white, moving worms, usually the size of a fingernail clipping, are frequently pinworms. If the child has pinworms, he should obtain medicine from the physician to kill them. The bed linen should be changed to prevent any further spread of the infection.

FERNANDO J. deCASTRO, M.D.
St. Louis, Missouri

My toddler is trying to have a bowel movement and is unable to move it past the rectal opening. He is in some pain. What can I do for him?

There are several possible solutions to this problem. Pain due to constipation is usually intermittent and will soon pass. You could give your child a mild, oral laxative such as Metamucil or mineral oil. He should then have a bowel movement twelve to twenty-four hours later. If you think your child needs immediate relief, lubricate one of your fingers with warm soap suds and insert it into his rectal opening, breaking up the hard stool in his rectum with gentle sweeping motions with your finger. Still another solution would be to give him a rectal suppository such as Durolax. This should result in a bowel movement within an hour.

It is easier to prevent constipation than to treat it. If your child has frequent trouble with constipation, provide a diet that includes such foods as cabbage, corn, lettuce, bran cereals, prunes, and other dried fruits. Toilet training should be done in a gentle, nonthreatening manner. Some toddlers will "hold onto" their stools because they are afraid of the toilet. The bowels then become impacted with hard stool. It will be much easier for your child to have a bowel movement if his feet are touching either the floor or a platform.

SUSAN T. EDWARDS, M.D.
Hanover, New Hampshire

What causes red streaks in my baby's stool?

When parents report red streaks in their babies' stools, there are always two major problem areas to be investigated. First, there is the problem of determining the cause of the unusual color in the stool. Second, and probably more important, there is the problem of the great degree of fear and anxiety that seeing a red stool will cause. As adults, we have been taught to think of any unusual bleeding as a potential sign of cancer or other catastrophic disease. From the pediatric point of view the presence of a red stool never indicates the presence of cancer and almost never indicates the presence of a severe or life-threatening disease. The cause is almost always benign and treatment, if needed at all, is usually easy.

When a pediatrician is first told that a baby is passing red stools, he or she asks the question "Is it blood?" It is surprising to find how often a child, especially one with mild diarrhea, may pass a stool that looks frankly bloody when in fact it is simply colored by dyes found in food or medication. Common offenders in this area include raspberry or cherry gelatin, red-tinted medications such as ampicillin or pyruvinium pamoate (used for treating pinworms), and natural foods such as cherries or beets, especially when they are eaten in large quantities. Whenever in doubt, and when the stool is available to test, a simple examination with a material called guaiac may demonstrate that the red substance is, in fact, not blood. At that point it becomes a simple matter to counsel and reassure the parents.

If the red material in the bowel movement is proved to be blood, especially if it appears as streaks and if the stool is very hard and/or the child appears to be in pain during passage of the bowel movement, then there is probably an anal fissure, which is a small tear or cut of the skin and membrane around the anus, the opening into the rectum. In fact, this is the most common cause of true bleeding associated with a bowel movement. Fissures are almost always due to constipation or hardness of the bowel movement and tend to cause more problems because of pain from subsequent bowel movements than from the bleeding itself. Children usually respond well to a combination of warm baths and dietary and medication maneuvers to soften the bowel movement. The use of mild laxatives at times and a change to a diet containing more fruits and vegetables will produce a softer stool, which will allow the fissure to heal. In extremely rare cases, several fissures may be seen at the same time in children with unusual forms of colitis. These problems are almost never seen in the infant and toddler.

The third common group of causes for finding blood in a child's stool is the group of many different causes of infectious diarrhea. This is diarrhea that is caused by viruses or bacteria that produce a usually brief but dramatic course of bowel movements that may be bloody. The child can be quite feverish and may look quite ill; not only blood but occasionally pus, mucus, and undigested food might be found in the stool. When pediatricians see such children, they look carefully for signs of dehydration and sometimes get laboratory studies to determine not only the cause of the diarrhea and bleeding but also blood counts. Stool cultures and smears of the stool are taken to look for microscopic evidence of particular infections. Fortunately, in almost every case the diarrhea is short-lived and resolves itself without treatment. Certain of these forms of diarrhea do respond to treatment with antibiotics and therefore all such patients should be seen and evaluated by a physician. Bacteria with such exotic names as Salmonella, Shigella, Campylobacter, Yersinia, and E. Coli may require specific medical treatment and examination of other family members to be sure that an infection has not passed to them.

There are other, *very* rare causes of blood in the stool, such as the hemolytic uremic syndrome and various forms of inflammatory bowel disease, but a pediatrician would almost never consider these as possibilities in a child who is having blood in the stool for the first time. Finally, polyps may occasionally be present in the child under two years of age and may cause acute bleeding from the rectum. This is usually seen in a child closer to five or seven years of age, but it would be considered in a child with severe unexplained bleeding from the rectum.

If your child does pass a stool with a streak of red, the pediatrician should be called, but you can take comfort in the fact that the answer is almost inevitably simple and the treatment short and easy.

STEPHAN R. GLICKEN, M.D.
Boston, Massachusetts

My infant has diarrhea. What can I do for him?

Having determined that the cause of the infant's diarrhea is secondary to nonspecific gastroenteritis and that the infant is well hydrated and can manage oral fluids, the following is suggested:

Offer your child only clear liquids for the next twenty-four hours. Ready-to-feed solutions such as Pedialyte or Lytren may be given, supplemented by apple or cranapple juice diluted equally. You may also give beverages such as Seven-Up and ginger ale, weak tea, or Jell-O water. Do not give milk or solids. After twenty-four hours, please check with the doctor, but you may begin solids such as rice cereal, applesauce, and bananas. Continue this bland diet for a day or so before gradually resuming your baby's normal diet. Cow's milk should be withheld for at least a week.

JAMES M. BURGIN, M.D., F.A.A.P.
College Park, Maryland

My toddler is lethargic. She has had diarrhea off and on for a week now and seems to have no energy. Should I be concerned?

Diarrhea is defined as a sudden increase in the frequency, looseness, or volume of bowel movements. Most episodes of diarrhea are due to a viral infection of the intestines. These episodes usually last for several days to a week. The main goal of treatment is to prevent dehydration by giving enough oral liquids to replace the fluids lost through diarrhea. Your child's doctor will be able to tell you how to do this.

Your pediatrician should be consulted as soon as possible if your child has symptoms of dehydration or severe diarrhea. The symptoms of dehydration include crying without tears, a decrease in urine output, a dry mouth, and lethargy. Severe diarrhea is signaled by frequent watery stools, pus or blood in the stools, persistent temperature greater than 101°, and markedly decreased activity.

If your child is lethargic and has had diarrhea off and on for a week, her doctor should be contacted as soon as possible so as to discuss the situation.

CHRISTOPHER A. KUS, M.D.
Canaan, New Hampshire

Is my infant too young to be given an enema?

Enemas are not recommended for infants or children at any time. If you think your baby needs an enema, consult your doctor, who will have other recommendations that may be more appropriate.

AVRUM L. KATCHER, M.D., F.A.A.P.
Flemington, New Jersey

My toddler has had loose bowel movements for three days. She doesn't seem sick otherwise. What should I do?

First, you need to answer a few questions: Is there any blood or pus in the bowel movements? Does your child have a fever? Is she urinating in normal or just slightly reduced amounts? Does anyone else in the family have diarrhea? Has your child been sick and on any medicine or antibiotics that might cause loose stools? Has she been eating any high-fiber (roughage) foods such as bran or spinach, which might cause loose stools?

If these questions can be answered in the negative, she probably has a mild viral intestinal infection. The main goal in treatment is to prevent dehydration by giving enough fluids to replace the fluids lost in the loose stools. She will get better faster if you follow the following dietary regime: Give your child clear liquids for twelve to twenty-four hours (e.g., dilute sweetened tea, Jell-O water [use twice the usual amount of water], Gatorade, Seven-Up). Do not give your child any milk or milk products *for one week.* Give only clear fluids. If after twenty-four hours of clear liquids the stools have decreased in number or become more solid, you may start a low-fiber, bland diet, gradually going back to a normal diet.

Some bland foods that may be given as the child improves are: canned applesauce, fresh banana, rice cereal or rice, noodles, white dry toast, white boiled or baked potato without butter or margarine, cooked carrots, lean meats, and bland soups.

If at any time your child gets worse instead of better, please notify your pediatrician.

ALICE MARSH, M.D.
Kansas City, Kansas

My baby's bowel movements are very loose and have a strong odor. Does this indicate that something is wrong?

If the child is alert, contented, free of fever, not vomiting, voiding well, and vigorous, he or she may just have a tendency toward loose stools. If you are in doubt, call your doctor.

AVRUM L. KATCHER, M.D., F.A.A.P.
Flemington, New Jersey

My infant strained a great deal while having a bowel movement, and the stool was hard and had blood on it. What does this mean?

Most infants who strain a great deal are usually slightly constipated; this results in stools that are harder than usual. When these stools are passed, they distend the tissue around the anal opening, producing small tears or fissures that usually bleed and coat the stool with streaks of blood. Occasionally, these fissures can easily be seen with careful observation. This problem is easily corrected by adding more fluids or fruit to the diet, and also by applying Bacitracin around the anal opening for three or four days after each bowel movement. Only rarely is the short-term use of laxatives required. Once the stools are softer, the problem is usually resolved.

Should bleeding become more severe and persistent, your physician should be notified immediately to rule out any potentially serious problem.

GILBERT A. NORWOOD, M.D.
Beverly, Massachusetts

My toddler's rectal area is still very itchy and raw even though he is taking medication for pinworms. Can I use a cortisone cream?

No. If your child is still itching after he has taken a full course of treatment for pinworms infection, other causes of anal itching should be considered. The itching could be due to coarse or wet undergarments or to an anal fissure, which is a small crack in the skin in the anal area, or to local inflammation. Clean the anal area with mild soap and keep it dry. Your child should see his pediatrician for an examination.

INDIRA B. REDDY, M.D.
Dayton, Ohio

CHAPTER 8

Convulsions

My infant just had an episode in which his arms and legs twitched a lot and then stopped. Was that a convulsion?

Twitching may or may not be a convulsion, depending on the age of your child, the circumstances under which the twitching occurred, and the nature of the twitching movements. Newborns and young infants are commonly jittery and react to stimulation with a startle or tremulous movements. Sometimes these may occur spontaneously. When young infants are asleep, there may be twitching movements of the face, arms, or legs as part of the active phase of sleep, which is similar to the dream phase of sleep that occurs in adults. Typically, these tremulous or twitching movements are of very brief duration, lasting only a few seconds, and are easily recognized. Convulsive movements, on the other hand, are generally more violent than twitches and last for a longer period of time. Frequently, the child will be awake when the convulsion begins and will then lose consciousness. Stool or urine may be passed during the episode, and once the convulsion has ceased the child is generally sleepy and difficult to arouse. To determine whether a seizure actually has occurred, you should take your child to see a doctor, who will examine him and take a detailed history. You should do this as soon as possible after the episode. Laboratory tests and an electroencephalogram may be required to help determine whether a convulsion has really occurred. The more details you remember about the episode, the easier it will be for your doctor to answer your question.

PHILIP MARKOWITZ, M.D.
Richmond, Virginia

My infant had a convulsion from a fever last month. Will she always have convulsions with fevers? Is this a form of epilepsy?

The answer to your question depends on whether your child had a febrile convulsion or a convulsion with fever. Febrile convulsions or fits are common in childhood, occurring in approximately 3 percent of all children. They are generally not a cause for concern, as the vast majority of children who have them will outgrow them and not develop epilepsy. Frequently, other members of the family also experienced febrile seizures as children. These seizures generally are of short duration, lasting only a few seconds or minutes, and involve both sides of the body equally. They typically begin between six months and three years of age and generally resolve themselves by age six. Most children will experience only one or two seizures, although some will have more.

Convulsions with fever, on the other hand, are epileptic fits that are brought on by fever and occur in a child with a predisposition to epilepsy. They are less common than febrile convulsions and they frequently occur without fever as well. Children with this condition are considered to have epilepsy and may continue to have convulsions for the rest of their lives.

Your doctor is in the best position to determine which of these conditions your child has. He or she will also decide whether medication is necessary.

PHILIP MARKOWITZ, M.D.
Richmond, Virginia

My older child had convulsions with high fevers. Is there any chance that my newborn will have them, too?

Yes, that certainly is possible. When considering convulsions or seizure disorders, it's known that the febrile kind of convulsion is the most common of all, occurring as it does in about 2 percent to 5 percent of children under five years of age. The peak age of occurrence is usually between one and two years of age.

We also know that in one out of every five cases of febrile seizures, there is a history of one or more members of the immediate family having had febrile seizures early in life. Therefore, it can be said with some degree of certainty that a subsequent child in a family where one child has had febrile seizures has a higher risk than the population at large of also having febrile seizures.

The risk, though small, warrants that attention be given to the subsequent child each time he or she has a febrile illness so as to attempt to forestall the occurrence of a convulsion. Your pediatrician can help greatly with the management of prevention in each individual case.

JOSEPH ZANGA, M.D.
Richmond, Virginia

Is there any medication to prevent convulsions?

There are many medications that are used to prevent convulsions. Each of these has a specific place, and their selection, combination, dosage, and dosage schedule needs to be very much individualized for the child and for the type of seizure. These decisions are best left to an experienced pediatrician, most often with the assistance of a pediatric neurologist.

As a point of general information, however, the two most commonly used drugs for convulsions in children are Phenobarbital and Dilantin. Of the two, Phenobarbital is the older and probably still the more widely used. When used as directed for the right kind of seizure, both of these drugs are safe and very effective.

One thing that should be realized is that the prevention of convulsions is not something that you can do at home at the time you recognize signs in your child that a convulsion might be coming on. Most of these drugs, given by mouth, require multiple doses and often for several days there is a sufficient amount of drug circulating in the child's blood to prevent a seizure. Because seizures are often easier to prevent than they are to stop, it's important that the medicine prescribed be given exactly as directed.

JOSEPH ZANGA, M.D.
Richmond, Virginia

CHAPTER 9

Diapers

My baby cries after wetting his diaper. What does this mean?

As a general rule, this means nothing more than that your child has a soggy piece of cloth or paper wrapped around him that is making him feel uncomfortable. On the other hand, if this does seem to be a fairly frequent occurrence, and if there is no other cause for irritation such as an inflamed diaper rash, the baby should be kept exposed for a short while to see whether or not he seems to be having difficulty in actually passing urine. That might indicate an infection or obstruction to the urinary flow, and should be reported to your pediatrician promptly.

SPENCER G. WEIG, M.D.
Fall River, Massachusetts

Can my baby get a bladder infection from wearing a dirty diaper too long?

Most likely, yes, especially if your baby is a girl. It is difficult for male babies to get bladder infections. A dirty diaper or even a wet diaper may result in some irritation to the end of the penis and may cause some scarring and closure of the opening of the urethra. This is particularly evident in circumcised infants. However, it is difficult for organisms to travel up the male baby's rather long, tortuous urethra and cause a bladder infection. In the female, however, where the urethra is relatively short, straight, and open to the vulva, it is quite possible to get a bladder infection from exposure to a dirty diaper.

In addition to infections, there is the problem of diaper rashes resulting from the baby's body being next to a dirty diaper for a long time. It is strongly recommended that infants who are susceptible to diaper rash have their diapers changed frequently. A drawback of plastic pants or paper diapers covered by plastic is that it is difficult to perceive when the baby has wet or dirtied the diaper. Parents should be aware of the sensitivity of the baby's skin and the possibility of urinary tract infections due to dirty diapers. Also, if there is an "ammonia" smell when changing the wet diaper, a simple treatment prescribed by your doctor can cure this condition.

RICHARD A. GUTHRIE, M.D.
Wichita, Kansas

My newborn's outer vaginal area is reddened. What should I do?

The skin of the newborn's outer vaginal area is very sensitive and may be easily irritated by urine, stool, chemicals, paper diapers, soaps, detergents, or local infections. Initial treatment would involve placing the baby in an open diaper in front of a sunny window. When the diaper is closed for the night, a soothing cream such as zinc oxide, A&D ointment, Desitin, or Balmex should help ease the discomfort of the irritation. If the redness persists, it may help to avoid all soaps, baby wipers, and heavily perfumed paper diapers. If the redness has not improved after several days, an infection may be the cause and a physician should be consulted.

ALAN R. RUSHTON, M.D., Ph.D.
Flemington, New Jersey

What causes a diaper rash? What should I do for it?

Diaper rash is caused by ammonia irritation (caused by bacteria from the stool interacting with the urine after it is passed), fungal infection of the skin (aggravated by wet diapers, especially if they are covered by air-tight plastic or rubber pants), or by food sensitivity. Occasionally, bacterial infections of the skin or, very rarely, a virus can be the cause. Treatment should be appropriate to the cause. Changing wet diapers promptly can often both prevent and cure diaper rash.

MERRITT B. LOW, M.D., F.A.A.P.
Ashfield, Massachusetts

My baby's diapers have an ammonia-like odor. Is this normal?

Yes, it is normal for a baby's diaper to have ammonia-like odor because the normal composition of urine contains trace amounts of ammonia. In some cases, for example, when the baby's metabolic status is acidotic, the ammonia content in the urine is much higher, and you will smell a heavy ammonia odor.

TSUN-HSIN LIN, M.D.
Akron, Ohio

How can I tell if my baby has a bladder infection?

A baby or toddler with a bladder or urinary tract infection may develop a fever without obvious reason. Sometimes he or she will have a poor appetite, vomit, and seem to have abdominal pain. The baby may cry because of pain when passing urine, and may urinate more often than usual. Sometimes the baby will just be listless and fail to gain weight normally. The urine may be cloudy or pink or may have an unusual odor. On the other hand, many bladder infections in infants are completely silent and produce no symptoms or signs. This is one of the reasons your doctor examines a urine sample during your baby's periodic checkups. Because of the shortness of their urethras (the tube carrying the urine from the bladder to the exterior of the body), girls are more susceptible to bladder infections than are boys.

JEAN F. KENNY, M.D.
Greenville, North Carolina

My child's diaper has a pink stain on it. Is there something wrong?

The pink stain is probably from altered urine color. Foods like beets, blackberries, and vegetable dyes used in food color, candy, and soft drinks can give a pink or red color to the urine. Certain laxatives containing phenolphthalein can also color the urine pink or red. Some drugs can give a pink, red, or orange-red color to urine. The presence of blood or muscle pigment due to several causes could color the urine pink, red, or brown. Metabolic disorders involving blood pigment metabolism could also color the urine pink or red. When you see a pink stain on a diaper, try to collect a urine specimen. Keep track of the baby's diet and medications, and bring the baby to your physician for a urine test and physical examination.

INDIRA B. REDDY, M.D.
Dayton, Ohio

My newborn has a brown vaginal discharge. Should I be concerned?

No, you should not be concerned. Even though a brown vaginal discharge may seem unlikely in a newborn girl, and quite understandably it has prompted your question, it is a normal, benign event. The explanation for this is as follows:

While your daughter was in the womb, she received from you the different substances that your body usually makes. Among these are the sex hormones, which have the capacity to stimulate the sex organs of a normal newborn. One of the things that may result from this stimulation in a newborn girl is a vaginal discharge. The discharge may be white or, if mixed with some blood, brown. And, occasionally, a certain amount of vaginal bleeding may occur as in a menstrual period. The amount of blood lost is so small that it causes no anemia or any other problems.

The vaginal discharge, as well as swelling of the breasts or genital organs that may accompany it, represents a limited reaction that will disappear completely by the tenth day of life, because by that time your daughter will have eliminated from her body all the sex hormones that she initially received. The benign episode will have no recurrences or untoward effects.

MARY C. PEREZ, M.D.
Oklahoma City, Oklahoma

CHAPTER 10

Ears and Hearing

Is an ear infection contagious?

An ear infection resulting in a blocked ear with fluid in the middle ear is an isolated infection and is not contagious. If, however, the infection is a complication of a respiratory infection, then it is communicable and contagious.

JAMES A. O'SHEA, M.D., P.C., F.A.A.P., F.S.C.E.
Lawrence, Massachusetts

My child just finished taking medicine for ten days for an ear infection and is now complaining of ear pain again. Does this mean the medicine didn't work?

Acute ear infection (otitis media) is one of the most common infectious diseases of childhood. Three different studies in the United States have shown that 76 percent to 95 percent of all children will have at least one ear infection, and that 20 percent to 26 percent of all children will have six or more ear infections by six years of age.

Most ear infections are caused by bacteria, and usually ten days of an appropriate antibiotic will cure the infection. However, 10 percent to 15 percent of young children will have infections that recur after ten days of an antibiotic or soon after stopping the medicine. There are three major causes for this failure of treatment. First and most commonly, the medicine was not given in the appropriate dosage or for the time period prescribed. It is no secret that it is extremely difficult to assure that a young child receives three or four doses of medicine for ten full days. Children often mount impressive resistance to taking medicine despite the wiles used. In addition, misunderstood directions, busy schedules with children at day-care centers or school, and old-fashioned forgetfulness often contribute to inadequate treatment. Second, it is possible that your child's ear infection is caused by an organism not controlled and killed by the antibiotic given. Some infections may be caused by viruses or germs not affected by antibiotics. More probably, the culprit is a familiar bacterium, but one that has become an increasing problem in recent years. Third, there are numerous factors in some children that contribute to the development of ear infections and that make cure more difficult. Such factors include inadequate drainage from the Eustachian tube, from the middle ear to the back of the throat; scarring from previous ear infections; allergic disorders; enlarged adenoids, and, possibly, abnormal infection-fighting mechanisms (immunity). It is well known that some children are "otitis-prone," with frequent infections that tend to persist. It is of some comfort to parents to know that this condition generally improves as the child gets older.

To answer the specific question, any child complaining of ear pain deserves a medical examination. There are other causes of this complaint, such as a toothache, but if your child has had a recent ear infection and now again has symptoms, chances are the ear pain signals a persistence of the infection. Again, remember that this will happen in 10 percent to 15 percent of young children who have had an ear infection. It is exactly for this reason that many pediatricians recommend an "ear-check" visit seven to fourteen days after diagnosing an ear infection to look for resolution of the signs of infection. If a persistent ear infection is noted in your child on the repeat examination, the physician should ask you how thoroughly the previously prescribed medicine was given. This is important information, and honesty on your part is always best. Most doctors will opt for one of three choices: continuing the same antibiotic for a longer period and checking for healing before discontinuing it; switching to a different antibiotic, thinking that perhaps the responsible germ was not effectively killed by the previous antibiotic; or a drainage procedure, whereby a small slit is made in the eardrum, allowing any accumulated pus to drain. In some cases, this drainage procedure is followed by placement of small tubes through the eardrum to allow for long-term drainage. Chronic ear infections can lead to persistent hearing defects, so it is especially important to work closely with your child's doctor until the ear infection is completely cured.

JANET ENDRESS SQUIRES, M.D.
Fort Worth, Texas

My toddler seems to have trouble hearing. Could that be caused by an ear infection?

Toddlers frequently have ear infections that cause a temporary decrease in hearing. In fact, about half of normal children have at least one ear infection in the first two years of life. Even for the health practitioner, diagnosing ear infections is often difficult because of the presence of earwax, the small size of the ear canal in a young child, and the frequent irritability of a child ill from any cause.

Parents should always have children suspected of a hearing loss evaluated thoroughly, since apparent hearing problems in children are also often due to conditions other than ear infections. These other situations include excessive earwax, earlier injuries to or infections of the brain, and even an unwillingness on the part of the child to communicate.

JOHN S. O'SHEA, M.D.
Providence, Rhode Island

My toddler has tubes in his ears, and one just fell out. Should it be replaced?

The paracentesis tubes were placed in your child's ears to permit the resolution of fluid in the middle ear cavities. This was felt necessary to improve his hearing and to prevent recurrent ear infection (otitis media). These tubes may remain in place for a variable period of time and do fall out spontaneously. (If they do not fall out in one to two years, an ear, nose, and throat specialist should remove them.)

The fact that one of your child's tubes fell out is not necessarily a cause for concern. If examination by your pediatrician or ear, nose, and throat specialist reveals normal movement of the eardrum, normal hearing, and the absence of infection, the tube need not be replaced. Your child should have periodic examinations, with attention to these conditions. If there are recurrent problems of reaccumulation of fluid or ear infections (which do not respond to antibiotic treatment), the tube will probably need to be replaced.

MELVYN B. LEVINE, M.D.
Medford, Massachusetts

I noticed a small amount of blood on the sheet and inside my infant's ear when I took her out of the crib. Is this bad?

The first thing you should do is make sure this is not just earwax. Earwax can be very dark brown at times and can also be soft enough to come out of the ear in a good-sized lump. If what you think is dried blood feels slimy or greasy and is yellowish brown in color, it is probably earwax. Blood is reddish brown; when it dries it is crumbly and flaky.

If it is dried blood in your child's ear, look for a scratch or cut on the outside of the ear. Blood can drip into the ear canal from the outer ear. A small scratch on the outer ear would be treated like any other scratch. Blood from inside the ear can also be from a scratch within the ear. Never put anything inside your baby's ear canal. If the blood is coming from the ear, your pediatrician will have to look inside the ear canal to inspect it and the eardrum to make sure they are all right. The pediatrician needs an otoscope (an instrument for examining inside the ear) to do this.

ELIZABETH M. SPECHT, M.D.
Akron, Ohio

My toddler has had many ear infections. Will he have fewer infections as he grows older?

The course of ear infections in any particular child is difficult to predict. Generally, as children grow older, ear infections become less frequent.

Ear infections are generally the result of obstruction of the Eustachian tubes, the small passageways that connect the middle ear with the back of the nose and throat. When these tubes are obstructed, fluid collects in the middle ear and eventually becomes infected. The obstruction may be the result of a cold, allergy, or other factors. However, as a child grows older, the Eustachian tubes grow in size and they are less likely to become obstructed. The frequency of ear infections, regardless of cause, is markedly reduced in most children by the time they reach their sixth birthday.

MARK D. WIDOME, M.D.
Hershey, Pennsylvania

Can an ear infection cause permanent damage?

Ear infections are a common problem in young infants and children. Parents are frequently concerned about the possibility of permanent damage to the ear or permanent hearing loss. However, this almost never happens with an ordinary ear infection. Indeed, many children have repeated ear infections throughout their childhood years and as older children and adults have no detectable abnormalities in either the appearance of the eardrum or their ability to hear. The biggest problem with an ear infection is the amount of discomfort that it causes and the necessity to take medication. Most ear infections heal quickly, but many children have fluid remaining in the middle ear for a variable length of time, often for several months. For young infants, this can impair the hearing and if this is unrecognized, many experts in the field worry about later language development. Older children with fluid in the ear, a condition called serous otitis media, are usually able to recognize their hearing loss and convey this to their parents and teachers so that these adults can speak louder to them or speak in a way that ensures that the child will hear.

Parents do not need to worry about permanent ear damage or permanent hearing loss if their child has an ear infection. However, they do need to recognize that during the actual episode of an ear infection and often for several weeks thereafter, their child may have a temporary, mild hearing loss. For this condition, they should adjust their speech to ensure that the child hears adequately.

PAUL C. YOUNG, M.D.
Burlington, Vermont

I have to keep repeating myself to my toddler. Is he hard of hearing? He seemed fine a month ago.

Everyone wonders at times whether a child is not hearing—or just not listening. The answer *may* be found by visiting the child's doctor. Sometimes by merely looking into the ear canal, a wax or ear infection can be discovered that could affect hearing. Or, the doctor might be able to see how the eardrum moves (and thus conducts hearing) by means of a little puff of air or with an instrument called a tympanometer. There are also more elaborate ways to find out if a child has a hearing loss, and what part of the hearing pathway might be involved. Many of these problems are resolved spontaneously, some require medical treatment, and a few require surgery. Occasionally, a child needs therapy with people trained in teaching the deaf. In any case, a visit to your child's doctor is the first necessary and important step. A child learns what he hears. If he hears poorly, he is already a few steps behind.

ROBERT EASTON, M.D.
Peoria, Illinois

What can I use to get rid of the water in my toddler's ears after she swims?

Most of the water will run out of the ear if the child's head is tilted down. The corner of a small towel will frequently absorb most of the fluid if it is inserted into the external ear. As a last resort, if the child jumps up and down with the head tilted to the side, trapped water can be dislodged.

Cerumen (earwax) in the ear canal may expand when exposed to water. To avoid complications, it is important that no rigid object, such as a Q-tip, should ever be inserted into the ear canal.

MILTON GRAUB, M.D.
Philadelphia, Pennsylvania

My toddler just stuck a bead in her ear. How can I get it out?

A toddler with a bead in her ear should visit the doctor within a day or two to have the eardrum examined for infection and to have the bead removed.

Often, children troubled by ear pain will place objects in their ears. Attempting to remove the bead at home usually causes it to be pushed further inside the ear, where, if left in place, it will cause swelling and irritation.

GRETCHEN FRAUENBERGER, M.D., F.A.A.P.
Needham, Massachusetts

My infant pulls at his ear and sometimes rolls his head from side to side. Could he have an ear infection?

He could have, but there are several points in the question that indicate that this behavior is more habitual or ritualistic. The question, as posed, suggests that this behavior has been going on for some time and is recurring. Children with acute ear infections most often have fever, are irritable, and frequently have a preceding cold. Head rolling and ear pulling are common manifestations of otherwise healthy children who develop ritualistic mannerisms when tired, sleepy, or anxious. This type of behavior is entirely normal and is akin to the need for the security blanket or the thumb-sucking and eye-rubbing activities of many children. If this behavior precedes sleep or occurs when he is obviously tired, then this is most certainly a ritualistic mannerism and should be ignored. You should, however, consult your pediatrician to be certain of the diagnosis.

C. WARREN DERRICK JR., M.D.
Columbia, South Carolina

Can constant loud noises or music damage my baby's hearing?

Yes, constant loud noises and music can damage a baby's hearing. A baby's hearing is very well developed and very acute in the early months of life; it is probably best developed then. There is now a growing body of evidence that constant exposure to loud music results in damage to the hearing of adolescents and that constant loud noises, including industrial noises, can result in damage to the hearing of adults as well. Industry has recognized its liability in this regard and now provides ear covers for individuals exposed to loud noises.

We have not recognized the danger of loud noises to newborn infants, however. The problem remains as great, and perhaps even greater, because their hearing is more acute and sensitive than that of older individuals. Loud noises and loud music are, therefore, discouraged for babies. Soft music is beneficial and soothing to the baby, as it is to other individuals.

RICHARD A. GUTHRIE, M.D.
Wichita, Kansas

What is swimmer's ear? How can I prevent my toddler from getting it?

Swimmer's ear, the lay term for external otitis, is caused by an accumulation of water and bacteria in the inside of the ear canal. This sets up an area of infection. It generally occurs after a child has been swimming and does not get enough water out of the ears. By using the corner of a towel to absorb excess water and by tilting the child's head to one side to drain out any water from the ear, you can help prevent your child from getting an ear infection. Swimmer's ear is generally manifested by a fair amount of pain in the ear and by extreme soreness in the external area of the ear when it is touched. Children with this condition or those who are suspected of having it should see their doctor.

JEROME E. KWAKO, M.D.
Duluth, Minnesota

Is it harmful if my toddler goes swimming without earplugs?

Earplugs while swimming are not necessary for a healthy child under two years of age as long as the child has no concurrent disease worse than a mild cold.

Opinions vary as to whether children with plastic tubes in the eardrums, placed for chronic ear infections, should swim at all. If these children do swim, they should wear earplugs. Usually the physician who has placed the tubes has custom-made earplugs, which work much better than the over-the-counter products.

V. WAYNE LOWE, M.D.
Madisonville, Kentucky

Can my toddler go swimming if he has an ear infection?

There are two types of ear infections: otitis externa, an infection of the external ear; and otitis media, an infection of the middle ear. Otitis externa may be caused by excessive swimming and is then referred to as "swimmer's ear." This develops when excessive moisture in the ear canal interferes with the protective function of the earwax. An immoderate amount of moisture also encourages the growth of many organisms.

If your child has otitis externa, it is better for him to avoid swimming. If your child has otitis media, he would probably have pain, fever, and loss of hearing. He should be on medication for pain and temperature and should have bed rest. Swimming and other forms of exercise must be avoided.

KANIKA CHAUDHURI, M.D.
Nashville, Tennessee

My children were fooling around, and a straw was pushed into one child's ear. He's crying and holding his ear now. Could the straw have punctured anything?

Yes. The straw could have punctured the eardrum. The eardrum was probably not ruptured if there is no bleeding from the ear. Although it is not an emergency, your child's ear should be examined by a physician to find out whether or not the eardrum is punctured.

If the eardrum is punctured, it will probably heal without requiring surgical repair. Even more important than a hole in the eardrum are the possibilities that one or more of the middle ear bones (ossicles) could be damaged, or that the inner ear could be damaged. Therefore, if your doctor says that your child's eardrum is not punctured, you should make sure that the child has no difficulty hearing. If he complains of or seems to have difficulty in hearing, you should request that your child have a hearing test. You should not be told that he is too young to have a hearing test—all children can have their hearing tested.

If there is a hole in the eardrum that does not heal, or if the middle ear bones are damaged, the hole can be closed and the hearing can be restored by means of surgery. Although a punctured eardrum itself is not a serious emergency, damage to the inner ear is. If your child has imbalance or dizziness soon after sustaining an ear injury, take him to a doctor immediately.

KENNETH GRUNDFAST, M.D.
Washington, D.C.

My toddler's ear is draining a light, yellow-colored fluid. Is this serious? What should I do?

The conservative and safe approach in dealing with drainage from a child's ear is to view it as abnormal. It may not always be abnormal, but this approach will cause a parent to have the ear checked, thereby possibly preventing later complications.

Sometimes the parents mistake earwax for ear drainage. Earwax is normal and is really of no concern unless it becomes impacted. Sometimes an adult will observe ear drainage shortly after a bath. Some of the warm water may have mixed with the wax and is draining out of the ear. This is not really a problem, but parents should try to keep water out of a child's ear. Moisture in the external ear canal can lead to ear problems, such as swimmer's ear.

A draining ear can be the sign of a number of problems. The most common is an infection of the outer ear. This can be caused by bacteria or fungus and sometimes a combination of organisms. Sometimes children pour liquids into their ears. Obviously, this is uncommon in children younger than one year of age, but it becomes more common in children in the one- to two-year age group. There is also the possibility that an insect may have gotten into the ear, causing some sort of irritation that could produce drainage. Or the child could have placed something in his or her ear; this, too, could cause an irritation. Another consideration is that the child may have had a middle ear infection that caused rupture of the eardrums and drainage of fluid. A number of relatively serious problems, such as trauma, may also show up as ear drainage.

The first step for the parent who notices ear drainage is to have the ear examined by the family physician or pediatrician.

DON C. VAN DYKE, M.D.
Atlantic City, New Jersey

My baby-sitter's son has an ear infection. Is there any danger to my newborn?

The usual germs that cause ear infections in young children are generally not a problem for the newborn. The infection in question is in the middle ear, which is essentially a closed space. The germ in the ear may well be in the nose and throat of the affected child. It would seem prudent to limit exposure of the newborn to any child with a cough or runny nose, at least in the early stages of the illness. It would likewise be inadvisable to cloister a newborn from all children, since the germs may be carried by the completely asymptomatic child. The risk of infection to the newborn is really small.

V. F. BURRY, M.D.
Kansas City, Missouri

How can I tell for sure that my infant hears?

You can usually tell if your infant can hear by the type of responses you get from your baby when various sounds are made. The infant's response can be anything from eye movement to a head turn to a startle. As you spend more time with your baby, you will get to know his or her responses to certain stimuli and in this way determine if your baby hears. Short of sophisticated testing, it is very difficult to tell for sure if a baby hears when he or she leaves the newborn nursery. Testing is not indicated unless the baby falls into a high risk group, that is, if the baby has jaundice, infection, anoxia, or birth defects; was premature; was born to a mother who used drugs; or if there is a family history of deafness. Be assured that, with a little experience, you will be able to tell whether your infant is hearing the normal sounds around the house, especially your own soft, loving voice.

ROBERT FOMALONT, M.D.
Princeton, New Jersey

Why does my child get earaches? How can I ease the pain for him?

Earaches are usually the result of infections in the middle ear in the cavity behind the eardrum. When a child has a cold, congestion prevents the normal functioning of the Eustachian tube (the canal leading from the back of the throat to the middle ear) and allows fluid to accumulate. This, plus the effects of infection from bacteria that may be present, creates fluid pressure in the middle ear. The pressure distends the eardrum, which is very sensitive to painful stimuli, and an earache develops. It appears that some children are particularly prone to ear infections and will repeatedly suffer such episodes, especially during the winter and spring. Allergic children may also be susceptible to middle ear infections. Complaints or signs of ear pain, such as pulling at the ears, are evidence that an ear infection may be present.

If the earache is due to an ear infection, it is best treated by proper diagnosis and therapy, usually with antibiotics. Some physicians will attempt to reduce swelling in the throat with a decongestant. Until the antibiotic has had an opportunity to act, ear pain can be eased with a mild analgesic such as aspirin or acetaminophen. In addition, a number of commercial products are available as ear drops. Be sure that the ear is not draining before instilling any solutions into the ear canal. Warmed vegetable oil is probably as effective as commercial preparations for this purpose.

LLOYD C. OLSON, M.D.
Kansas City, Missouri

My toddler is screaming and holding his ear. Could this mean he has an earache?

This is the classic picture of an earache, especially if there is a cold or fever present and if it persists for an hour or more despite soothing and distraction.

MERRITT B. LOW, M.D., F.A.A.P.
Ashfield, Massachusetts

What is ear lavage? Can it be done routinely to keep the wax out of my child's ears?

Ear lavage is the irrigation of hardened or impacted earwax in the external ear canal. This requires flushing the canal with a stream of water, warmed slightly to ensure comfort. This is usually accomplished with a large ear syringe, which is a plunge device with a blunted point. It can also be done with a Water Pic, directing a stream of water into the canal. There are also chemical agents that may soften the wax in the ear canal prior to lavage. These should be used only on advice from your doctor. It should be mentioned that, although this lavage can be done routinely to keep the ear canals clear, in most cases the normally secreted wax is flushed automatically during the course of bathing. Ear lavage is used routinely only in those cases where the wax is very hard, dry, and impacted, and unusually resistant to nature's way of cleaning.

ROBERT FOMALONT, M.D.
Princeton, New Jersey

How soon can I get my infant's ears pierced?

There is no special age for piercing an infant's ears, so the answer would be anytime during infancy.

However, this procedure is often done around the third month. The physician or nurse marks that area of the earlobe most acceptable to the mother, and, using a sterile ear-piercing instrument with sterile gold-plated studs, does the job quickly.

Avoid cheaply made earrings or those of small design, which can become embedded in the earlobe. When there is chronic inflammation or drainage, the earring should be removed.

E. JAMES ANDERSON, M.D., F.A.A.P.
Metairie, Louisiana

CHAPTER 11

Eyes

My child keeps rubbing her eyes, and I have noticed that the whites of her eyes are red. How long will it take before her eyes are clear again?

Rubbing the eyes is common in children. Many children rub their eyes when they are tired or sleepy. If a child has hay fever or allergies, he or she will have a runny and stuffy nose, postnasal drip and cough, and itchy eyes, which cause the child to rub them. The solution to this problem is best directed at the allergies, not the eyes.

Any irritant that comes in contact with the eye can produce redness and reflex-rubbing. This happens after swimming, from dust or airborne chemical pollutants, or from irritants such as soap suds that get directly into the eye. The rubbing itself causes no harm and therefore should not be forbidden.

When the irritant is removed, the redness and the urge to rub should disappear spontaneously within several hours. If irritation persists, then some other explanation should be sought.

JOSEPH H. CALHOUN, M.D.
Philadelphia, Pennsylvania

I am giving my toddler an ointment for an eye infection, but the infection still doesn't seem any better. What is the correct way to put the ointment in her eye?

To place an ointment correctly in an eye, several procedures should be performed. First, place the toddler comfortably on her back. Attract her attention so that the eyes roll up, allowing more of the white of the eye to show. Place a finger on the toddler's lower lid and gently pull the lid down, slightly everting it. A small cul-de-sac or pouch on the inner area of the lid will be created by this maneuver. In this pouch, a small amount of ointment should be placed. It is important to remember that if an eye infection is not improving with an ointment, it may be due to an inadequate ointment rather than improper placement.

LEONARD B. NELSON, M.D.
Philadelphia, Pennsylvania

What is the easiest way to remove an eyelash from my toddler's eye?

Take a piece of cotton that has been soaked in either cold or warm water and draw it over the closed eyelid several times with a slight downward and inward movement. If this does not work, do not worry—the eyelash will soon find its way to the side of the eye nearest the nose.

MARY C. BUCHANAN, M.D.
Hicksville, New York

My toddler gets styes in the corner of her eyes. Are styes contagious?

A stye is a localized infection of one of the many glands contained in the eyelids. Most toddlers have germs (bacteria) that are continually present around their lids as well as on other areas of the body. Most of the time these germs cause no harm. Occasionally one of them will cause an infection of a gland in the lid. Children who rub their eyes frequently seem to get styes more frequently. Even though styes are not usually spread to other people, it is important to care for them as you would any other infection. Wash your hands after handling the child and use separate, clean washcloths to keep the area around the eye clean. If it seems to be getting worse, consult your pediatrician. Careful treatment may present further styes from developing.

ROBISON D. HARLEY, M.D.
Philadelphia, Pennsylvania

How can I care for a stye, and how long will it take for it to clear up?

The most effective therapy for a stye is the frequent application of warm, moist compresses. This will help decrease the swelling and promote drainage of the pus from within the stye. To make a warm compress, take a clean washcloth and soak it in warm water. Place it on the affected area until it begins to cool. This should be done approximately four times a day. If the stye is not getting better after several days, the child should be taken to your pediatrician who may prescribe an antibiotic ointment or drop. The stye will usually clear up within several weeks. However, it may leave a small, hard lump that may take several months to resolve completely.

DOUGLAS A. FREELEY, M.D.
Philadelphia, Pennsylvania

While I was changing my baby's diaper, he urinated. Some urine hit him in the eye. Will this hurt his eye?

Urine in the eye acts as a mild irritant, similar in effect to soap in the eyes. The protective blinking or lid-closing reflex will allow only a few drops of urine to come in contact with the eyeball itself. A mild irritant will have two effects on the eyeball: It will cause the blood vessels in the white part of the eye to be more prominent, creating a "pink eye," and the irritant urine will cause reflex tearing, which dilutes and washes the urine away. The eye may remain red and tear for several minutes but will gradually return to normal appearance. No treatment is necessary.

JOSEPH H. CALHOUN, M.D.
Philadelphia, Pennsylvania

Will my baby's eyes become more sensitive to light as he grows older?

Some babies' eyes are more intolerant of light for no known reason. The light sensitivity may remain unchanged or may increase or decrease with time. However, light sensitivity in a baby may indicate an eye problem, occasionally of a serious nature. Therefore, this condition should be brought to the pediatrician's attention early.

LEONARD B. NELSON, M.D.
Philadelphia, Pennsylvania

I do not think my toddler sees well. Is she too young to have her eyes tested?

Estimating how well a child can see can be done from birth. The older a child gets, the easier it becomes to determine the level of his or her vision. Some indications that your child might not be seeing well are: (a) jerky movements of the eyes; (b) eyes that cross or turn out; (c) inability by the age of three months to hold a gaze on the mother's face for short periods; (d) holding all objects right to the face to see them; (e) frequent bumping into objects; or (f) a history in the family of eye diseases that occur early in life.

Any of these things should alert you to have your child, no matter what the age, checked by your pediatrician.

DOUGLAS A. FREELEY, M.D.
Philadelphia, Pennsylvania

My toddler has yellowish drainage accumulating in the corners of his eyes. What should I do?

Yellowish drainage in the corners of the eyes of a toddler may represent accumulation of the secretions from the glands of the eyelids. However, if this drainage is associated with bloodshot or pink eyes, it may indicate an inflammation of the eyes (conjunctivitis). The pediatrician should be consulted in order to make the diagnosis. If an eye infection is present, then the use of an antibiotic eye drop or ointment will be necessary.

LEONARD B. NELSON, M.D.
Philadelphia, Pennsylvania

I've heard that oxygen can permanently damage a baby's eyes. I'm very worried while my baby is in an oxygen tent because of pneumonia. Will she be all right?

Many babies, including those who are premature or who weigh less than five pounds at birth, may receive oxygen shortly after birth. These children can develop an eye disease called retinopathy of prematurity, which can severely affect vision. Babies born at full term and who weigh more than five pounds have a minimal risk of damage to their eyes from oxygen. Once any infant, whether premature or of low birth weight, reaches approximately four months of age, the risk of oxygen damage to the eye diminishes. If your child is at risk of having damage done to her eyes, your pediatrician will have your child's eyes examined prior to her leaving the hospital.

ROBISON D. HARLEY, M.D.
Philadelphia, Pennsylvania

Is conjunctivitis contagious? For how long?

Conjunctivitis is present when the whites of the eyes become bloodshot or pink. It may be associated with itching and a watery or pus-like discharge. Conjunctivitis can be highly contagious. Parents should wash their hands thoroughly after caring for their child, as the germs can be passed from person to person. Since the germs can be found in the eyes for as long as fourteen days, the child should be considered infectious during this period.

LEONARD B. NELSON, M.D.
Philadelphia, Pennsylvania

My toddler's right eye turns inward now and then, especially when he is tired. Should I be concerned?

A child's eyes should always be straight. If his eyes are crossed (or turned out), he may have an eye disease or may develop a lazy eye, that is, an eye that does not see well. Many children seem to have eyes that cross because the bridge of their nose is flat and wide. The eyes of many tiny infants wander. However, all children whose eyes do not seem straight should be checked by their pediatricians.

DOUGLAS A. FREELEY, M.D.
Philadelphia, Pennsylvania

CHAPTER 12

Feeding

When can I start my infant on regular milk? Must I introduce it slowly? Should it be whole milk or skim milk?

For the best in nutrition and other benefits, babies should breast-feed for their first year, if possible, and have solid foods started after they are four to six months old. If breast milk is not available, the second best milk is infant formula with iron. Formula has a built-in vitamin and mineral supply along with protein, unsaturated fats, and other essential nutrients. About one can (twenty-six to thirty-two ounces) every twenty-four hours will supply the infant with most of the nutrients needed during the first year. Whole and skim milk lack iron and are not as easily digested as breast milk or formula, so they are not suitable for infants younger than one year of age. If your infant is twelve or more months old, you can begin feeding whole milk in a cup or glass. This can be started gradually, one or two times each day. Unless your family has a strong history of allergy, whole milk is usually adequate. Getting a child used to a cup will make it easier to skip bottles altogether.

Fats are needed by the infant for development of the nervous system. So don't be in a hurry to give skim or low-fat milk during the first two years, while growth of the brain, spinal cord, and nerves is continuing. During the second year, your baby could drink about sixteen to twenty-four ounces of whole milk each day by cup. Your toddler will have an appetite for solid foods and a decreased chance of developing cavities in the front incisor teeth from prolonged bottle-feeding.

BETTY OSEID, M.D.
New Orleans, Louisiana

My toddler is putting on a lot of weight. Should I put him on skim milk?

Children grow very rapidly in the first two years of life. The average baby doubles his or her birth weight by four months of age and triples the birth weight by twelve months. Adequate nutrition is extremely important during these growing phases if normal development is to occur. A proper balance of carbohydrate, fat, and protein is just as important as the total amount of food eaten each day. Parents sometimes are concerned about rapid weight gain in a young child, when this may in fact be a quite normal phase of rapid growth. Before any attempt is made to reduce or alter the child's size, the physician should be consulted. Evaluation of the child's rate of growth in height and weight will indicate whether he or she is too chubby. Skim milk lacks the fat that is present in whole milk. This is a very important material for normal development of muscles, nerves, and skin. Very rarely, a child may be unable to digest fats properly and his or her intake of fat each day must be limited. Special diets for these children should be carefully supervised by the physician. The average child should not receive skim milk as a major dietary component. Obesity in children is certainly something to be avoided.

ALAN R. RUSHTON, M.D., Ph.D.
Flemington, New Jersey

Can my baby be harmed if he is exposed to a microwave oven that is in operation?

All currently manufactured commercial microwave ovens are generally considered to be safe. There is very little leakage of radiation while the oven is in operation, and this should present little danger to infants and children. Nevertheless, there is some controversy about the effects of exposure to low levels of microwave radiation.

Some children have suffered burns because they have come in contact with foods that have been heated in microwave ovens. Usual parental precautions for keeping infants and children at a safe distance from hot dishes should prevent any difficulties. Children and their parents can be fooled about the temperature of food that is heated by microwaves because the container may be much cooler than the food inside. Parents should check the temperature before feeding any heated food to an infant. The simplest way to do this is to taste the food yourself. The classic technique of placing a few drops of warmed formula on your wrist is also an effective way to prevent burns.

MICHAEL B. SHEEHAN, M.D.
Kansas City, Missouri

My toddler never seems to have enough to eat. Could he have a tapeworm?

Tapeworms are very rare in children. Expenditure of excess energy or the child's natural metabolism would be much more likely causes of your child's constant desire to eat. If he is not gaining excessive weight, it is probably a good healthy appetite.

MERRITT B. LOW, M.D., F.A.A.P.
Ashfield, Massachusetts

My husband occasionally gives our toddler beer. Is this all right?

It can be very dangerous to give an alcoholic beverage to a toddler. Small quantities can intoxicate a youngster. Children who have ingested as little as one to five ounces of beer have died as a result. Alcohol can also cause the sugar in a child's bloodstream to become so low that he or she could pass out or have a seizure.

The habits formed by offering alcoholic drinks to a toddler can be equally dangerous. One or two sips of beer will probably not harm a toddler. If the child assumes that the offering of beer is a sign that it is acceptable to drink beer, he or she might drink a larger and more dangerous amount at another time.

Alcoholic drinks should be considered poisonous to children. Beer should not be offered, and alcoholic beverages should always be placed in a safe spot, out of reach of toddlers.

STEVEN W. KARIYS, M.D.
Hanover, New Hampshire

Should I boil water before giving it to my newborn? For how long should it be boiled?

Almost all municipal water supplies are safe as far as bacteria are concerned. The receptacle is more important than the water. The bottle or cup should be clean, preferably sterilized, and water should not be stored or kept around for later use, but used fresh each time. If you are in doubt about the water you use, boil it for ten to fifteen minutes.

MERRITT B. LOW, M.D., F.A.A.P.
Ashfield, Massachusetts

When can my infant start on baby foods?

Few questions have as much potential to arouse controversy between mothers, mothers and grandmothers, and mothers and doctors. This is because over the years patterns of infant feeding have varied widely, but have tended toward the early introduction of solid foods. In recent years, however, there is increasing evidence that delaying solid foods until at least four months of age is more beneficial for the infant. As your baby approaches this age, there are several rules of thumb to help you make this decision. First of all, the American Academy of Pediatrics currently recommends starting solids at four months of age for formula-fed infants and six months of age for those who are breast-fed. Alternatively, if your baby is taking more than 32 ozs. of formula or breast milk a day, you may consider adding solids. You may also begin to think about solid foods if your baby doubles his or her birth weight before four to six months of age.

There is also no evidence that adding cereal to an infant's diet helps him or her sleep through the night, or improves his or her disposition. In fact, giving solid foods to an already colicky infant may worsen the situation and lead to more frustration and anxiety. However, withholding solids for an undue length of time may deprive an older infant of nutrients necessary for growth.

NANCY deTORA, M.D.
Worcester, Massachusetts

Should my infant lie on her back or on her stomach for sleep after a feeding?

If your infant tends to be spitty or to vomit after feedings, keep her in a supported, semi-upright position for one-half hour after feedings. Otherwise, it is probably better to place her on her stomach.

MERRITT B. LOW, M.D., F.A.A.P.
Ashfield, Massachusetts

Should I be concerned if my newborn son spits up after each feeding?

Many normal infants overindulge and then regurgitate the excess. Spitting up seems to be more common in bottle-fed babies than in breast-fed infants, but it can happen with any normal newborn. If your infant is thriving and spits up only small amounts that end up on his chin, your shirt, his clothes, or the adjacent blanket, you need not be concerned. If, however, the baby has projectile vomiting of an entire feeding shortly after the feeding is completed (that is, if he spits up the entire amount and projects for a distance of a foot or so), then he may have an obstruction to the outlet of the stomach (pyloric stenosis) or a neurological problem. Projectile vomiting that represents a serious problem is repetitive rather than occasional and does not usually correct itself until the infant receives appropriate medical attention. If your baby simply spits up a little after each feeding, don't worry. If your infant has episodes of projectile vomiting, you should contact the doctor. Many normal infants who spit up continue to do so for many months. When your son begins to crawl or cruise, you may have to clean up after him as he moves about the house after his meals.

WILLIAM J. CASHORE, M.D.
Providence, Rhode Island

My baby gags during feedings. Why? Is he full?

Infants can gag during feedings because they have eaten too much, but they also can gag when the normal muscle that closes the opening of the stomach doesn't close all the way and produces a so-called gastroesophageal reflux. Children with moderate-to-severe gastroesophageal reflux may gag without eating too much. Also, rarely, children may gag because there is only a small or narrow passageway between the esophagus, the tube that goes between the mouth and the stomach, and the trachea, the breathing tube that goes to the lung.

FERNANDO J. deCASTRO, M.D.
St. Louis, Missouri

After my baby has started on cereal, when can I start her on strained fruits, vegetables, and meats? What should I give her first?

There is no generally agreed upon time at which solid foods, fruits, vegetables, or meats, should be introduced into an infant's diet. Many pediatricians suggest withholding solid foods until at least two months of age, and preferably until the infant no longer seems content with only milk. Nutritionally, breast milk or formula is clearly the best food for the child during the first six months of life.

Children who have not been offered solids by the age of six months will usually start themselves on these foods by snatching them from the parent's dinner plate if the plate is within arm's reach.

Assuredly, there is no set time at which all children need to be started on solid foods.

J. CROSSAN O'DONOVAN, M.D.
Baltimore, Maryland

Does the color of the new foods I give my infant affect the color of her bowel movements?

The color of an infant's bowel movements can indeed be affected by certain foods. Beets are the classic example, causing a red color. Some parents immediately assume this is blood. Other foods, especially green ones like spinach and chard, can also color the movements. This is less noticeable with yellow foods, since most normal bowel movements are yellowish. In addition, excess fats sometimes cause greenness. If your baby's bowel movement looks peculiar, check for possible causes.

MERRITT B. LOW, M.D., F.A.A.P.
Ashfield, Massachusetts

My toddler's baby-sitter lets her chew gum. Should I put a stop to this?

When more than one caregiver is involved with a child, it is important that consistent rules be established. These rules need to be agreed upon and consistently implemented.

When you employ a baby-sitter, you should inform her about the most important household rules and routines. Clearly, no baby-sitter will care for your child *precisely* as you do, but the sitter should attempt to follow your usual routines as closely as possible. Minor differences are perfectly acceptable, and children usually are flexible enough to adapt to different caregivers without difficulty.

However, if there are any specific rules imposed by your child's sitter with which you disagree, or if you have a specific rule that she does not implement with your child, this should be discussed with her. In almost every instance, just making your sitter aware of your own practice and your wish for this to be carried through consistently will be enough to achieve your purpose. In rare cases, disagreements will occur. In these situations, parents generally should have the most to say about rules for their child, by virtue of their authority as parents, and because the baby-sitter is in their employ. In addition, the experience and maturity of the sitter may be an important consideration.

If a solution or compromise is not easily achieved, you have two choices. First of all, you can tell your children that a given policy is different when they are at home or at the sitter's ("Mrs. Smith has gum at her house, but we do not chew gum here"). If the children's care is reasonably consistent in other ways, a small difference in caretaking patterns should easily be accepted by most children. Another choice is to seek the services of a different sitter, one with whom there is more consistent agreement.

Reasonable questions to ask yourself are, "*Why* do I want to change this practice of the baby-sitter? Is it for valid health reasons?" If in doubt, ask your pediatrician. "Is it because of personal preference, or cultural difference? Is there any reason *not* to allow a given practice?" In the end, one question remains, "How important is this one issue to me?" If you feel strongly about a particular policy, then it probably should be changed. If it is not of utmost importance, then compromise seems reasonable. Since you are the parent, the final decision remains yours.

BETSY BUSCH, M.D.
Boston, Massachusetts

I have run out of baby cereal. Can I give my two-month-old regular cooked cereal?

No, it would be inadvisable to feed such a young baby regular cooked cereal. The infant variety of cereal is specially prepared (it is precooked) for easy digestion, whereas the variety prepared for older individuals may not be wholly suitable for such a small baby. The cereals prepared for infants also contain essential vitamins and iron.

Ideally, children should be fed milk alone for the first three months of life, because milk provides all of the necessary building blocks of growth in this period. However, many young parents feed their infants cereals as early as six weeks of age without adverse results.

KATHERINE M. KNIGHT, M.D.
New Orleans, Louisiana

When should I stop my baby from using a bottle?

There is no definite time when a baby should be weaned from the bottle. Many factors, including emotional, nutritional, and neural development, determine when an infant is able to drink exclusively from a cup. The practice of putting the infant to bed with a bottle of sweetened liquids, milk, or formula should be condemned. This leads to the "nursing bottle syndrome," which results in the destruction of the baby's teeth.

STEPHEN E. WALLACE, M.D., F.A.A.P.
Springfield, Illinois

When can my baby drink unboiled water?

If your water is from a safe, treated city water supply and if it is taken from a free-flowing tap source and fed to the baby immediately, there is no need to boil the water for a child of any age. On the other hand, if your water supply is from your own well or spring, or if the water will be standing in the bottle for any period of time before the baby drinks it, as would occur when you are visiting or traveling with the baby, the water should be boiled and placed in a sterilized container. This procedure should be followed until your child is at least three to six months old.

FRANK M. SHEPARD, M.D.
Johnson City, Tennessee

My baby seems to have a lot of gas. How can I help her?

Gas itself should cause no concern in an otherwise healthy baby. It is not dangerous and, therefore, will cause your baby no harm.

Gas in the intestinal tract comes from swallowed air or, more rarely, from the action of bacteria in the intestinal tract upon undigested food. Also, air will be swallowed when the baby cries a lot.

To reduce the swallowing of air, first make sure that your baby's bottle and nipple are working properly. When you invert the bottle, a few drops of milk should run out freely, and then the flow should cease. If too little milk runs freely, your baby may have to suck too hard to get the milk. This may cause the swallowing of excess air around the nipple. If the milk runs too fast, the baby may have to gulp. This will also result in the swallowing of excess air.

After air is swallowed, it may become trapped in the baby's stomach if she is put on her back during or immediately after feeding. You should burp the baby frequently during feeding. In addition, it may be helpful to sit her up often during feeding and to lay her on her stomach after feeding.

The second cause of excessive gas is the fermentation in the intestine of undigested food. This may be a temporary problem that is the result of an acute infection. (In such circumstances diarrhea will also be present. The diarrhea will often cause a "burning" type of diaper rash.) Your pediatrician may recommend a formula containing a more easily digested sugar. More rarely, the gas may be a sign of a significant problem. In that case, it would be exceedingly unusual for gas to be the only or even major symptom.

It should be emphasized that there are signs the pediatrician looks for to determine if your baby is healthy. If you feel that gas is causing your baby pain, you should consult with your pediatrician. His or her first concern will be, "Is she growing and thriving? Does she appear to be healthy?" Your pediatrician will want to know whether the baby is eating and gaining weight and whether she is inconsolably fretful. The pediatrician will also probably want to know about any change in bowel habits such as diarrhea or constipation. If the baby's weight gain is good and her examination is normal, then it is extremely unlikely that gas is a sign of significant problems.

In summary, gas by itself is usually of little medical significance. If the baby is otherwise well and thriving, gas should be of concern only if it is accompanied by pain and diarrhea. In such cases, attention should be centered on the cause of the pain or diarrhea.

NEAL S. LeLEIKO, M.D., Ph.D.
New York, New York

My toddler always wants to eat. Should I stop him from doing so? He is not overweight.

The rapid growth experienced during the first twelve months of life slows down considerably when a child becomes a toddler. During this period a child has an opportunity to explore his or her environment completely, and every new thing that is encountered goes through the "taste test." Every child goes through several psychosocial-sexual stages of development. The oral stage is very strong during the first eighteen months of life and is, unfortunately, marked by a high incidence of accidents and poisonings. Toddlers are not aware of the limits and dangers of their environment.

Many parents mistakenly think that because toddlers put everything into their mouths, they are hungry. They quickly offer food, which is more often rejected than accepted. It should also be remembered that toddlers are still teething, and their gums alternately itch and ache. Consequently, many of the items going into the mouth may be an attempt to alleviate this discomfort. Toddlers are known to create havoc in their households over their eating patterns. They may be very selective about what they eat. The color, size, and shape of food play a more important role in their selection process now than during infancy. Imitative behavior becomes more apparent; if there are older siblings, the toddler may follow their patterns. Toddlers also enjoy food items that they can pick up and put into their mouths. Parents are encouraged to offer only a nutritious variety. Parents are also advised not to despair because no toddlers have starved themselves this way, and most will not become overweight. It is during this phase of a child's development that pediatricians spend a lot of time allaying parental anxieties and, through anticipatory guidance, preparing them for other surprises that await them during this period.

LILLIAN McLEAN BEARD, M.D.
Potomac, Maryland

My toddler does not seem sick, but she has lost interest in food. She eats "like a bird." Is this normal?

Healthy children have a way of eating as much as they need for energy and growth. Their needs, however, do not always coincide with their parents' expectations.

In the first year, children grow rapidly and generally eat quite a bit. It is typical for an infant to gain about fourteen pounds in the first year of life. After the first birthday, it is normal for growth to slow down. Children typically gain about seven pounds between their first and second birthdays and even less in subsequent years.

It is common for parents to observe a decline in appetite after the first birthday. Toddlers are typically picky eaters. Some eat only two meals a day. Others seem to live on only three or four foods, totally avoiding some foods that their parents may feel are important for their nutrition. However, most toddlers are pretty good at selecting a nutritionally complete diet when they are offered a reasonable variety of food.

If your child is not gaining weight or seems ill in some other way, her eating habits may reflect a problem. Lack of interest in food in the face of good growth and normal activity seldom reflects an underlying problem.

MARK D. WIDOME, M.D.
Hershey, Pennsylvania

My newborn is fussy and has no appetite. What could be wrong?

A long labor, difficult delivery, or excessive maternal sedation may cause poor sucking or fussiness during the first forty-eight hours or so of life. The infant then begins to improve slowly. In some infants, this period is more prolonged. A well-grown and mature infant should experience little harm. But persistent fussiness or apathy and loss of appetite may be a manifestation of a more serious underlying problem.

A lack of appetite, a failure to feed, and excessive crying, after a period of normal feeding and behavior, should be regarded as danger signals. In the absence of technical reasons such as enlarged breasts, inverted or insufficiently protractable nipples, or an inadequate or blocked hole in the nipple of the bottle, the cause lies in the infant and must be actively sought. These symptoms may herald congenital heart disease, the start of an infection, metabolic problems, and so forth, particularly if they are associated with fever, vomiting, jaundice, difficulty in breathing, and so on. The concurrence of several symptoms or the persistence of a single symptom may be a warning signal of a serious problem.

J. S. SURPURE, M.D., F.A.A.P.
Oklahoma City, Oklahoma

My toddler recently became a very picky eater. Should I try to force him to eat?

Toddlers should not be forced to eat certain amounts of food nor specific kinds of food because the changes in the toddler's eating patterns are the result of normal changes in growth and development. As your baby becomes a toddler, his rate of growth decreases considerably. During the first year of life, a baby gains a pound or more a month. After that, the toddler gains considerably less, and thus needs less food. At the same time that the need for food is decreasing, toddlers are learning that they have certain likes and dislikes, that they can make choices, and that in making choices they can have an effect on those around them. It is thus normal for toddlers to begin picking and choosing whenever they have the opportunity, and they have no greater opportunity to pick and choose than at mealtime.

Forcing a child to eat certain amounts of food or certain kinds of food interferes with the child's appetite, which is presumably regulated by the need for food in order to grow, as well as by the child's freedom to pick and choose. Also, forcing a child to eat provides the child with a wonderful opportunity to rebel and thus effectively "control" those around him. This usually results in frustration for the parents and havoc at meals.

Parents should see that the foods available to the toddler are nutritious and varied, and that junk foods simply are not available as a choice. If it is important to the family that meals be at certain times, then food should be available only at those times. Whatever is not eaten in a reasonable time is simply put away without comment. If strict adherence to mealtimes is not important, then the toddler can be given food when he wants it. The only important consideration for the parent is that all food provided be nutritious. The second method of feeding is probably more in line with the needs of the toddler than is the first; however, the toddler who eats frequently may appear to eat less than the toddler who eats three meals a day because the amount of food eaten at any one time will be small.

Parents who are concerned about their child's food intake can allay their fears by keeping a check on their child's growth. Having the child weighed and measured at the physician's office or local health center every three or four months allows the parents to plot their child's growth on standardized growth tables that physicians and health centers keep. As long as the child's growth plots normally for the child, parents need not worry about their toddler's eating patterns.

FOSTER H. YOUNG JR., M.D.
Kingstree, South Carolina

My two-month-old baby takes his feedings well, 8 ozs. every four hours, day and night, but still cries for more after he has been fed. Why?

Everyone knows that babies cry when they are hungry. But babies also cry when their tummies are full. It is clear that 8 ozs. every four hours is too much formula for a two-month-old. This adds up to 48 ozs. every twenty-four hours. Even at four, five, or six months and older, a baby needs only somewhere between 24 and 26 ozs. of formula per day.

A baby's stomach is just so big. Too much milk in it causes some stretching. Imagine an extra large chicken egg or, maybe, a small to medium-sized lemon when you think about the size of a baby's stomach in the first few months after birth. Now, try to imagine how much milk could fit in a stomach about that size. It doesn't take much imagining to see that 8 ozs. won't fit without lots of stretching.

Why does a baby gobble up too much? It's a vicious cycle. To start with, a baby often gulps down air with feedings. This air occupies space in the stomach and, in fact, may cause a tummy ache, so the baby cries. But he cries because he has too much in his tummy, this time air, not because he's hungry.

Here comes some milk. In go a couple of ounces. He doesn't feel any better so in goes some more, and more, and 8 ozs. are in, and he still cries.

So the answer to your problem is to give less rather than more formula. We are probably talking about 4 ozs. or so, five times in twenty-four hours. Don't be too concerned about exact amounts or schedule. Do what works, but more than 26 ozs. at any age is too much, and even less than this at an earlier age is too much if the weight gain is excessive.

Sometimes you can bubble the air out. Burping a baby over your shoulder is fine, but a more efficient way is to push on the left side of the baby's tummy under the ribs with four flattened fingers. While you are pushing with your right hand, raise his head up with your left hand. This little maneuver lets the air go up and out in a hurry. Push the air out before—and after—each feeding and any time your baby is fussy.

GLEN C. GRIFFIN, M.D.
Bountiful, Utah

Do I need to worry about high-cholesterol foods for my infant?

The answer to that question is not a simple one. The reason for concern is the link between cholesterol and a type of heart disease called atherosclerotic heart disease. Below is a description of what is known about cholesterol and heart disease and recommendations regarding low-cholesterol diets for infants.

Plaques, or fatty deposits, develop in the lining of arteries supplying the heart. These plaques restrict and may ultimately block the flow of blood to the heart muscle, thereby causing a heart attack. The plaques contain high amounts of cholesterol. Extensive research has shown that the higher an adult's blood cholesterol level, the greater chance there is of developing heart disease. This is presumably because of greater deposition of cholesterol into arteries and the formation of larger, thicker plaques. It is also known that in cultures in which the people eat low-cholesterol foods or in which they are vegetarians, atherosclerotic heart disease is much less common than it is in the United States. Other factors such as cigarette smoking also play very important roles. Thus, cholesterol cannot be blamed entirely for the high incidence of heart disease.

Despite improvements in the treatment of atherosclerotic heart disease, heart attacks remain one of the leading causes of death in adults. Therefore, many physicians believe that some method of preventing heart disease must be devised. It is known that the process of forming plaques, called atherosclerosis, frequently begins in childhood. It is known also that it is possible through diet, exercise, or drugs to reduce the blood cholesterol level at any age. All this knowledge leads many doctors to believe that lowering the cholesterol in the diet of all people probably is good and that it will result in fewer heart attacks. Proof of this theory still requires decades of research.

In the absence of proof, what recommendations are there for infants under two years of age? First, infants who come from families having a high frequency of heart attacks probably should have their cholesterol levels measured by two years of age. Those families should seek advice from physicians and dietitians regarding their diet and how it might be changed to reduce cholesterol intake. Second, once an infant is older than twelve to eighteen months, high-cholesterol foods can safely be reduced. Third, current recommendations do not include a low-cholesterol diet for infants younger than twelve to eighteen months of age. Cholesterol is used in brain growth, which continues to about eighteen months of age. Furthermore, breast milk is relatively high in cholesterol, and pediatricians are reluctant to recommend a diet that might be different from what is accepted as the model food for infant nutrition.

In summary, moderately low-cholesterol diets appear safe in infants older than eighteen months of age. Certain infants will probably benefit from more significant restrictions in cholesterol intake. Before embarking on any major change in family diet patterns, you should seek advice from physicians and nutritionists with experience in pediatric nutrition.

KENNETH K. GOERTZ, M.D.
Kansas City, Kansas

My infant has been refusing to drink milk lately. Is this all right? Will she get rickets?

Milk or milk-based formulas are major sources of the proteins, minerals, and vitamins required for the normal growth and development of infants. Young children need 24 to 32 ozs. of formula each day. Deficiency of calcium or vitamin D produces a softening of bones and cartilage. This condition is called rickets. Infants need about 400 units of vitamin D and 500 milligrams of calcium each day for normal bone development. Both formula and cow's milk are supplemented with vitamin D and are rich in calcium.

A child who refuses to drink milk may well develop serious problems due to malnutrition. Milk products such as cheese, yogurt, pudding, or cottage cheese may be substituted. The physician should be consulted and may wish to prescribe liquid vitamin or calcium supplements to ensure normal bone growth and development.

If the child is allergic to milk, egg yolk and dark green leafy vegetables do contain needed calcium.

ALAN R. RUSHTON, M.D., Ph.D.
Flemington, New Jersey

My baby vomits quite forcefully after eating. What should I do?

There are several causes for forceful vomiting in infancy, especially if it occurs after eating. One of the most common causes is overfeeding an infant. This is less frequently seen in children who are breast-fed because they themselves can stop when they are satisfied. In bottle-fed babies, mothers usually try to feed a certain amount of formula or milk and continue to offer this to the baby even though he or she may have been satisfied with a lesser amount. The best solution for a bottle-fed baby who possibly may have this problem is to stop feeding the baby as soon as he or she slows down and does not show any more interest in eating.

If overfeeding does not seem to be the cause of forceful vomiting, perhaps the cause is due to the fact that the child is not burped adequately during the feeding. It is advised that the mother should burp this child more frequently and therefore relieve some of the gaseous stomach distension that can result from feeding. Once again, this problem is seen more frequently in children who are bottle-fed than in those who are breast-fed.

Another major cause of vomiting after eating is a mechanical obstruction in the gut. The most common obstruction in infancy is pyloric stenosis, which is a blockage between the stomach and the gut. Once the child is fed, the food cannot pass through readily and there is backup of the food and the child vomits. If a child continues to vomit forcefully after the mother is sure that she is burping adequately and the child is not being overfed, it is advisable to contact a pediatrician.

JEANNE M. FULBERG, M.D.
Kansas City, Kansas

When should my baby be on a three-meal-per-day schedule?

One cannot generalize about this. Babies are individuals. Determining factors are age, desire to eat, adjustment to breast-feeding or to formula, hunger and satisfaction, and family wishes and patterns. Probably no harm results regardless of how an eating schedule develops.

MERRITT B. LOW, M.D., F.A.A.P.
Ashfield, Massachusetts

Is it safe to leave my two-month-old alone in his crib with a propped bottle?

The answer to your question is "no" for several reasons. Propping is a bad idea for an infant of any age. It could lead to aspiration, that is, the inhaling of milk in the baby's windpipe. This could cause choking and even lead to pneumonia. Milk could also get into the baby's Eustachian tube and cause ear problems. In the older infant the slow drip of milk from a propped bottle could cause severe dental caries. Thus, holding the bottle is advised when feeding your baby.

EDWARD J. FEROLI, M.D.
Gaithersburg, Maryland

When should I give my newborn water, and how do I fit it into her feeding schedule?

Newborn infants do not require extra water except in very unusual circumstances. Both breast milk and all properly mixed formulas provide all the water a baby normally needs. Giving water with a bottle to a breast-fed baby may make breast-feeding more difficult because it might decrease the baby's hunger and sucking power, which directly affects the production of breast milk. The baby may also become confused about using two different kinds of nipples.

Some circumstances may require that extra water be given, but this should only be done under medical guidance and when related to a specific problem.

MICHAEL B. SHEEHAN, M.D.
Kansas City, Missouri

Is it possible to make my own baby food, using the food I make for the rest of the family and putting it through the blender?

Yes, it is perfectly possible for a parent to make baby food by putting food prepared for the family through a blender or food mill. Preparing food in this fashion is economical and safe.

One word of caution should be mentioned, however. The reason many parents began making their own baby foods was that sugar, salt, and food additives were added to prepared baby foods by the manufacturers. Consumer pressure has forced the manufacturers to take sugar, salt, and additives out of most baby foods. One recent study has shown that homemade baby food actually contains more salt and sugar than do commercial preparations. If the family demands that seasonings be added to the table food, they should be added after a portion has been set aside for the infant.

J. CROSSAN O'DONOVAN, M.D.
Baltimore, Maryland

Additional precautions for preparing homemade baby food are:

1. Choose from the four basic food groups so that their nutritional contributions are complementary.
2. Thoroughly clean, wash, and trim all foods.
3. Cook foods properly to provide tenderness, inactivate undesirable enzymes, improve digestability, and destroy undesirable or dangerous bacteria—but cook no longer than necessary to avoid destroying heat-sensitive nutrients.
4. Avoid having to discard water-soluble nutrients by using as little cooking water as possible.
5. Use leftovers carefully since they may be contaminated with high levels of bacteria and may lose their nutrient values when reheated.
6. Add enough liquid to achieve a consistency that an infant can easily swallow.
7. Thoroughly clean utensils and kitchen surroundings so they do not

become a source of food spoilage organisms.
8. Store and prepare baby foods in amounts that can be fed at one meal. Avoid thawing and refreezing which can lead to bacterial build-up.

GERBER PRODUCTS COMPANY
Fremont, Michigan

CHAPTER 13

Feet and Walking

My eleven-month-old has just begun walking and he appears to be knock-kneed. Is this normal?

Sometimes babies with very fat thighs appear to be knock-kneed when they first start walking, but it is unusual for a child of eleven months to appear knock-kneed. The appearance of mild knock-knee deformity is normal in children from two to six years of age. The possibility of knock-knees should be discussed with your pediatrician at the child's next checkup.

FRANK M. SHEPARD, M.D.
Johnson City, Tennessee

When can I expect my infant to take her first steps?

Children vary a great deal as to when they begin to walk. First of all, walking must be defined. Walking is when a child can walk unassisted halfway across an ordinary-size room. Otherwise, every grandmother has her grandchild *walking* as soon as she stands momentarily on her feet at six months of age, and then plunges forward flat on her face after a couple of unsuccessful, daring forward steps. Some children can walk at eight months of age, and others not until they are eighteen months old and who later become athletes and graduate from college with honors. A lot depends on a child's initiative, encouragement, and environment. Some kids are just more daring; others more reticent. Some children are kept in playpens, to keep them out of trouble (and also keep them from walking). Some children are around a mob of other children, at home or in day-care centers, where they learn (as do all good *and* old soldiers) that the lower they crouch, the healthier it is; so walking is an invitation to disaster. Pushing around a little cart with wheels accustoms your child to move in various directions. But, just as with training wheels on a bike, she does not get used to the art of balancing herself. At any rate, you will wait anxiously for your first child to walk, but you will pray that the next ones will be content to sit!

ROBERT EASTON, M.D.
Peoria, Illinois

My infant is in a spica cast for a hip problem. How long will this delay his walking?

A destined pattern for walking is not usually delayed by temporary casts and appliances, although these obviously produce some delay before the "catch-up" starts.

MERRITT B. LOW, M.D., F.A.A.P.
Ashfield, Massachusetts

When should I buy my infant's first shoes? What should they be like?

The only reason for buying shoes for any child is to protect the feet. Therefore, an infant's first shoes should be purchased when he or she is mature enough to be moving outside the home and getting into areas that are potentially dangerous to bare feet. The best assurance of good arch and foot formation is to let the child go barefoot or in a very soft slipper around the house. What should a child's first shoes be like? Choose a high-top shoe for the first few months of walking, and then a good sneaker. That is certainly a lot more economical and just as good as a fancy, expensive shoe.

A. E. REARDON, M.D., F.A.A.P.
Duluth, Minnesota

Is it harmful for my baby to go barefoot?

Children need shoes only to protect their feet from injury and temperature extremes. For most children, the best shoe is a properly fitted one that allows the foot to move naturally. Shoes do not promote walking skills or healthy foot development. Instead, infant shoes with stiff soles may decrease foot flexibility and, by restricting movement, limit the strength of the supporting muscles.

The young infant, just beginning to walk on carpeted floors, does well in soft, moccasin-type shoes. When protection against the pavement and other hard surfaces becomes necessary, thicker but still pliable soles are recommended. High-topped shoes may keep toddlers from stepping out of their heels. Children outgrow shoes rapidly, and expensive footwear is unnecessary and uneconomical. A child's shoe should be of adequate size, well-ventilated, and have a flat, flexible sole. Inexpensive canvas sneakers fulfill these requirements. Furthermore, they have rubber soles that provide good traction and minimize falls.

DANIEL W. DUBNER, M.D.
Chelmsford, Massachusetts

Will my baby be bowlegged if she tries to stand too early?

Mild bowlegs are normal in the infant and young child. Gradual, spontaneous correction is the natural course of bowlegs, and the great majority are straight by the time the child is two years of age. In most children, no treatment or special shoes are necessary.

Several illnesses can produce severe bowlegs that need to be treated, but this is a very rare occurrence. These illnesses cause disturbances in the growth and the strength of the bones, which may become more bowed when the child puts weight on the legs or begins walking. One disease is rickets, caused by a lack of vitamin D. Another is Blount's disease, and is seen in children who are overweight and begin walking at an early age. However, it has not been proven that early walking is the actual cause of bowlegs. If your child's bowlegs become worse after she begins walking, whether early or late, you should consult your pediatrician.

JAMIE HEWELL, M.D.
St. Louis, Missouri

My baby has a blister from his shoe. What can I do for it?

If your baby has developed a blister from his shoe, most likely the shoe does not fit properly. I would return to the store with the shoes and the infant and have the size and fit rechecked. In the meantime, I would suggest keeping the blister clean with soap and water and not using shoes on the infant until it heals (in about seven to ten days). If you find it necessary to cover the feet for warmth or protection, cover the blister with a Band-Aid after washing it and use slipper socks, soft leather shoes, or moccasins, which are unlikely to irritate the blister.

EDWARD C. SAEF, M.D.
Concord, Massachusetts

Is it true that the purpose of high shoes is to give the baby's feet support?

It certainly is *not*. Whatever support the foot gets from the shoes comes from beneath the shoes and not from the sides. As a matter of fact, sneakers are perfectly acceptable footwear for toddlers. The baby's first shoes should have soles that are semisoft. Walking barefoot on a soft rug, or in warm weather, on grass or sand helps exercise little feet.

SYDNEY WALDMAN, M.D.
Philadelphia, Pennsylvania

My son has started to walk and his feet turn outward. Will this correct itself? Is it anything to worry about?

Pronated feet, or "flat feet," are very common in children and completely normal in infants up to two years of age. When an infant first begins to stand and walk, the feet are spread wide apart for balance as the child grasps for support. At this age the infant's arch is filled with a fat pad that disappears when the child has mastered walking.

Flat feet appear normal when weight is not applied to them, but turn outward when they bear weight because of a shift of the center of gravity; an older child is able to "toe in," or turn the foot in, while walking. This shifts the center of gravity to the center of the foot.

Parents need not be concerned unless this turning outward persists to three to four years of age or if the child has pain in the foot, excessive wearing of the inner side and heel of the shoes, or a poor arch when asked to stand on tiptoe.

STEPHANIE W. PERRY, M.D.
Nashville, Tennessee

My infant's feet are very wide. Will they stay that way?

No, the feet will become relatively less wide across the toes as your child's feet grow longer. Obviously, some infants have fatter, wider feet than do others and will probably have a relatively wider foot as an adult, but an infant's and toddler's foot is wide in relation to its length.

M. E. SYMONDS, M.D.
Mountainside, New Jersey

My toddler toes-in when he walks. Should he see an orthopedic specialist?

Most babies, as they begin to walk, tend to turn their toes in. They also at first walk with their feet rather far apart. This is to give them a broader base on which to balance. As they improve their walking skills, they bring their feet closer and closer together and point their toes forward or even toe-out. Thus, they do not trip over their own toes. Your pediatrician will tell you if your child is toeing-in excessively and causing inward torsion of the leg bones, and will, if necessary, refer you to an orthopedic specialist.

M. E. SYMONDS, M.D.
Mountainside, New Jersey

Can my infant wear his sister's old baby shoes if they fit?

Shoes for infants serve two important functions: to protect the feet from sharp objects and to keep them warm. Basic requirements for infants' shoes include proper fit, flexibility, and durability. Many infants outgrow their shoes before they have worn them out. Therefore, an infant may indeed wear his sister's old shoes. However, certain questions should first be answered: Does the shoe fit properly in the heel, and are the length and width correct? The infant's heel should fit firmly into the heel counter without being too snug. The shoe should extend approximately one-half inch farther than the big toe and be wide enough at the widest portion of the foot to allow squeezing a pinch of shoe between the fingers. Has the shoe retained its shape? If the shoe is lined, is the lining still good enough to avoid pressure areas and blisters? If the answers to these questions are "yes," pass down the shoes and save money!

PAUL H. DWORKIN, M.D.
Farmington, Connecticut

What kind of shoes do you recommend for a child who has just started to walk?

Shoes should be chosen only for the protection of the feet. Where appropriate, *no* shoes are best.

STEPHEN S. NASON, M.D.
Washington, D.C.

My baby is one year old and is not walking. Shouldn't she be walking?

Many babies are walking at one year of age; however, it is not at all unusual to see a baby not begin to walk until fifteen months of age. Assuming all of the child's other developmental milestones are within the normal range, you should not be overly concerned just because the child has not begun to walk by one year of age.

DAVID J. TEPPER, M.D.
Chattanooga, Tennessee

CHAPTER 14

Formula Feeding

I will not be breast-feeding my baby. Should I add an iron supplement to her formula?

It depends on the type of formula you choose to feed your baby. Ideally, you should give her one of the "maternalized" formulas: Similac with iron, Enfamil with iron, or SMA. These formulas all have more than adequate iron to meet your baby's needs. If, however, you should choose evaporated milk formula, you will need to add an iron supplement in the form of iron drops.

Dairy milk from the carton is not recommended for infant feeding. Under certain circumstances it may be necessary to feed infants a soy formula. The soy formula, however, contains adequate iron, so that iron supplements are unnecessary. Occasionally it is necessary to use goat's milk for infant feedings; goat's milk needs to be supplemented with both iron and folate.

It was once thought by many pediatricians and mothers that iron produced abdominal discomfort in a child, causing increased crying, colic, or even constipation. Two very good studies have demonstrated that the small amounts of iron present in the commercial formulas have no effect on the baby's stomach, and do not cause vomiting, diarrhea, constipation, colic, or gas. Iron supplements may make a baby's stools appear darker than usual.

At six months of age both breast- and formula-fed babies should be eating baby cereal, which is also a good source of iron.

JANICE L. COCKRELL, M.D.
Richmond, Virginia

What is the difference between ready-made formula and homemade formula? How do I prepare the latter? Which is better for the baby?

Both homemade and ready-made formulas are liquid sources of food for young infants and contain ingredients that provide the baby with protein, sugar, fat, minerals, and some vitamins. The major differences between homemade formula and ready-made formula are these:

1. Homemade formula uses a mixture of water, evaporated cow's milk, and Karo syrup. There are many ready-made formulas with different ingredients from which to choose. Some have ingredients similar to those in homemade formula. Others try to imitate breast milk. Still others have special ingredients for infants unable to digest a cow's milk formula; these use soy protein instead of cow's milk protein.

2. Homemade formula may not contain extra vitamins, as do all ready-made formulas. It does not contain extra iron, which is in some ready-made formulas.

3. Homemade formula leaves the correct mixing of several ingredients to the mother and, therefore, it may be subject to mistakes. Most ready-made formulas are either ready-to-feed or need only to have water added.

4. Homemade formula may be less expensive. The most common ingredients for homemade formula are: one 13-oz. can evaporated milk; 2 tablespoons (1 oz.) Karo syrup; and 17 ozs. freshly boiled water. Wash the top of the can of milk with hot water and soap, rinse it with hot water, and punch two holes in it. Then mix the milk with the Karo syrup and freshly boiled water. Pour the formula into presterilized bottles or into clean bottles, which are boiled in a water bath for twenty-five minutes. The bottles may finally be stored in the refrigerator until used.

Homemade formula and ready-made formula are equally good for the baby if the homemade formula is properly mixed, extra vitamins prescribed by your doctor are given, and your baby can digest a cow's milk formula well.

Check with your baby's doctor about the use of vitamins and the choice of formula for your infant.

DEBORAH L. MADANSKY, M.D.
Worcester, Massachusetts

Should I give my infant a bottle when she goes to bed either for a nap or for the night?

Because a bottle presumes to provide both nourishment as well as some amount of emotional security, it is often used indiscriminately as a convenient pacifier for babies. If the baby usually has a bottle before bedtime or at naptime as part of the total daily food intake, a bottle certainly can be given at those times. It is likely, however, that a bottle at those times would no longer be required by a child of one year of age.

The question does not address bottle-propping, but bedtime and naptime often lend themselves to such a practice. This should be discouraged, if not completely avoided, for several reasons. It precludes the emotional benefits for the infant that come from being held. The caregiver also derives satisfaction from this closeness with the baby. Bottle-propping also allows the child to swallow air along with the fluid, possibly resulting in abdominal discomfort. The parent or other caregiver should hold and cuddle the infant, giving the bottle in an unhurried manner.

GRACE E. HOLMES, M.D.
Kansas City, Kansas

Ever since I switched my infant to formula, I have noticed that his bowel movements have changed in color and consistency. Is this to be expected?

Children who are breast-fed will frequently have yellow, somewhat loose, unformed stools. These stools will be more frequent in the first several weeks of breast-feeding. When a breast-fed infant is a few months old, however, his stools may occur less frequently—even once a day or once every other day. When switching a child to a cow's milk formula, the stools frequently become firmer in consistency. In fact, some cow's milk formulas may cause some constipation.

Cow's milk feedings usually result in stools that range in color from yellow to brown. They are firmer than the stools of a breast-fed baby and may have more of a fecal odor. Infants fed commercial formulas usually have one or two stools a day, whereas breast-fed infants may have from two to four stools a day during the first four or five months of life. As the child grows older and has a diet of more food and less milk, the stools take on the consistency of adult stools. Usually at around two years of age the stools become firmer. Some mucus can normally be seen in the stools of an infant. This frequently does not represent a problem, but it might in an older child.

MURIEL WOLF, M.D.
Washington, D.C.

When should I teach my infant son to drink out of a cup?

Drinking out of a cup can be started usually by six or seven months of age, although some mothers try to train their babies as early as four months. The infant should be able to sit or be propped up comfortably before such training is begun seriously. A spouted or pitcher-lip cup sometimes works well, but most people feel that, if you don't start too early, a regular cup is best. One thing to remember is that it is always easier to start with the cup by introducing a new fluid in it. It's sometimes hard to teach a baby to drink something out of a cup that he or she is used to associating with a bottle. If you are changing from breast milk or formula to cow's milk, or if you're starting a new juice, that's a golden opportunity to begin with a cup.

MERRITT B. LOW, M.D., F.A.A.P.
Ashfield, Massachusetts

My infant drinks out of a cup but refuses to settle down at night in the crib without the bottle. What should I do?

Putting a baby to sleep with a bottle is not recommended because it leads to very severe dental cavities. Give the baby a bottle while you are talking, singing, or playing games just before putting the child into bed. Tell the child what you are doing and that there will be no more bottles that night. Then leave the child alone. In most cases, after a few nights of complaint, the baby will settle down.

AVRUM L. KATCHER, M.D., F.A.A.P.
Flemington, New Jersey

I have run out of formula. Could I use condensed or evaporated milk until I get more formula?

An interim formula can be prepared using evaporated milk. One recipe involves mixing 13 ozs. of the milk in 17 ozs. of water and then adding 3 tablespoons of corn syrup. This solution is placed in glass bottles and steam-sterilized for fifteen minutes. This formula requires refrigeration, and any remainder should be discarded after twenty-four hours. The final mixture has adequate protein, fat, and carbohydrates for a normal infant's growth. It does not contain the proper amounts of fluoride and vitamins, however. The physician can prescribe a vitamin preparation for a child who receives such a formula.

ALAN R. RUSHTON, M.D., Ph.D.
Flemington, New Jersey

CHAPTER 15

Growth and Development

When will my newborn see?

A brand new baby has the ability to see and is able to distinguish between light and dark. By two weeks of age, infants notice large objects more intensely than small ones, and by two months of age follow a moving object with their eyes. If you watch your infant, you will notice very early that he or she will look at your face with interest during feedings.

KATHERINE M. KNIGHT, M.D.
New Orleans, Louisiana

Does my newborn see colors, or just shades of gray?

Infants apparently cannot differentiate between colors of the same brightness at birth, but most can make this distinction by approximately ten weeks of age. The question of what infants can see is obviously a difficult one, since babies cannot tell us exactly what they do see. The major methods employed to determine what infants may see have been to examine what they prefer to look at and how they react to repeated presentations of the same or similar patterns. Infants have the ability to "tune out" boringly repetitive presentations of the same stimulus. If a picture is placed in front of an awake, alert infant, he or she will look attentively at the picture. However, if the same picture is repeatedly presented and removed, the baby's attention will decrease until he or she pays essentially no attention to the same picture. Studies of infants' visual abilities repeatedly present objects or patterns with only one aspect of the pattern changed. For instance, a yellow line may be placed in front of the infant several times until the infant no longer glances at the line. A green line of the same size and shape is then substituted. If this change does not regain the infant's attention, it is then assumed that the infant cannot see the difference in color. Studies such as these suggest that by the age of three to four months, infants can discriminate colors almost as adults do.

Although newborns may not be able to discriminate colors, they are certainly able to turn to visual stimuli and to see areas of high contrast between light and dark, such as the upper part of the face (hairline, eyebrows, and eyes). Newborns prefer to look at the edges of patterns and at curved rather than straight lines. They like simple rather than complex patterns and enjoy seeing moving patterns.

As early as two to four months of age, infants begin to prefer more complex patterns and to perceive colors. Babies then begin to examine the whole of a picture, not just eyes, for instance; and by four to five months of age they can recognize an individual face despite changes in facial expression.

Thus, although infants may not be able to see different colors, their visual ability certainly goes beyond seeing the world only as gray.

LINDA J. MORGAN, M.D.
Hanover, New Hampshire

When will my infant start to fear strangers?

Not every infant goes through the phase of what is commonly known as strangeness reaction. Although many infants do show this reaction at about six to nine months of age, it is now recognized that this is not a necessary step in normal infant development. This is based on the demonstration that each baby is born with its own pattern of behavior or temperament. Although this can be modified by environment, mainly parental reaction, it will play a role in determining whether an infant ever develops fear of strangers or manifests this fear early and consistently throughout infancy and early childhood.

Some babies have temperaments that are characterized by an ability to approach new things and to adapt quickly to change. Such infants very probably will not show a strangeness reaction. On the other hand, some babies are difficult. This is *not* the mothers' fault. These babies are born with a behavior pattern of withdrawing from new things and taking a long time to adapt to change. Such infants may react strongly to strangers by crying vigorously. Between these two extremes are infants who may react to strangers in some intermediate fashion, as by a wary look.

So whether your infant will react to strangers with fear depends on what sort of behavior pattern he or she has developed. Discussion with your physician may help you analyze your baby's temperament and how you can best react to it.

T. F. McNAIR SCOTT, M.D.
Philadelphia, Pennsylvania

When will my baby start to crawl?

Your baby can start to crawl when he or she is anywhere from six to fifteen months of age. Crawling is not one of the major milestones that pediatricians look for in children. The reason is that there is great variation in the type of crawling and the time at which a child crawls. Some children never crawl. They merely go from sitting and rolling to walking. If your child has not begun to crawl, there is no reason to be concerned that he or she is delayed. Children have many different types of crawling, all of which are normal. Crawling is frequently a step between sitting and walking, but it is not a required step.

JEANNE M. EULBERG, M.D.
Kansas City, Kansas

When will my infant son start reaching for objects?

Your child sees from birth, although he may comprehend little. He will close his eyes at bright light from the moment he is born. He will follow your light-colored blouse across his field of vision (an area of ninety degrees at one month of age), and when he is two to three months old, he may look directly into your eyes, even though it is your lips that are moving. Therefore, sight is necessary for him before he reaches for objects (although some blind children will reach out toward sound). Usually this development takes place around four to five months of age, and by six months of age, the baby can transfer an object from one hand to another. Obviously, if he has some disorder with his eyes, muscles, nerves, bones, or brain, or was premature or some serious illness retarded his physical and/or mental growth, this milestone could be postponed.

Among the most frequent injuries pediatricians see are those caused by burns, often coffee burns. These so often happen when mom is holding her four-month-old child on her lap while she is watching television and drinking her coffee. The child reaches out and pulls over the cup of coffee. So, either put that cup out of reach, or drink milk instead.

ROBERT EASTON, M.D.
Peoria, Illinois

I can almost lift up my infant if he grasps my fingers. Is this good for his muscles, or can it hurt his arms?

Lifting an infant in this manner may generally be harmless. But in rare instances, it can result in painful dislocation of parts of the elbow joint. There is no benefit to be gained by this type of exercise and certainly there are safer ways of entertaining the child.

ALVIN EDELSTEIN, M.D.
Wayne, New Jersey

My infant's abdomen is hard and distended. What can I do for him?

A distended abdomen is associated with various clinical conditions. These disorders result from the structures within the abdomen, such as the kidney, adrenal gland, sympathetic nervous system (nervous tissue), muscles, liver, intestine, and bladder. Tumors arising from the kidney, adrenal gland, and sympathetic chain are frequently associated with distension of the abdomen, as are intestinal obstructions. Intestinal obstruction means that the flow of intestinal contents is diminished, reversed, or arrested; the result is constipation or vomiting. This obstruction is usually caused by growths, fecal impaction, foreign bodies, malrotation (twisting) of the gut, or obstructed inguinal hernia. A perforated appendix or a duodenal ulcer (perforation of the small intestine) also cause tenderness and distension of the abdomen. Growth in the liver and spleen, a distended urinary bladder, and many other conditions also cause distension of the abdomen.

Most of these conditions can have very serious consequences and require early medical or surgical intervention. Early diagnosis and intervention will certainly make the difference to your child. So, contact your physician immediately for treatment.

CHURKU MOHAN REDDY, M.D., F.A.A.P.
Nashville, Tennessee

My infant has an undescended testicle. What caused it? Is surgery necessary to correct this condition?

The male testes are formed during fetal development in the vicinity of the kidneys. The maturation process requires the testes to migrate into the scrotal sac. By the thirty-second to thirty-sixth week of gestation, the testes usually appear in the groin area. The migration should be complete at the time of birth of a full-term male. About one in three premature males, born prior to a gestational age of thirty-two weeks, has one or both testes undescended. Only 3 percent to 4 percent of all full-term male babies are born with undescended testes. Maturation, however, continues, and by age one, only three to four males in 1,000 have undescended testes.

Undescended testes means that the testes cannot be seen and palpated within the groin area. On occasion the mother may see the testes high up in the scrotum just below the inguinal canal, the groin. During a warm bath the testes may move into the scrotal sac. A male child with this condition is normal.

If the testis is still not completely in the scrotum after one year of age, the child needs special attention because an undescended testis is in 90 percent of such cases associated with a hernia (a rupture) on the same side of the groin. An undescended testis also has a fifteen-fold higher probability of becoming malignant than does a normal one. Infrequently, an undescended testis is not completely functional in a grown male. The ability to function as a man and to produce children is practically normal, since the other testis will produce enough sperm.

There is still debate about when and how to treat an undescended testis. However, agreement exists that action should be taken prior to age four or five. An attempt may be made to bring the testis into the scrotal sac by hormone injection. If this fails, surgery is indicated in order to bring the testis downward and to repair the possible rupture or hernia. The success rate with this treatment, measured by a sperm-producing testis, is about one in three.

EDUARD JUNG, M.D.
Chicago, Illinois

When should my infant be able to focus on an object or face?

Even a newborn infant is able to see, albeit poorly. The newborn can fixate on an object if it is in contrast to the surroundings. An infant can also focus on his or her mother's face, especially during feeding. Most infants are six to eight weeks of age before they are able to follow a moving object, such as a finger or a light. During the first three months of life, an infant's eye may be seen to "wander" in its attempt to focus. This is of no concern unless it is constant or if it persists past that time.

ROBERT E. GLENN, M.D.
Little Rock, Arkansas

My baby's eyes are blue. Will they stay that color?

Most white infants have blue eyes at birth although occasionally infants are born with brown eyes. Infants born with brown eyes (which includes most black children) will not have a change in eye color. Infants with blue eyes may have a color change some time during the first six months of life as the pigment of the iris (the colored part of the eye) further develops. Parents can get some idea if their child's eyes will change color by the presence of dark flecks in the iris.

Eye color is determined by two genes, one inherited from each parent. The gene for brown eyes is dominant; the gene for blue eyes is recessive. If a child inherits genes for blue eyes from both parents, he or she will have blue eyes. If, however, a child inherits a gene for brown eyes from either parent, he or she will have brown eyes. Therefore, two blue-eyed parents will have only blue-eyed children. If one or both parents have brown eyes, they can still have a blue-eyed child as long as both parents carry the recessive gene for blue eyes.

HOWARD SPIVAK, M.D.
Boston, Massachusetts

When should my baby be able to hold on to her rattle and other objects?

Babies are usually able to hold on to rattles and other objects from birth because they have a normal grasp reflex that results in their grasping anything that is put in their hands. Babies are unable to release voluntarily what is being grasped until they are about six or seven months of age. It is not uncommon for young infants under four or five months of age to grasp whatever is placed in their hands and then to see them banging to try to get rid of the object because they are unable to release it.

FERNANDO J. deCASTRO, M.D.
St. Louis, Missouri

When will my newborn start to recognize different faces and voices?

Infants can see as soon as they are born. They can differentiate light from dark and can perceive some colors. They examine faces and other objects, and are attracted by lights, windows, and other bright objects. Newborns will study faces, but are unable to get a clear image if a face is too far or too close. Eight to ten inches away from the baby's eyes is about right. Babies can hear before they are born.

As for differentiating between different faces and voices, babies around three months of age start to recognize familiar objects, and sounds begin to have more meaning. Infants between three and six months of age notice differences between the lower voice of father, higher voice of mother, and the very high voices of children.

Newer studies have shown, however, that by two or three weeks of age, newborns recognize and respond to their parents' individualized ways of relating to them, and can express their love and acknowledge this special relationship.

SHARON POHORECKI, R.N., C.P.N.P.
Toledo, Ohio

When should my infant be able to roll over by herself?

This is very variable. Some babies can roll over within a few months, but other normal babies may not be able to do so for a year or more. Rolling over is not a particularly accurate measure of a child's development.

AVRUM L. KATCHER, M.D., F.A.A.P.
Flemington, New Jersey

When will my baby smile back in response to smiles and words?

You should expect your baby to smile in response to social contact by the time he or she is eight weeks old. Sixty percent of all infants will be smiling by four weeks of age.

STEPHEN E. WALLACE, M.D., F.A.A.P.
Springfield, Illinois

My toddler has a bulge in his lower abdomen, and the skin covering the bulge is bluish. Should he see a doctor?

How long has the bulge been present? Is it on one side or right in the middle? Is it sore, painful, increasing in size, intermittent? Also, is there a break in the skin? Was there an injury? Are there similar bumps elsewhere?

These are the things the doctor should know so that he or she can tell whether a visit is necessary.

MERRITT B. LOW, M.D., F.A.A.P.
Ashfield, Massachusetts

My son crawls backward but not forward. Is this all right?

When babies first get up onto their hands and knees, they often move backward before they learn to crawl forward. If your baby continues to move only backward by the time he is ten months of age, he should be checked by his pediatrician to make sure his motor development is otherwise normal.

M. E. SYMONDS, M.D.
Mountainside, New Jersey

When will my infant sit up by herself with no support?

Generally, a baby can sit up by six or eight months of age.

AVRUM L. KATCHER, M.D., F.A.A.P.
Flemington, New Jersey

At what age should my infant be able to raise his head and chest off the mattress, supporting himself with his arms and hands?

A few infants will raise their heads and chests off a mattress or table in the prone position (lying on abdomen) by one month of age. Most infants should be able to do this by three months.

If your baby is not raising his head and chest off the table by four months, this should be brought to the attention of your doctor.

JAMES T. HARTFORD, M.D., P.C.
Beaverton, Oregon

CHAPTER 16

Immunizations and Vaccines

My infant has been crying for two hours since the DPT injection and he seems to have a fever. What should I do?

The problem can be solved by administering one-fourth to one-half of a baby aspirin every four hours as needed. This may help with any pain and also decrease the fever that may follow the DPT injection. The same advice may be followed after each DPT injection. For the two-year booster shot, the dosage of aspirin should be increased to one and one-half baby aspirins every four hours. (Tylenol in the proper dosage could be substituted for the aspirin.)

HUGH B. SPENCER, M.D.
Tulsa, Oklahoma

Is there a chance that my baby will get measles, mumps, or rubella before she is immunized?

The American Academy of Pediatrics recommends that measles, mumps, and rubella immunizations be administered at fifteen months of age. If, between the ages of six to fifteen months of age, your infant is exposed to measles or rubella (and mumps to a lesser degree), you should contact your physician. Antibody or immunity is transferred to the baby while in the womb and lasts for some months after the child is born. There is some chance that the amount of antibody transferred to the baby was not enough to render that baby immune. If a mother has not had measles, mumps, or rubella, there is a chance that her child could contract one of these diseases prior to immunization. With the advent of the immunizations for these three illnesses comes a whole new set of questions as to what will happen to the offspring of immunized mothers. It would appear that the protection afforded by the wild virus as opposed to that given by the immunization virus is more lasting. Therefore, there is a chance that mothers who have been protected from the diseases since the vaccines have been available may not pass on as much immunity to the infant in the womb as those who were rendered immune by an infection with the wild virus. This remains to be seen, as the vaccines have been available only since 1963.

In summary, the answer to the question is yes, but protection lasts for only six months or so, and if there is exposure, check with your pediatrician.

THEODORE I. PUTNAM, M.D.
Buffalo, New York

Can my infant still get whooping cough even though she has been immunized?

Although this is remotely possible, it is highly unlikely. The pertussis (P) or whooping cough component of the DPT vaccine is effective in its ability to induce protection but is also the component associated with the most reactions. Since your child has completed her initial three DPT shots (plus a booster at age eighteen months), you can feel comfortable that she will not get whooping cough. Sometimes, however, viral infections can occur that closely resemble the symptoms of whooping cough. Actual whooping cough is caused by a specific bacterium.

There is most concern about very small infants who have not had any immunizations against whooping cough since it is highly communicable and can be very serious. Even one or two immunizations is of considerable help in developing protection.

DOUGLAS S. HOLSCLAW JR., M.D.
Philadelphia, Pennsylvania

My infant had the DPT injection in his leg, and now, five hours later, he has a lump there that feels warm and seems awfully tender. What can I put on the area? Is this a normal reaction to the shot?

This is a frequent reaction with many infants. It is a local reaction to the ingredients within the shot and it often causes pain and warmth in the area. The best thing to do now is to apply a cold washcloth to the area and continue to do this for a few minutes, three or four times a day until the redness and tenderness seem to be disappearing. This should only take a day or two. Most likely, though, your child will possibly be left with a pea-sized little knot under the skin in the area where the shot was given. This is nothing to worry about and it eventually will go away, but may take many months.

BRUCE P. MEYER, M.D.
Columbus, Ohio

My husband and I need some immunizations for traveling abroad. Our newborn will go with us. Will he need these shots, too?

In most developed countries of the world (for example, Australia, Canada, Great Britain, Japan, New Zealand, and the European countries), the risk of an infant's acquiring an infectious disease is probably no greater than the risk incurred while traveling in the United States. However, for travelers in underdeveloped countries, such as those in Africa, Asia, South America, Central America, and the Middle and Far East, the risk of certain infections is significantly increased, particularly for travelers venturing to small cities or off the usual tourist routes. Nevertheless, only rarely is it advisable to alter the standard immunization schedule recommended for all infants living in the United States. One circumstance might be for families traveling to certain areas where the risk of contracting whooping cough (pertussis), polio, or measles is very high. In such areas it may be appropriate to *initiate* routine immunizations at an earlier age, for example, giving DPT (diphtheria, pertussis, tetanus vaccine) and oral polio vaccine in the immediate newborn period instead of at two months of age, and giving measles vaccine at twelve months of age (or occasionally earlier) instead of at fifteen months of age. (Booster immunization with these vaccines should then be continued according to the standard schedule for infants in the United States. The doses administered to the newborn should not be counted.) Because these vaccines are often less effective and occasionally more hazardous when given at an earlier age than usually recommended, one needs to weigh carefully the possible benefits of early immunization with the potential risks. The distribution of different infectious diseases varies widely in the world. Therefore, one should consult a pediatrician or public health authority for recommendations about immunization and/or gamma globulin treatment for prevention of diseases specific to a particular area.

Finally, probably the most frequent and potentially severe infections in infants traveling abroad are gastrointestinal illnesses that are not prevented by currently available vaccines. The most convenient way to minimize this risk is for the mother to continue to nurse her baby for as long as possible (preferably for the entire first year). Alternatively, sterilization of infant formula, tap water, and bottles, and strict attention to good hygienic practices will also lower the risk.

LINDA K. MYERS, M.D.
DAN M. GRANOFF, M.D.
St. Louis, Missouri

I understand that most vaccines are grown on eggs. My baby is allergic to eggs. Can she still receive her immunizations?

Babies who have true allergic sensitivity to eggs manifest this by hives, wheezing, or worsening of eczema. These infants should not receive vaccines grown directly on eggs for such diseases as yellow fever and influenza without having a skin test with the vaccine before administration.

However, the active immunization with measles and mumps virus vaccines usually poses no problem for the child who is allergic to eggs. These vaccines are grown on chick embryo fibroblasts and probably do not contain significant amounts of egg antigen. It has been shown that administering a live measles virus vaccine to children with a severe clinical reaction to egg protein did not result in unusual reactions. Also, allergic sensitivity to feathers does not necessarily indicate allergic sensitivity to virus vaccines derived from chick embryo cultures. Infants who are sensitive to feathers should also be able to receive measles and mumps vaccine.

In general, if an infant can eat eggs without problems, egg-grown vaccines are acceptable.

DONALD E. KLEIN, M.D.
Providence, Rhode Island

Why are immunizations given to my baby in his thigh?

Immunizations are given in the form of injections into the muscle. Over a period of days, the injected material is carried away by the bloodstream and circulated throughout the body. The needle must not damage any important structures such as nerves or blood vessels. All injections do hurt, but the pain is lessened if the injected material is placed deep within a large muscle mass. Babies have a large amount of muscle in the buttocks. This is not a good injection site, however, because many important nerves run from the spinal cord down to the legs just beneath this muscle group. Serious damage to these nerves can be caused if they are punctured by a needle. The outer portion of the baby's thigh is another muscular area. Here there are no major nerves or blood vessels and this is the safest location for an immunization injection in infants and young children.

ALAN R. RUSHTON, M.D., Ph.D.
Flemington, New Jersey

Why are smallpox vaccines no longer one of the required immunizations for my baby?

Smallpox vaccination is no longer required for two reasons: the likelihood that a person might develop a serious or even fatal reaction to the vaccination itself is much greater than the likelihood that a person might contract smallpox; and, as of 1977, there have been no known cases of smallpox.

Routine vaccination of children against smallpox was stopped in the United States in the 1960s because serious illness or death from the vaccination was more likely than contracting smallpox itself. (The last case of smallpox in the United States occurred in the late 1940s.)

It now appears that smallpox has been completely eradicated worldwide. Since 1977, no one is known to have contracted the illness as a result of infection with the "wild" smallpox virus. There have been several laboratory workers infected as a result of laboratory error. It is believed, however, that as long as no new cases of smallpox occur, this will be a disease of the past. This is the first such illness of mankind to be totally eradicated!

FOSTER H. YOUNG JR., M.D.
Kingstree, South Carolina

Are there any risks or dangers to my child from immunizations and vaccines?

Two major types of immunizations are used to protect children from serious infectious diseases. Live virus vaccines are made from attenuated (weakened) strains of the virus. They produce very mild forms of polio, mumps, measles, or German measles (rubella). The body's own immunization system is stimulated to generate protective antibodies to block future infection by the natural virus that causes each disease. There may be some minimal tenderness around the injection site immediately after a vaccination. About one or two weeks later, a low fever, joint pains, and a flat red rash may develop. These symptoms are easily controlled with aspirin or acetaminophen, and they disappear within a few days.

The second type of vaccination is "DPT." This is manufactured from whole bacteria (whooping cough), or from toxins made by a bacteria (tetanus and diphtheria). Adverse reactions are more common with this type of vaccination. About 50 percent of children will have some pain, swelling, and redness at the injection site. Within the first twenty-four to forty-eight hours after the vaccination, 25 percent to 50 percent will also develop a fever, fussiness, or drowsiness. The great majority of such symptoms can be controlled easily with aspirin or acetaminophen.

Serious side effects of vaccines are rare, but they do occur. A few children have been reported to be unable to fight viral infections very well. When such children are immunized with live virus vaccines, they may become very ill. In these children, inactivated (killed) vaccines are safer than attenuated (weakened) ones.

The whooping cough vaccine in the DPT injection may produce high fever. These occur within twenty-four hours of the immunization. Careful follow-up examinations of such children have shown that they then develop normally. Permanent brain damage or even sudden death may also result from this type of vaccination, but this is extremely rare and occurs with approximately 1 out of 310,000 children.

The rapid decline over the past twenty years in the frequency of serious childhood illnesses such as polio, whooping cough, diphtheria, measles, and mumps is clearly related to extensive use of vaccines to produce immunity in children. Several countries in Europe halted routine immunizations, and a dramatic increase in the incidence of these diseases quickly followed. The viruses and bacteria that cause the major childhood diseases are still present in our society. The risk of serious injury from a vaccination is very small compared to the benefits of avoiding infections with these potentially serious diseases.

ALAN R. RUSHTON, M.D., Ph.D.
Flemington, New Jersey

Does my child have to be immunized? What shots should he get, and when?

No young infant or child *has* to be immunized, although the law requires certain immunizations before a child goes to school, unless there is a medical exemption request signed by a doctor. You should be aware of the definite risks involved in all immunization procedures, which most pediatricians feel are far outweighed by the benefits. You should also be aware of the dangers from the diseases themselves. Your consent for the immunizations is required. Statistics prove the points regarding risks. Forty years ago in the United States, there were 900,000 cases of common contagious diseases that are now preventable. Now each year there are 30,000 cases, one-thirtieth as many.

Consult your physician about the schedule. DPT (diphtheria, whooping cough, tetanus) and MMR (measles, mumps, rubella) are the usual shots—plus polio "drinks." Others may be advisable in individual situations. Polio "shots" are sometimes given instead of "drinks."

MERRITT B. LOW, M.D., F.A.A.P.
Ashfield, Massachusetts

CHAPTER 17

Infant

My infant is constantly moving and kicking his feet. Is he nervous?

Not necessarily. Some babies, just like some adolescents and a few adults, seem to be full of energy and more active than others. A nervous baby or child tends to be tense and sometimes fidgety. Your baby is just busy and active. You might find this "busy" trait in close relatives if you inquire. Mention this activity next time you see your pediatrician, but you probably have no reason to worry.

HENRY J. KONZELMANN, M.D.
Springfield, Illinois

My infant only catnaps during the day and sleeps for only three hours at night. Should I give her medicine that will make her sleep?

The answer is a definite no! Although the parents may become exhausted from such a schedule, an infant should not be sedated so that the parents can sleep. The child will generally sleep as much as she needs to, provided she is left undisturbed during her sleep periods. If the baby is fussy or crying during the night when she is not sleeping, then she may have colic, may be teething, or may be getting secondary gain from the fussy behavior (this type of child is the so-called trained night crier). Treating colic is frustrating and often unsuccessful, but babies do outgrow it. Behavior modification may be necessary if the baby is a trained night crier; you may want to consult your pediatrician for help. (Some pediatricians may prescribe temporary, mild sedatives if an infant is a severe night crier or has prolonged bouts of colic or teething.)

There are studies being done that suggest that a baby's sleeping patterns are determined by a maturing process of the nervous system that takes place in all infants, but not at the same rate in any two children, and, to a lesser degree, by the infant's individual temperament. There are obvious temperamental differences in children, and certain types of temperaments seem to be associated with shorter periods of sleep and less total sleep during the day.

LINDA C. LONEY, M.D.
St. Louis, Missouri

Should I leave a night light on for the baby?

Yes. If the baby should awaken, he or she will feel more secure with a light on.

JAMES R. McNIEL, M.D.
Fort Dodge, Iowa

Is a playpen too confining for my baby? Will it lessen his spirit of exploration and thus retard his development?

The answer to this question is a qualified no. The question of whether to use a playpen or not is still a controversial issue among various authorities and some parents. Certainly young infants and toddlers can be safe and move about freely in this confined area. A playpen is a rather useful piece of equipment because not only does it allow the baby to view and explore the environment, but it also gives you a safe place to put your baby. Whether indoors or outdoors, it keeps him off the ground and allows him to view the world around him relatively free of danger. Some babies respond better to confinement in the playpen area if they are introduced to the playpen at an early age (three to four months) so that when they begin to sit and crawl, they have the feeling they can do so without the restrictions of having to be picked up and removed from hazardous situations. This theory establishes the playpen as the infant's special area and seems to meet with less resistance in various stages of development. There is no clinical evidence to suggest that the playpen itself will retard the child's development; however, keep in mind that personal contact is very important in the overall development of your child, so direct stimulation to the child should be carried out.

BONITA L. SETTLE, M.D.
Nashville, Tennessee

My baby has to have a chest X ray. Will this be harmful to him?

Current radiological techniques produce very minimal radiation exposure from chest X rays. Therefore, a chest X ray would not be harmful to your baby. If your child's history and physical findings dictate a need for a chest X ray, do not hesitate to allow this to be done. It means that certain conditions need to be ruled out that can be done only be obtaining chest X rays. You can depend upon the radiologist to minimize any radiation exposure.

WILFRED Q. COLE, M.D.
Jackson, Mississippi

When and how should I cut my baby's nails?

A baby's nails grow at the rate of about 0.1 mm a day. This means they grow about ⅛ of an inch each month. The major problems with nails are caused by overzealous trimming. Nails should be trimmed every three to four weeks or when scratching becomes a problem. Nail clippers or blunt scissors should be used, and the corners should not be rounded. Rounding the corners damages the groove in which the nail grows and promotes the possibility of infection or ingrown nails.

GAIL H. GALLEMORE, M.D.
Johnson City, Tennessee

141

Sometimes my infant cries for no apparent reason but stops when I pick her up. Will this spoil her?

It is not appropriate to speak of spoiling a young infant. Spoiling implies excessive gratification on the part of an adult of the wishes and whims of the child. Young infants who cry or fret are in some distress, either physical or psychological, and primarily need to be comforted. It is not until the end of the first year of life and especially into the second year that one can begin to speak of "spoiling." Even at this stage, it requires sophisticated analysis to determine whether the child is in need or is being excessively demanding. In general, the younger the child, the more attentive and gratifying you must be, and the older the child, the more gradually and slowly and empathetically depriving you must be.

JAMES EGAN, M.D.
Washington, D.C.

My infant's cry has been very high-pitched for the past two days. What does this mean?

A high-pitched cry can be a serious symptom of various types of disorders. Occasionally, it occurs after a baby has had a routine DPT shot. However, whenever a baby has a high-pitched cry, it is a good idea to contact your doctor or take the baby to the doctor's office for an examination.

DAVID J. TEPPER, M.D.
Chattanooga, Tennessee

Should I let my one-year-old child keep toys in her crib at night? If so, what kind?

Most children develop special attachments to objects (e.g., dolls, stuffed animals), and separation from these objects at night may be very difficult. There is generally no reason for concern, and the child can be permitted to take toys to bed as long as they conform to simple safety guidelines. Safe toys would include sturdy rattles, washable squeaky toys, large beads on a cord (but be absolutely certain that objects attached by loose string, wire, or plastic cannot become entangled with your child), and stuffed animals that do not have glass or button eyes that the child might remove. Mothers can make soft, pillow-like stuffed animals with bright-colored cloth and fire-retardant filler. Unsafe toys would include those small enough or with removable parts that may be swallowed, flammable objects, or objects that a child could use as a toehold to climb out of the crib.

Above all, it must be recognized that attachment to toys is a normal part of child development and should not be discouraged.

GERALD B. HICKSON, M.D.
Nashville, Tennessee

My infant does not have any tears when she cries. Is this all right?

Although it is unusual, 1 percent or 2 percent of all children will cry with few or no tears. The overwhelming majority of these children are perfectly normal. There are rare diseases that are associated with an absence of tears. In some of these cases, the eye will appear unusually dry and such children should be seen by a physician. Even if your child is not having other medical problems and she still cries without tears, her pediatrician should be made aware of this condition on the next routine visit.

J. MARTIN KAPLAN, M.D.
Philadelphia, Pennsylvania

When should I expect my baby to sleep through the night?

From the perspective of social development, children in the first four weeks of life usually awaken twice during the night for feeding. By eight weeks of age, they usually have one nighttime feeding. By the time a child is approximately three months of age, he or she is sleeping through the night.

An important consideration is the family's adjustment to the child's sleeping pattern. In one study, 7 percent of mothers surveyed felt that at five weeks of age their infants' sleeping should be proceeding better. This figure had decreased to 2 percent to 3 percent by three to six months of age. Most families appear to adapt well to the sleeping patterns of young children. When their children were five weeks of age, only 18 percent of families surveyed noticed significant changes in their family patterns. This figure decreased to 7 percent by the time the child was three months of age.

Some mothers feel that they can prognosticate their children's temperaments from their sleeping patterns. Some studies done on this subject, however, demonstrate that it is difficult to do this in the first six months of life. An infant regarded as difficult at one point in the early months may not be so at a future point.

DON C. VAN DYKE, M.D.
Atlantic City, New Jersey

My baby's hands and feet are often cold. Is this normal?

Many young babies have relatively poor blood flow in their hands and feet. This is particularly evident in cold rooms, where the hands and feet may become blue and cold. When the baby is in a warm room, blood flow increases, and color and temperature in the hands and feet improve. Rarely, a baby may have narrowing of the arteries supplying blood to the hands and feet. In this case, the hands and feet would be cold or blue all the time. A physician can easily check the baby's circulation at a regular office visit if parents are concerned.

ALAN R. RUSHTON, M.D., Ph.D.
Flemington, New Jersey

What kind of mattress (foam or felt) and crib are best for a baby?

There are specific federal recommendations for full-size to non-full-size cribs that went into effect August 10, 1976. Non-full-size cribs must have a label stating they meet U.S. Consumer Product Safety Commission regulations. Recommendations from the American Academy of Pediatrics for cribs and mattresses are as follows: Cribs should have slats no more than 2⅜ inches apart. No lead-based paints should be used anywhere on the crib. No plastic bells or balls should be used as ornaments. The end panels should be made of a material that will not splinter. There should be no cross bars on the sides. The sides, when lowered, should be four inches above the mattress. The sides should be operated with a locking, hand-operated latch. The mattress should be the same size as the crib so there are no gaps to catch arms or legs.

MILTON GRAUB, M.D.
Philadelphia, Pennsylvania

CHAPTER 18

Infections

Can my son go outside even though he has chicken pox?

In moderate climates, in good weather, there probably is no harm in children being allowed to go outside to get some fresh air, provided they feel well and have no fever. However, because chicken pox is so contagious, they should not be allowed to play with other susceptible children. And, because of the dangers of secondary skin infections, they should not be allowed to play in the dirt or otherwise contaminate the exposed skin.

JOHN D. MORONEY, M.D.
Tampa, Florida

Can a child get chicken pox more than once?

A single, well-documented attack of chicken pox confers lifelong immunity to the disease, so that a second case of chicken pox would be extremely rare. Some people think they have had chicken pox when they have not, and following an exposure to it in adult life, they develop a classic case of the disease. In nearly all such situations, the original disease that they thought was chicken pox was something else. However, the chicken pox virus can live for many years without symptoms in an infected patient and then become reactivated. Because the virus migrates to the nerve roots, the secondary attack is not a single case of chicken pox, but rather an attack of shingles or herpes zoster. This is a reactivation of a slow virus infection, and presumably not a reinfection with a new strain of chicken pox virus. Attacks of acute herpes zoster may follow exposure by an older person to a fresh case of chicken pox, or more commonly, may accompany some type of other infection or serious stress. Active herpes zoster is mildly contagious for other people who have not previously had chicken pox, and close family contacts may occasionally cause chicken pox to develop through exposure to a person in the family with active herpes zoster. However, the reactivation infection with herpes zoster is not as infectious as classic chicken pox. Incidentally, approximately 85 percent to 90 percent of all adults will have a positive serum test for antibodies to chicken pox even though they cannot recall a history of the disease.

WILLIAM J. CASHORE, M.D.
Providence, Rhode Island

Can chicken pox become infected?

Yes, but infections do not occur very often. Itching can be formidable with chicken pox, and it is therefore surprising that more children do not infect their pox. Sometimes physicians prescribe medicine to help with the discomfort. A few tablespoons of baking soda in a tub of cool water can also help relieve itching. As with other childhood illnesses, careful handwashing can help retard the spread of the infection to other children. It also helps to prevent infected pox.

A. W. SIMINGTON, M.D.
Keene, New Hampshire

My son was with a friend who broke out with chicken pox today. How soon will my child break out with it?

Sometimes children have so few lesions while they have chicken pox that the disease is unrecognized. If your son had unrecognized chicken pox, he is immune and protected from developing chicken pox. Otherwise, if he was infected by his friend, he will break out with chicken pox within two weeks, plus or minus three days.

HERBERT A. WENNER, M.D.
Kansas City, Missouri

Are there any symptoms that appear before chicken pox show up?

Chicken pox is an acute, contagious, viral disease that is transmitted from person to person only. The incubation period is from two to three weeks, and the infant or child who is exposed may develop symptoms as early as two days before the spots of the chicken pox actually appear. These symptoms include fever and, sometimes, a slight runny nose. The fever may be as high as 103° or 104° during that time. In some cases, the infant may develop the lesions of chicken pox, not just on skin surfaces, but on mucous membranes such as those in the mouth and in the vaginal area in little girls, and these spots or lesions may show up during the forty-eight hours prior to the time that the skin spots show up. Other symptoms, such as cough, vomiting, or diarrhea, should make you suspicious that there is something else going on and make the diagnosis of chicken pox less likely.

Remember that chicken pox is usually not a life-threatening illness in infancy and childhood, but the child should be kept away from persons who are susceptible to severe complications. Such persons are those with leukemia, or those who are taking steroids for other illnesses whose immunity might not be good and therefore would be susceptible to a possible life-threatening situation. The infants and children who develop chicken pox are contagious for two or three days prior to the time that the actual skin lesions show up.

DONALD F. JOHNSON, M.D.
Kalamazoo, Michigan

Can my child give chicken pox to anyone before he breaks out with them? How long is he contagious to others?

Chicken pox is an illness that is both airborne and carried on objects such as clothing. Your child is contagious with chicken pox from the time he develops the upper respiratory symptoms, three to four days before the eruption of the pox, until there are no new spots and the oldest ones are well dried out. This usually takes approximately seven to ten days.

A. E. REARDON, M.D., F.A.A.P.
Duluth, Minnesota

Is there a vaccine for chicken pox?

No, there is no commercial vaccine available for chicken pox in the United States. The Japanese have been working for several years on such a vaccine, and it is being tested on an experimental basis. The vaccine has not been tested in the United States, however. It will require several years of testing before it becomes commercially available.

RICHARD A. GUTHRIE, M.D.
Wichita, Kansas

My toddler has some chicken pox in his throat. How can I relieve the discomfort for him?

There are no good medications to relieve throat pain in the toddler, but changes in the diet may be helpful. Encourage the child to try to eat Popsicles (the cold may help numb the pain) and to drink clear liquids such as soda, Kool-Aid, or water. It is often wise to avoid dairy products such as milk and ice cream with any sore throat, since they may cause increased formation of mucus in the back of the throat and may cause the child to cough or gag, thus adding to the discomfort. Acid fruit juices such as orange juice may cause a stinging sensation and are best avoided, as are spicy, salty, or crunchy foods, such as potato chips or corn chips.

K. LYNN CATES, M.D.
Farmington, Connecticut

My daughter has a few chicken pox around the genital area. She's very uncomfortable because of this. What can I do to help her?

The chicken pox may be so few as to escape diagnosis, or they may be so many and so severe as to make Grandma think your daughter has the extinct disease of smallpox. When they are numerous in the panty area, especially in a diapered child, they are quite troublesome because the moisture of urine keeps them open, and the bacteria from bowel movements can then infect them. The salty urine may burn on the sores so much that the child may hold back her urine to a most uncomfortable stage.

You can help decrease the incidence of your daughter's scratching her chicken pox and alleviate her itching by clipping her fingernails closely, so that there won't be so much to scratch with. Wash her nails and hands frequently to keep down the germ population. Bath water to which either starch or baking soda has been added can coat the body with a fine layer of dust and cut down on the itching. Blot her body dry, don't wipe. Various calamine types of lotion or creams on the itchy areas may help. If your daughter is afraid to urinate because it hurts her chicken pox in the genital area, put her in a tub of warm water and coax her to urinate (remember, you may have scolded her in the past for doing just that, so be patient if she heeds her earlier training). Occasionally, an ointment that has an anesthetic in it, such as Nupercainal, will remove the sting of the sores when urine comes in contact with them. It will be well to leave the area exposed to air—if she doesn't scratch them open.

The sores should heal best this way. But most children will scratch the pox, so a cloth diaper, without a plastic cover (so air can circulate), is best placed snugly over the diaper area till the chicken pox have dried up.

ROBERT EASTON, M.D.
Peoria, Illinois

My toddler has chicken pox and has developed a high fever and sore throat. Is this to be expected?

High fever and sore throat can develop with chicken pox, which, after all, is a systemic viral illness that affects the whole body. The sore throat can be due to chicken pox lesions inside the mouth, making the child rather uncomfortable and unable to drink enough fluids to keep the temperature normal. Nevertheless, these symptoms should alert the parent to a possible complication of chicken pox, namely a secondary bacterial infection. This development during the course of chicken pox should be reported to your physician. Remember, acetaminophen (Tylenol, Tempra, Liquiprin), not aspirin, should be used for the fever or discomfort of chicken pox. However, this is only if needed in addition to fluids and relief from itching, as prescribed by your doctor.

ROBERT FOMALONT, M.D.
Princeton, New Jersey

My son has a lot of chicken pox on his face. Is this going to cause scarring?

Chicken pox often causes scars, but these have a remarkable tendency to disappear by the time the child has grown up.

AVRUM L. KATCHER, M.D., F.A.A.P.
Flemington, New Jersey

Can my child get strep throat from chicken pox?

No. Chicken pox is caused by the varicella virus. It is characterized by the appearance of crops of topical sores on the skin and somewhat less obvious lesions on the membranes of the mouth and throat.

The rash begins on the trunk and spreads to the arms, legs, face, and scalp. After twenty-four to forty-eight hours, the lesions of chicken pox may be seen in all of the different stages at one time, from the beginning red spots, through the raised bumps, to the fluid-filled blisters, and finally to the dried scabs. Chicken pox is no longer contagious when most of the sores have become scabs.

The illness is accompanied by fever during the first three to four days, when the rash is erupting. The patient may have a sore throat due to chicken pox-related lesions in the mouth and throat. This throat pain is usually not due to streptococcal infection, which is a bacterial infection separate from chicken pox.

One doesn't get strep throat from chicken pox. The patient with chicken pox could, of course, have caught strep throat by coincidence from someone else, but this chance occurrence is uncommon.

ALAN P. DeMAYO, M.D., F.A.A.P.
New York, New York

What causes strep throat? Is strep throat contagious?

Strep throat is caused by a bacterial infection. The name and group of the bacteria most commonly responsible is Group A beta hemolytic streptococcus. It is a contagious disease and may be transmitted by sneezing, coughing, or by using the same eating and drinking utensils used by someone with the disease.

KATHERINE M. KNIGHT, M.D.
New Orleans, Louisiana

My child just finished taking some medication for strep throat and I noticed that her fingers and toes are peeling. Is this because of the medication or the strep?

Your child's peeling skin is most likely due to the strep infection and not to the medication.

The bacteria that cause the inflamed throat and/or tonsillitis commonly known as strep throat are called Group A beta hemolytic streptococci. Group A streptococci not only cause strep throat but also cause scarlet fever, which is tonsillitis with fever and a rash. It is important to remember that both strep throat and scarlet fever are manifestations of the same disease and that one is not more serious than the other. Seen another way, strep throat is scarlet fever without the rash.

Peeling of the skin is a characteristic feature of the skin rash seen with scarlet fever. Those particular streptococci produce a substance called a toxin, which causes the changes in the child's skin, including the redness, sandpaper roughness, and subsequent peeling. It is important to note that this toxin does not cause the sore throat or fever, but only the skin manifestations of the disease. Taking antibiotics eliminates the bacteria in both strep throat and scarlet fever. The child's fever goes down and she feels better. But the antibiotics cannot neutralize or remove the toxin produced by the bacteria before they are killed. Therefore, the skin changes of the strep infection are unaffected by the medication. The peeling of the skin characteristically occurs during the second week of illness and can last anywhere from three to eight weeks. The peeling is a self-limiting process, and normal skin will replace it.

In conclusion, it appears that the peeling of the fingers and toes of your child after a course of antibiotics (which is usually ten days) is secondary to her strep infection.

JO-ANN S. HARRIS, M.D.
Kansas City, Kansas

One of my older children has strep throat. Can my newborn catch it? Does my newborn have any natural immunity to strep throat?

Strep throat occurs most commonly in the school-age child. It is caused by bacteria, Group A beta hemolytic streptococci, that can infect all age groups. In general, however, the incidence of strep throat is lowest in infancy, gradually rising during childhood, and peaking at adolescence.

In newborns and young infants a strep infection is indistinguishable from the common cold. The infant has a runny nose, a mild fever, and a decrease in appetite. Strep infections of the skin, called impetigo, are common in the preschool child. Tonsillitis or strep throat occurs most commonly in the preschool child. The strep bacteria sometimes make a toxin that can cause a rash called scarlet fever.

Newborns do not have immunity against many strep bacteria, but they do have immunity against the toxin that the strep bacteria make; therefore, they rarely acquire scarlet fever. Rheumatic fever, which can cause damage to the heart, is a complication of a strep throat infection. It is caused by the body's response to the strep infection and, too, is rarely seen in newborns or very young children.

JAMIE HEWELL, M.D.
St. Louis, Missouri

Will my toddler always have a fever if she has strep throat?

Not necessarily. Although a low grade fever usually accompanies strep throat, each person responds differently to the illness. One child may be very sick, with a fever of 104° to 105°, whereas another may not be. The ultimate diagnosis of strep throat is always positive results of a throat culture.

EVELYN BAUGH, M.D.
Toledo, Ohio

My son is always getting strep throat. Does this mean the medication is no longer working?

It is extremely unusual for your son to get strep throat unless he is in intimate contact with an older child who has it. The great majority of sore throats are due to viruses, which will produce more complaints of pain than will a strep throat. When he complains of soreness, a throat culture can be made to diagnose whether or not the infection is strep throat.

LAWRENCE PARK, M.D.
Torrance, California

My child has a hivelike rash that started on her face and is spreading. What could cause this?

The successful management of a skin rash on an infant or child depends on accurate diagnosis. It must be considered that the rash may be infectious, allergic, traumatic, or symptomatic of some metabolic or physiologic disorder. Hives, or urticaria, are skin eruptions characterized by red or pale raised areas called wheals. These areas are usually itchy and often rapidly change form. A variety of factors can bring on hives, but in only 10 percent or 20 percent of these cases can one pinpoint the specific cause in a particular child. Some forms of hives are truly allergic in that they are mediated by the reaction of an allergen such as a food or an inhalant and an allergen-specific immunoglobulin or allergic antibody. The classical acute hives due to an allergy may occur following the ingestion of a food such as eggs, chocolate, milk, nuts, peanuts, strawberries, fish, and shell fish, or drugs such as penicillin, sulfa, tetracycline, aspirin, and codeine. Hives may occur as a result of insect bites from fleas, bees, wasps, yellow jackets, and hornets or after contact with certain animals such as dogs, cats, cows, horses, rabbits, or hogs. Hives also occasionally result from excessive exposure to environmental allergens such as pollens. When horse serum antitoxin was used for the treatment of tetanus and pneumonia, hives occurred in 10 percent of immunized patients.

Hives may result from exposure to cold, the sun, direct heat, pressure, or water. Cholinergic urticaria, a distinct red rash with small, well-demarcated lesions, appears within a few minutes after exercise, general overheating, or emotional stress.

Certain infections seem to produce a hivelike rash. Some viral infections as well as some fungal infections and even various parasitic infections have been documented as causing hives. Certain forms of inflammatory diseases, such as juvenile rheumatoid arthritis, occasionally appear as a hivelike rash.

The incidence of hives is extremely high. More than 20 percent of the population have had hives at some time in their lives. Acute hives occur most often in children and last from a few hours up to forty-eight hours. Many times the exact cause is never determined.

Acute hives usually can be controlled symptomatically with antihistamine medications and with the elimination of any known inciting factors. Most often hives are self-limited, and usually no underlying cause can be identified. However, adequate documentation of the child's diet, health, and environmental conditions at the time of the onset of the rash will be most helpful if the hives are recurring and require medical attention.

When part of a general allergic reaction (stuffiness, wheezing, weakness, nausea), hives need immediate attention.

ROBERT J. DOCKHORN, M.D.
Kansas City, Missouri

My toddler's baby-sitter has hepatitis. Is it contagious? When can she baby-sit for my family again?

If the baby-sitter has the infectious type of hepatitis, it most likely would be contagious. However, there are other types of hepatitis, and what needs to be ascertained is the type she has. This generally will not be known until the doctor does enough studies. If it is the infectious form, it certainly is contagious, and you need to discuss with your doctor the exposure of your baby to the sitter. She can baby-sit for your family again after she is completely cleared of her disease. The baby-sitter will be able to determine that by talking with her own doctor about when she would be completely cured. It is very important that she also contact any other persons for whom she was baby-sitting shortly before she was diagnosed as having hepatitis.

JEROME E. KWAKO, M.D.
Duluth, Minnesota

Can my child's liver be permanently damaged if he gets hepatitis?

Yes, but as a general rule children fortunately make excellent and complete recoveries from hepatitis.

MERRITT B. LOW, M.D., F.A.A.P.
Ashfield, Massachusetts

My baby-sitter has mononucleosis. Can my newborn or toddler get it?

Infectious mononucleosis is a disease caused by a virus known as the Epstein-Barr virus (EBV). The disease is usually characterized by a sore throat, swollen lymph glands in the neck, skin rash, and mild hepatitis. The disease is most commonly seen in teen-agers and college-age students, but occasionally is encountered in younger children. Part of the reason for this appears to be that infection in young children produces either few or no symptoms, whereas in older individuals the symptoms are more severe. Infectious mononucleosis is, in addition, not very contagious. Thus, it is unlikely that an infant or young child would be infected by a baby-sitter, and, even if infection occurred, symptoms would probably be mild, at most. Moreover, in a young infant, immunity to infection acquired from the mother before birth would likely be present and act to prevent infection.

LLOYD C. OLSON, M.D.
Kansas City, Missouri

What is scarlet fever? Is it contagious? For how long?

Scarlet fever is a red rash that accompanies infection with strep germ. This rash usually begins on the trunk and extends out to the arms and up to the face. With the fever, the lines in the folds of the elbows and behind the knees are somewhat darker than normal. The child will usually have fever and the typical red, "boiled lobster" type of rash. The scarlet fever itself is not contagious; however, the strep germ that causes it is contagious and will remain so usually for forty-eight hours after antibiotics have been begun.

DAVID J. TEPPER, M.D.
Chattanooga, Tennessee

Is there any medication to prevent my toddler from getting hepatitis?

There are inoculations that may be given after intimate exposure to hepatitis, such as gamma globulin, which is similar to what is used for children exposed to measles before they have had the permanent measles vaccine. Such inoculations are only temporarily protective, lasting from four to six weeks, and are given to get a person over a specific exposure. Long-lasting vaccines are not yet available for infants and small children, although they may be used by some older persons, at special risk.

MERRITT B. LOW, M.D., F.A.A.P.
Ashfield, Massachusetts

What does the rash for scarlet fever look like? How long does it last?

The rash of scarlet fever usually appears within twelve hours after the illness begins. It first appears on the skin opposite the elbows and in the groin area, usually spreading over the body within twenty-four hours; it can, however, be delayed for forty-eight hours. The forehead and cheeks are smooth, red, and flushed, but the area around the mouth is pale. The rash is a red, pinpoint eruption that fades on pressure. Since the pinpoints are raised above the surface of the skin, they cause the skin to have a rough, sandpaper-like feel when touched. The rash looks like a sunburn with goose pimples, and is most intense on the neck, under the arms, in the groin region, and behind the knees. The pinpoint red rash fades after the first week. Shortly thereafter peeling occurs, first on the face, then body, arms and legs, and finally on the hands and feet, which peel and flake between the second and third weeks after the start of the illness.

STEPHEN GLASER, M.D.
Riverdale, New York

CHAPTER 19

Inherited Traits

Arthritis runs in my family. What symptoms should I look for in my child and at what age can the symptoms be found?

The predominant types of arthritis involving children are rheumatoid arthritis and septic (infectious) arthritis. There are also rare types of arthritis associated with certain metabolic diseases. Therefore, the type of arthritis that runs in the family should be determined. If it is rheumatic, it does not occur in children under three years of age, and since it usually follows a streptococcal throat infection, early treatment of the infection prevents it. If arthritis occurs in older persons in the family, it is most likely osteoarthritis, which does not affect children. Rheumatoid arthritis, which has its peak onset between one and three years of age, is, therefore, our chief concern.

The polyarticular type of rheumatoid arthritis, which involves multiple joints, is seen in both sexes, sometimes even in the first year of life. There is a second peak, at nine to twelve years of age, with three times more girls than boys having the disease. Symptoms at any age are fever and swelling of the knees, feet, hands, and ankles. Initially, the arthritis may be migratory, moving from one joint to another. In some cases, it may take a considerable time before a diagnosis can be made. There is pain, of course, and movement and the ability to use the affected joint are diminished. These symptoms are persistent, so that eventually a diagnosis is made.

There is another form of rheumatoid arthritis in children, called Still's disease, which consists of high fever persisting two weeks or more, with a characteristic rash and joint pain that lasts for six weeks or more. Boys are more usually afflicted and half of the cases occur before five years of age.

Any child with an unexplained fever and joint pain or swelling should be seen by a pediatrician.

Acute septic, or infectious, bacterial arthritis, on the other hand, may occur in the first two years of life and, of course, would be accompanied by symptoms of infection: fever, pain on movement of the joint, swelling, and perhaps redness of the joint. Usually only one joint is involved. The joint cannot be used and is unable to support weight. Early diagnosis and treatment are important because of the damage that can occur to the joint.

WILLIAM M. BRUCH, M.D.
Richmond, Virginia

Both my husband and I are blond. Why does our baby have dark hair?

Experience demonstrates that hair color seems to be passed on from parents to their children more often than not. This tendency is seen most dramatically in redheads. However, there is not any obvious genetic pattern identified, and it remains unknown why some children inherit a parent's hair color and why others do not.

MARK S. HARRIS, M.D.
Bradford, Vermont

What is the cause of arthritis? Can a child outgrow the disease or will it worsen each year?

The cause of arthritis remains unknown. Frequently mentioned possible causes are infections resulting from some as yet unidentified organism or perhaps an allergic kind of reaction to an unknown stimulus. Research is currently focused on determining the cause of rheumatoid arthritis. A slow, virus type of infection is suspected. It is known that children with immunodeficiencies may be predisposed to autoimmune disease, which is thought to be a factor in rheumatoid arthritis. There also appears to be a genetic component to this deficiency of some components of the immune system. Patients with autoimmune disease build up antibodies against

159

tissues and joints in their own bodies. There are several theories to explain the presence of these antibodies, but their cause is still unknown.

Certain types of arthritis are less likely to be associated with severe joint disease. The most crippling arthritis usually involves multiple joints. This type, however, usually starts in late childhood and affects girls in 80 percent of all cases. Up to half of these children will have severe arthritis. Other types of rheumatoid arthritis—the pauciarticular or monoarticular, involving fewer joints or even one joint, and the systemic type associated with high fever—may cause progressive arthritis but in only 15 percent to 20 percent of the patients. It is certainly not progressive in all patients, and yet one does not outgrow this problem. Long-term management is indicated for the many cases that become worse each year.

WILLIAM M. BRUCH, M.D.
Richmond, Virginia

My first child had cystic fibrosis. Will my new baby be likely to develop it?

As a prelude to the answer, I would hope that someone would have counseled the parents of a cystic fibrosis child regarding the risk of their having other children with cystic fibrosis.

The chances are very high that a second child will have cystic fibrosis. The chance of this disease occurring spontaneously in a first child is about 1 in 2,000. However, if a couple has a child with cystic fibrosis, the likelihood of their having another child with that disease is one in four. This does not mean that if they already have one child with cystic fibrosis, the next three children will not have it. At the present time, there is no available test that is recommended by the Cystic Fibrosis Foundation that can detect the presence of the disease in utero.

About 10 percent of all infants with cystic fibrosis will have some manifestation at birth. This is usually in the form of a type of intestinal obstruction called meconium ileus and, if present, it indicates cystic fibrosis. Although some infants will be on the slightly smaller side at birth, they may have no manifestations of cystic fibrosis at the time they are born. It can be very difficult to establish the diagnosis at birth. There have been tests done on meconium, the newborn infant's bowel movement. These tests, however, are inconclusive and may be falsely positive or falsely negative in 20 percent of infants tested. The only good test that one can utilize to determine the presence of cystic fibrosis is the sweat test. Unfortunately, it is very difficult to collect an adequate amount of sweat from the newborn. Although one may test the baby at birth, it is frequently not until he or she is two to three months of age, when adequate sweat can be obtained, that a reliable sweat test can be done.

The infant who does not manifest cystic fibrosis with meconium ileus may not develop any symptoms for a number of months. Some infants will fail to gain weight and have abnormally large, foul-smelling stools. Indeed, the symptom triad of failure to gain weight, a voracious appetite, and steatorrhea (abnormal stools) is characteristic of cystic fibrosis. The infant may be several months old before manifesting the respiratory symptoms so typical of cystic fibrosis: a chronic cough, which is frequently diagnosed as chronic bronchitis, or asthmatic bronchitis; or milk allergy; or pneumonitis. It is not until this cough has persisted for some time, the diagnosis of cystic fibrosis is considered, and the sweat test is done that the diagnosis is confirmed.

DAVID A. DRAPER, M.D.
Richmond, Virginia

My husband's family has a long history of high blood pressure. Would my toddler have any symptoms that I should be looking for?

Most likely your husband's family has a history of "essential" hypertension. This is to say that high blood pressure runs in the family and is not caused by kidney disease or any other identifiable physical defects. This type of hypertension or high blood pressure usually begins in adulthood but can occasionally be identified in children. Essential hypertension tends to occur in families. It is also associated with obesity and hyperlipidemia (increased fats in the blood), both of which tend to occur in families.

Pediatricians measure blood pressure in all children three years or older. Sometimes an elevated blood pressure is noted during an office visit, but because it has not been demonstrated that children who have elevated blood pressure at one time would necessarily have it at another, the tendency is to follow these children and measure their blood pressure at intervals. The significance of elevated blood pressure in a child is interpreted in light of the family history.

All in all, your child should not show any symptoms during the toddler years, but I would strongly suggest that you avoid allowing the child to gain excess weight and that you encourage exercise and good eating habits. Fresh fruits and vegetables and avoidance of salty and fatty foods should be encouraged at an early age. Children can be trained to eat right and to enjoy exercise; diet and exercise may be the only ways we have to prevent high blood pressure.

JANICE L. COCKRELL, M.D.
Richmond, Virginia

Both my husband and I are carriers of the sickle cell trait. How soon will we be able to tell if our newborn has sickle cell anemia?

In considering sickle cell anemia, you must realize that there are two ways your child might be affected. One is if the parent is a carrier, as both you and your husband are. The other is if the parent has the actual disease, which in your case has only a 25 percent chance of occurring. The answer to your question depends on whether you live in a state where screening for sickle cell anemia is part of a newborn screening program. If you do, a blood specimen taken at birth will determine whether your child has either the trait or the disease. Otherwise, your doctor can obtain a specimen of blood from your newborn infant that will provide the same information. When your child is older, between six and twelve months of age, there are other less complicated means of testing whether the sickle cell trait or disease is present. This testing is available through most health clinics and doctors' offices. Someday, it will be possible to tell by amniocentesis, the testing of amniotic fluid aspirated from the womb, whether an unborn child has sickle cell anemia. This will allow for prenatal genetic counseling for that condition.

PHILIP MARKOWITZ, M.D.
Richmond, Virginia

CHAPTER 20

Injuries

What are the signs of a concussion?

Concussion is a transient loss of consciousness, occurring after trauma to the head and lasting from a few seconds to a few minutes. In other words, one receives a concussion when one gets knocked out. Usually a concussion does not produce a life-threatening situation; however, it does indicate a fairly significant trauma to the head and brain. Any child with a concussion should be examined by a physician to determine the possibility of a more serious brain injury.

FERNANDO J. deCASTRO, M.D.
St. Louis, Missouri

My toddler fell down a flight of stairs. He has no obvious injuries. How can I tell if he is injured internally?

If a toddler falls down a flight of stairs and is not noted to be initially unconscious and has no obvious injuries, observation alone is all that is required at first. The child should be examined for bruises, discoloration or swelling over his entire body area, especially the skull. As a result of the excitement and crying that usually result from an occurrence such as this, the child can be expected to act tired and drowsy. This is not necessarily cause for immediate concern. Should the child fall asleep, he should be awakened periodically to ensure that he is acting in his usual manner. The extremities should be observed for their equal use and the gait noted if the child is of walking age. Vomiting, unusual behavior, or drowsiness occurring somewhat after the injury would be symptoms of concern and suggest head injury. While these things would be expected to show up within the first few hours, periods of as long as several days may elapse before delayed signs of head injury are noted. Vomiting, loss of appetite, and abdominal swelling might indicate abdominal injury. The delayed appearance of bruising or failure to use an extremity would suggest the possibility of a fracture at that site.

Occurrences such as these can be minimized or prevented by carpeting the stairs and by providing sturdy, easily used gates at the head of stairs. Young children should never be left unattended.

PAUL C. SCHREIBER, M.D.
Brockton, Massachusetts

My infant just fell off the dressing table and hit her head. She's all right except for some drowsiness. Should I be concerned?

Drowsiness is a very common symptom after an infantile head injury. The infant may even fall asleep and should be aroused at two-hour intervals. Vomiting and irritability frequently accompany the drowsiness caused by a head injury. If the infant is not easily awakened, or if the symptoms mentioned persist beyond eight hours, medical attention should be obtained.

ALEXANDER V. FAKADEJ, M.D.
Morgantown, West Virginia

My infant was in his stroller when it fell off the cement curb. He now has a bump above his eye that is bruised and scratched. What can I do for it? Is it serious?

If your child did not lose consciousness after the fall, and after the initial period of surprise or crying he seems to be his usual self, you need not worry further. It is important to clean the wound with soap and water and perhaps apply cold compresses, which will help reduce any swelling. Please ensure that your child is up-to-date on immunizations, which are standard precautions as part of any wound care.

It is not usually serious for a child of less than two years of age to fall from a height equal to the distance between the sidewalk and the street, even if he strikes a hard surface. Nevertheless, if your child has lost consciousness, does not appear his usual self, or feels ill, and perhaps vomits several times after the fall, be sure and notify your pediatrician.

JOHN H. STUEMKY, M.D.
Oklahoma City, Oklahoma

I picked up my infant by the arms and now he is not moving one arm and he's crying a lot. What did I do to him?

You probably dislocated the head of the radius bone at the elbow. Wrist and shoulder dislocations are extremely rare in young children. This injury needs a physician's help, and usually the treatment is relatively simple, quick, and curative.

MERRITT B. LOW, M.D., F.A.A.P.
Ashfield, Massachusetts

My toddler fell down some steps and now he is holding his shoulder so that one side looks lower than the other. Should he be seen by a doctor?

Yes. When a child falls in this particular fashion, he could possibly have broken his collarbone. If the collarbone is cracked or broken, the characteristic result is the holding of the shoulder so that one side droops lower than the other. This is a very simple fracture and can be easily treated by your physician. It will not cause a great deal of discomfort to your child.

BETTY A. LOWE, M.D.
Little Rock, Arkansas

I've read that you can dislocate an infant's hip if you constantly pick her up by one leg when changing diapers. Is this true, and if so, what should I do if I think this has happened?

Actually, it is unlikely to dislocate an infant's hip by picking the child up by one leg. However, it is not a good practice because some injury to the hip can occur. If one thinks that the hip may already be dislocated, the child should be taken immediately to the physician, because the hip needs to be placed back in position. Usually children whose hips become dislocated are those who were born with a flat hip socket (congenital hip dysplasia).

FERNANDO J. deCASTRO, M.D.
St. Louis, Missouri

My toddler caught her fingers in the front door. They are very red and have a deep crease across them. She is able to move them. Should they be X-rayed?

It is unlikely that your child has fractured, or broken, any of her fingers if she is able to move them. It is therefore not necessary for them to be X-rayed at the present time. Her fingers will probably become very swollen, and she will have increasing difficulty moving them. You should encourage her to move her fingers. If they get very swollen and she is unable to move them at all, it is advisable for you to take her to a physician, who will determine whether an X ray is needed.

JEANNE M. EULBERG, M.D.
Kansas City, Kansas

When I picked up my infant from the baby-sitter, she had many bruises on her arms that were not there before. Should I be concerned?

Yes. The bruises may be indicative of child abuse. First, make certain you have the baby-sitter's true name and accurate home address. Second, take the baby to a doctor or to an emergency room. If there is suspicion of child abuse, laws usually require that the suspicion be reported. However, certain bruises can occur because of a blood clotting problem, but usually the distribution is not symmetrical. Certain injuries can result in symmetric bruises, but this is unusual and depends on the age of the child. The sitter's story should be obtained and noted down carefully for a transmission to a physician. Do little else until a physician has been permitted to see the child.

CHARLES WOLF, M.D.
West Bloomfield, Michigan

My toddler has suddenly become fearful of her baby-sitter. Could that be a sign of mistreatment?

It certainly could! If the toddler has been cared for by the same sitter in the past and suddenly becomes fearful, it may be evidence that the child has been mistreated by the sitter. It is certainly evidence that that particular sitter is not right for your child. Children usually enjoy the company of compatible baby-sitters whom they know and trust. Behavior such as that described in the question should serve as a warning for you to be on the lookout for another baby-sitter.

SYDNEY WALDMAN, M.D.
Philadelphia, Pennsylvania

My infant fell out of the crib and hit her head quite hard. Now she is vomiting a great deal. What should I do?

Keep calm. Try to evaluate the baby's general condition—color, breathing, general awareness and behavior, and presence of abnormal drowsiness. Do not give her anything by mouth for an hour or two, and then start only with sips of water. Watch for a secondary relapse after a complete or partial return to normal appearance and behavior. Try to estimate the time of loss of consciousness. Do her eyes focus well and does she comprehend adequately? Dilated pupils, if due to the fall, are usually associated with other serious signs. Soft bumps are deeper than hard ones and are more often associated with skull fractures. It is all right to put ice on bumps if the baby is not in shock. Keep the child awake for an hour or so, so that you can evaluate conditions better. If symptoms or signs persist for an hour or more, you should call the doctor. And you should in any event plan to watch the baby closely for at least eight to twelve hours.

MERRITT B. LOW, M.D., F.A.A.P.
Ashfield, Massachusetts

I noticed that my son is limping but I do not remember his falling. What could cause this?

It is quite possible that your son sustained some minor injury, and his limp may be secondary to this. However, there are so many other reasons for a limp that you should arrange to see his doctor. On the basis of an examination and perhaps some additional laboratory tests, the doctor will be able to better define the cause of the limp.

RALPH E. MOLOSHOK, M.D.
New York, New York

CHAPTER 21

Newborn

Is it normal for my newborn to lose weight after birth? If so, how much of a loss is normal?

It is very common for the newborn to lose weight. The newborn infant has a lot of body water, which constitutes 35 percent of the baby's total body weight. During the first few days of life there is an average loss of six to ten percent of the excess fluid due to the unusual intake of fluid. When this loss is excessive, there may be dehydration within three to four days.

Most full-term infants regain their birth weight by ten days of age. Then the weight gain averages approximately ⅔ oz. per day for the first five months and ½ oz. per day for the remainder of the year. The full-term infant will generally double its birth weight by five months of age and triple it at the end of the first year.

AJIT DAS, M.D.
Nashville, Tennessee

How many pounds should my newborn put on each month? How many inches should he grow each month?

Since weight gain and linear growth are influenced by both environment and heredity, it is dangerous to follow rules about either. Variability is usual. It is reasonable, however, to think in terms of averages.

Most full-term babies double their weight by five to six months of age and many will triple their birth weight by one year of age. Gain is not equal each month. Some babies may grow less than a pound one month and perhaps two or even three pounds the next month.

Full-term babies grow about nine inches in their first year, and here again some infants may show little change in one month and in other months may grow more than an inch.

Some babies who eat a lot remain thin in appearance, whereas others who eat less than average may appear plump. Besides hereditary factors, physical activities such as kicking, turning, and wiggling may explain this paradox. Parents who see great variations in weight or growth should mention this to their baby's doctor.

After the first birthday, growth is so variable that no rules are practical. Semiannual or annual visits to the doctor will nearly always tell if there is any cause for alarm.

HUGH A. CARITHERS, M.D.
Jacksonville, Florida

Are lotions safe to use on my newborn's skin?

Yes, it is usually safe to use lotions on your newborn's skin. It is rarely necessary, though, because the dry skin that babies have is not painful and will go away by itself. A few babies, however, will get a rash from the lotion.

G. EDWARD SHISSLER, M.D.
Oklahoma City, Oklahoma

How do I take an infant's or a toddler's temperature?

The definition of a fever is the rise of body temperature above normal. Every parent should be aware of what is a normal temperature and how to obtain a body temperature. The range of normal temperature is 98.6° to 100.2°, depending upon the child's age, level of activity, environment, and other factors. There are three different ways of checking temperatures: oral, axillary, and rectal.

The rectal method of taking the temperature is recommended most often for infants. When the child is one year of age or older, the axillary method is preferred. A child's temperature should not be taken orally until you are sure your child understands what is expected. A child may be four, five, or six years of age before a temperature can be taken orally.

There are two basic types of thermometers, the oral and the rectal. The bulb of a rectal thermometer is round and oval. The oral thermometer is long and slim. The markings on both thermometers are the same. Before taking the temperature, shake the thermometer well until the measuring line is below 96°. Don't give cold foods or liquids for half an hour before you take the temperature.

Rectal: In order to take the temperature rectally, coat the bulb end of the thermometer with petroleum jelly. Gently insert the thermometer into the rectum no farther than one inch. Keep the thermometer in place for two to three minutes and then pull it out. In good light read the thermometer where the mercury column ends. A normal temperature taken rectally is usually 1° higher than a temperature taken orally.

Axillary: Axillary temperature can be checked by either an oral or a rectal thermometer. Place the bulb end of the thermometer under the arm. The arm should be held against the body. Make sure the armpit is dry. Keep the thermometer in place for three to four minutes. A normal axillary temperature is 1° less than oral temperature.

Oral: To take the temperature orally, place the bulb end of the thermometer under the tongue. Tell the child to keep his lips closed and not to bite on the thermometer. Leave it in for two to three minutes and then pull it out. Normal oral temperature is 98.6° to 100.2°.

After you take a temperature, clean the thermometer with warm water and wipe it with rubbing alcohol. Keep the thermometer in the container to prevent breakage.

NEELAN GOEL, M.D.
Chicago, Illinois

My newborn has dark, fine hair all over his body. Will this disappear, and is it normal?

Many newborns have a fine, downy hair covering their bodies. It is normal and it will disappear in several weeks.

KATALIN KORANYI, M.D.
Columbus, Ohio

How long should it take before my newborn gains back the weight he lost after birth?

The average, healthy, full-term newborn usually regains birth weight by one to one and one-half weeks of age. Those children who recover their weights earlier are not necessarily healthier than those who take a few extra days. Many bottle-fed babies regain the lost ounces by five days of age, whereas breast-fed infants are usually among those who take a week or more to get back to birth weight.

Premature or sick newborns may take as long as three to four weeks to make up the initial weight loss, depending upon the severity of the illness and/or the extent of the prematurity. At the other extreme, a postmature infant (one who is born two or more weeks past its due date and who exhibits the thin scrawny body seen in such cases) may lose practically no weight and gain rapidly from the very first day of life.

LEONARD H. GREENE, M.D.
Minneapolis, Minnesota

Why does the pediatrician measure the head circumference of the newborn?

Accurate measurement of the head circumference is a vital part of an infant's first (and subsequent) physical examination. It is a simple procedure, doesn't hurt, and provides a great deal of information about the baby's health and development.

The bones of a newborn's skull are separate from each other and are not fused together. (They become fused when the infant gets older.) The separation can sometimes be felt as shallow depressions or small ridges. A small space between three of the large bones is the soft spot. This disappears when the three bones grow together, at approximately eighteen months of age.

Growth and development of the nervous system begins early after conception and continues throughout gestation, infancy, and childhood. The size of a baby's head depends upon two important factors: the length of gestation (whether the baby is premature or term) and the state of development of the brain and nervous system. However, there is a wide range of normal. Some babies' heads may be normally small or normally large. Regardless of the size of the head (unless it is extremely small or large), the normal baby's brain will grow at a surprisingly predictable rate. The first measurement gives the pediatrician a base line, and future measurements are all compared to each other to see if the head (and the brain) is growing too slowly or too fast. This will permit early detection of problems so they may be promptly treated.

Measurement of the growth and development of the head cannot predict how smart a child will be, but it is the best indicator of how well the brain is growing.

STEPHEN H. SHELDON, D.O., F.A.A.P.
Chicago, Illinois

Is it true that my baby should triple her birth weight at one year?

This is one bit of conventional wisdom that is true. Generally, the full-term infant will double his or her birth weight by five months of age, and triple birth weight by one year of age. Contradictory as it may seem, the heavier the infant is at birth, the greater the age at which the birth weight is doubled. Boys are slightly larger at birth and will show a slightly greater gain than girls.

CONSTANCE U. BATTLE, M.D.
Washington, D.C.

Will the marks from the forceps on my newborn's head be permanent?

Low, or outlet, forceps are occasionally used for completion of delivery. Forceps are applied to the infant's head and will on occasion cause small pressure marks on the skin of the head. Sometimes, a narrow pelvis or prominence of bones in the delivery canal may cause similar marks, even with a spontaneous delivery. These marks are red and can appear as bruises or small red spots called petechiae. They are most frequently found over the sides and front of the skull and occasionally across the face. These areas most often heal rapidly and without scarring, and no dressing is needed. At times one will see "deep forceps injury," which causes subcutaneous fat necrosis, or a breakdown of the fat between the skin and the skull. This usually becomes evident between the fourth and eighth day after delivery. On most occasions it, too, heals spontaneously in a matter of weeks, with no complications. Once in a great while, however, one will see a small abscess (pocket of pus) in the area of the fat necrosis.

In the majority of cases, marks made by forceps are quite temporary and rapidly disappear. As with any other skin injury to a newborn, warm compresses are not suggested because of the susceptibility of the newborn to water-borne bacterial infection and of the newborn skin to injury caused by heat. The majority of forceps marks will disappear by the end of the second week of life. Should they become further inflamed, appear tender, or bother the newborn child, the pediatrician should be consulted. Rarely one will note skull fractures and subsequent intracranial (within the brain) hemorrhage following a difficult forceps delivery. This is, however, extremely rare and should not be interpreted as a contraindication for the use of forceps in delivery.

C. TATE HOLBROOK, M.D.
Greenville, North Carolina

When will the soft spots on my baby's head close over?

At birth, there are two soft spots or fontanels that are easily felt on the baby's skull. Both are located in the midline of the skull; the larger one (anterior fontanel) is near the baby's forehead, and the smaller one (posterior fontanel) is near the crown. The anterior fontanel tends to enlarge for the first few months of life and then slowly closes, becoming completely closed when the infant is between nine and eighteen months old. The posterior fontanel usually closes between two and four months of life, and is often closed at birth. Although there is no bony skull protecting the underlying brain, there is no danger of harming the baby's brain by routine bathing of the fontanels. In fact, it is desirable to shampoo these areas while bathing the baby in order to prevent cradle cap from occurring.

C. WARREN DERRICK JR., M.D.
Columbia, South Carolina

I think the tip of my thermometer broke off in my newborn's rectum. What should I do?

Do nothing. If the glass scratches the inside of the rectum, there could be minimal traces of blood. There has never been a reported case of a puncture through the wall of the rectum from this kind of incident. As far as the mercury in the thermometer is concerned, don't worry, for mercury as a metal is not absorbed and will be excreted *in toto*. The broken end of the thermometer will be encased in rectal feces and excreted as such without any harm or damage done. So relax.

AUDREY J. McDONALD, M.D.
Chevy Chase, Maryland

My baby drools a lot. Is something wrong with her tongue or swallowing reflex?

There is wide variation in the amount of drooling that normal infants do, particularly from four to sixteen or eighteen months of age. If the baby is developing normally otherwise and does not have difficulty in breathing or does not vomit excessively, a lot of drooling is a perfectly normal, but annoying, occurrence.

FRANK M. SHEPARD, M.D.
Johnson City, Tennessee

My newborn sleeps almost constantly. Is this normal?

There is no absolute sleeping pattern for all newborns. Every child is an individual with special needs. Sleeping and waking hours are regulated by the baby's own built-in rhythm (biological clock). Usually a newborn "sleeps almost constantly" during the first few weeks of life. Slowly, with increasing age, waking hours get longer and longer. In the early days the newborn needs all the sleep he or she can get in order not to waste any calories on activities but to convert all the caloric milk energy into rapid body growth. A newborn who "sleeps constantly" is probably a very healthy, normal infant, provided the child is awake long enough to consume the required amount of milk for adequate weight gain and mental development. On occasion, breast-fed babies have a tendency to oversleep feedings if the mother's milk supply is not sufficient. The mother will notice a lack of milk flow and a softening of her breasts. The baby will not gain as much weight as would be expected. This ought to be brought to the attention of the baby's physician. It is imperative to report any sudden, drastic change in the infant's sleeping pattern, which is associated not only with poor feeding, but also with drowsiness, body temperature irregularity, or any other deviation from the child's normal behavior.

EDUARD JUNG, M.D.
Chicago, Illinois

Why are my newborn's breasts slightly swollen and tender?

Swelling of the breasts may occur in either male or female newborns. This is because the hormones that the mother generates during pregnancy are at a significantly high level and can pass through the placenta to the infant and cause the swelling. Swollen breasts in newborns is a common occurrence and may last for several weeks. There is no need for treatment.

JEROME E. KWAKO, M.D.
Duluth, Minnesota

My newborn's head is bruised and one section is slightly swollen from delivery. How long will it be before his head looks normal? Will his head look normal?

Three common findings may be present on the head after the normal birth of an infant.

Molding: Toward the last few weeks of pregnancy the infant's head settles into the mother's pelvis. During this time the infant's head takes on the shape of the pelvis (much like Jell-O taking on the shape of the Jell-O mold), a process called molding. This can happen safely because the bones of the infant's head are soft and moveable. As labor begins and progresses, the process of molding causes the head to be more elongated to allow it to pass through the cervix (the opening of the womb). If the pregnancy is the first, the molding is often accentuated, causing the head to appear banana-like. Molding does not harm the baby's brain and typically resolves in twelve to twenty-four hours, resulting in a normally shaped head. The top of the head acts commonly as the lead point as the head passes through the cervix.

Two different swellings may result as part of the normal birth process. *Caput:* The skin covering the top of the head may become swollen and bruised from the pressures of labor squeezing the tissues. This harmless swelling of the skin disappears over the first week of life. *Cephalohematoma:* A firm knot can be noted on either side of the back of the head and may range in size from that of a marble to that of an egg. This is a bone bruise on the outside of the skull. It may take weeks or months to slowly resolve. Very rarely it may leave a permanent, although insignificant, lump on the head. Other causes for bruising of the head occur less commonly. Some are related to rapid progress of delivery, forceps marks, tight opening of the birth canal, and so forth. These conditions will be evaluated by your baby's physician and explained to you.

LLOYD I. KRAMER, M.D.
Falls Church, Virginia

In what position should I place my newborn when he is sleeping—on his back, abdomen, or side?

It is best to let an infant lie on his stomach. This has many advantages. During feeding, an infant swallows some air, which causes discomfort to his stomach. Burping after feeding helps to expel some air; the rest will be expelled if the infant lies on his stomach. An infant also spits up occasionally. If he is on his back, the vomitus may go back to the air passage, which lies very close to the food passage, and may block it. This may cause pneumonia or may even cause sudden death. This will not happen if the child lies on his stomach.

In older children this is not a problem. It is best to let them lie in whatever position is comfortable for them.

KANIKA CHAUDHURI, M.D.
Nashville, Tennessee

What are the soft spots on the baby's head? How careful must one be with these areas?

There are two soft spots on a baby's head, the anterior and posterior fontanels. They are areas where several bony plates of the skull will eventually meet and fuse. The anterior fontanel is at the near junction of the frontal and parietal bones. The posterior fontanel is at the near junction of the parietal and occipital bones.

The anterior fontanel is the more important of the two and varies greatly in size, from baby to baby, from ¼ inch to nearly 2 inches. (1 inch = 2.4 cm.)

There is a certain elasticity to the normal fontanel, and when an infant is crying the fontanel bulges slightly. Several conditions causing increased pressure within the skull also may cause bulging and tenseness, but these are problems best evaluated by the pediatrician.

By placing the fingers on the anterior fontanel, one can sometimes feel a throb. This is caused by the pulse of blood in the vessels beneath the scalp. It is not abnormal.

It is difficult to injure the fontanel, which is actually rather resilient, and one need exercise only the normal caution in handling a baby's head.

The anterior fontanel tends to become smaller in the first year of life and is usually closed by eighteen months of age, although this, too, is variable.

THOMAS R. C. SISSON, M.D., F.A.A.P.
Perth Amboy, New Jersey

There is a bulge in my newborn's groin. What is it?

Several things can cause unusual swelling in the groin of a newborn baby. The most common would be a collection of fluid around the testicle of a baby boy. This occurs when the testes are being formed; they migrate down out of the abdomen into the scrotal sac, and sometimes the area from which they come does not close off completely, and fluid is allowed to gather around the testicle. This condition is called a hydrocele. Many hydroceles will resolve spontaneously and require no intervention. However, if one is associated with a hernia, it may need surgery. Another cause for a bulge in a newborn's groin could be an inguinal hernia, which is a muscle defect in the lining of the lower abdominal wall that permits contents of the abdomen to protrude into the groin. This usually will require surgery. A third cause of a bulge in a newborn's groin might be a lymph gland, which, if it is not associated with redness, inflammation, and infection someplace in the lower extremities, is harmless and will require no therapy. Hernias can occur in both baby girls and baby boys. In girls, one will sometimes find a hernia protruding with ovarian tissue in the hernia, producing a mass in the groin area.

A. E. REARDON, M.D., F.A.A.P.
Duluth, Minnesota

How do I wash my baby girl's genital area properly?

At the end of her bath, simply use a mild soap and wash her genital area with a washcloth or cotton balls. Always wipe from the front part of her genital area to the back area, so that you won't spread germs from her rectum up to the front area where her urethra (the opening to her bladder) is. If your baby is very sensitive to soap, use a fragrance-free one like Basis to avoid a rash. Be sure to rinse off all the soap and dry her diaper area thoroughly with a soft towel.

SUSAN GIFFORD LIEBERMAN, R.N., M.N.
Prairie Village, Kansas

Should my baby be circumcised?

The age-old ritual of circumcision of the male infant has recently been questioned by pediatricians as to its medical necessity. There is no real proof that circumcision provides protection against later cancer of the penis. Other than affording ease in keeping the organ clean, there is no proven advantage to circumcision. The risks, although slight, involved in the operation do not warrant the procedure unless there is a medical reason for it.

ROBERT C. FAIRCHILD, M.D.
Kansas City, Missouri

My newborn's cord stump has a foul odor and a yellowish discharge. What should I do?

The baby needs to be seen and examined by your pediatrician or family physician. A cord stump that produces a foul-smelling, yellow discharge is more likely than not to be infected.

It is normal for the cord to be bluish-white and moist at birth. It begins to dry within the first day of life, becomes yellowish-brown, then assumes a dull, dark brown appearance, and shrivels up. Finally, about one week or so after birth it sloughs off, leaving a moist stump that at first may produce a minimal, milk-white, watery discharge. This is not the yellowish and foul-smelling discharge described in the question. Abnormal discharges may be accompanied by swelling and redness around the stump, by which time there is no question that an infection is present.

Because an infection of the stump can carry a severe health consequence for the newborn, the baby should be examined by a physician who may either reassure you or take cultures of the discharge to look for infection and prescribe an effective management regime.

ANTOINE K. FOMUFOD, M.D., M.P.H., F.A.A.P.
Washington, D.C.

I was told my newborn has an umbilical hernia. Will he need surgery?

First of all, you should realize that an umbilical hernia is not a true hernia in the sense that usually nothing is coming out through it. The umbilical hernia is really a space in the wall of the abdomen, usually right about where the baby's navel is located. What has happened is that the muscles and other things that make up the wall of the abdomen haven't completely joined together. Because of this, every time the baby cries or strains to have a bowel movement and increases the pressure inside the belly, the skin over this space stretches and bulges outward. It looks painful but isn't.

Will surgery be required? Well, that depends. Very often these spaces will close by the time the baby is twelve to eighteen months of age. Sometimes they are so small that, even if they're not closed by that time, it really doesn't make sense to subject a baby to surgery. On the other hand, if it's large, with a lot of protruding skin, it's best to have the surgeon make a very small cut, sew the muscles back together, trim off the excess skin, and close the cut. That saves the child a great deal of potential embarrassment when he or she is swimming or taking physical education classes, and so forth. For young female babies, some doctors usually recommend surgery by two years of age even if the space is small, since it can expand during childbearing and cause some degree of discomfort and disfigurement.

One last note. There are many old wives' tales about umbilical hernias. Some parents tape coins to the navel in order to push it in and, presumably, to promote healing. Some parents just apply adhesive tape to push the navel in. None of this works, and doing it often causes serious irritation of the skin to the point where an infection sometimes occurs.

Will surgery be needed? Time and regular visits to the pediatrician for well-child care are really the best way of answering that question.

JOSEPH ZANGA, M.D.
Richmond, Virginia

My baby's umbilical hernia bulges out when he cries. Is this normal?

Yes. Umbilical hernias protrude or bulge more when a baby cries, coughs, or strains with a bowel movement. However, if a baby's hernia remains protuberant after the crying episode and does not resume its usual appearance, medical advice should be sought to be certain the hernia is not incarcerated (or stuck), which occurs rarely.

Umbilical hernias are due to the imperfect closure of the weak area around the navel, and contain portions of the baby's small intestine. These hernias are seen more frequently in black infants, and vary in size. Most appear before the age of six months and disappear spontaneously by three to four years of age. If a hernia persists after this time, surgical repair may be indicated.

SUSAN JAY, M.D.
Augusta, Georgia

My baby's umbilical hernia constantly bulges out, whereas it used to only when he cried. Is something wrong?

Probably not. An umbilical hernia occurs frequently in infants, especially in those who are premature, and is caused by failure of the ring where the umbilical cord came through the abdominal wall to close off after birth. Anything that increases pressure in the abdomen (crying, coughing, or straining) will cause the hernia to bulge out more. In contrast to a hernia in the groin, there is very little chance of an umbilical hernia strangulating. Umbilical hernias are not painful. Taping or strapping them does no good and only irritates the baby's skin. The ring in most umbilical hernias will close off by the time the child is three years of age. If the hernia persists until the child is five years of age, it may have to be treated surgically.

ROBERT C. FAIRCHILD, M.D.
Kansas City, Missouri

The umbilical cord was wrapped around my newborn's neck. How and when will I know if he is brain-damaged?

The umbilical cord is wrapped around the neck of the newborn in more than 20 percent of all deliveries. Occasionally it is wrapped two or three times around the neck. It is extremely unusual to have significant problems for the newborn associated with this condition.

One should be concerned only if, prior to delivery, the cord is pulled too tight and the blood flow in the cord is stopped. If this occurs, the baby's heart rate will change. This is one reason the baby's heart rate is checked so frequently during labor.

Another reason for concern is present when the newborn's Apgar score (evaluation largely of heart rate and breathing effort at one and five minutes after birth) is low.

If the heart rate has not changed during labor, or if the Apgar score is not low, there is no reason to consider any long-term problems such as brain damage associated with a cord around the neck at birth.

JUDITH E. FRANK, M.D.
Hanover, New Hampshire

How do I care for my baby's umbilical cord stump?

The umbilical cord originally nourishes the baby through the three blood vessels that travel through it to the placenta. After the baby is born, this source of nourishment is no longer needed, and the obstetrician generally puts a clamp of some sort on the cord and cuts the cord close to the baby.

This cord is moist for the first day or so, but then begins to dry up and eventually drops off anytime between one and three weeks. It is important to clean the navel area several times daily with Q-tips dipped in alcohol or with alcohol wipes. It is also important to keep the area dry by keeping the top of the diaper below the navel. These procedures help to keep an infection from starting. The signs of an infection are a foul-smelling odor and redness around the navel area.

The baby should be given sponge baths until a day or two after the cord drops off. Frequently you will see a few drops of blood in the navel area when the cord separates. This will dry and form a scab and should heal completely within a day or two. Once the navel area has healed, the baby can have a tub bath. You should make sure that the navel area has been dried completely for the first few times the tub bath is given. This is to prevent infection or delay in healing.

MARY R. BURGER, M.D.
Unionville, Connecticut

I've heard that hernias can recur. If I am very careful about caring for my baby, can we wait until he is older so he won't need two operations?

There is no need to wait until your baby is older in order to repair his hernia. Most infant hernias are inguinal, with swelling of the groin and/or scrotum. And in young children, they are frequently found on both sides. The chance of recurrence after surgical repair is about five in one thousand. But, the chance that a hernia may incarcerate, that is, cannot be reduced by ordinary means, is about one in five. These figures reflect a fortyfold increase in risk. If your child has an incarcerated hernia, your physician will usually be able to reduce it. Normally, surgical repair will be done within two days of such a reduction. One-fourth of babies with an incarcerated hernia, however, require immediate surgery, for, as long as the hernia is incarcerated, the blood supply to the testis or ovary, as well as the bowel, is impaired. Thus there is little reason to wait.

DAVID C. HITCH, M.D.
Oklahoma City, Oklahoma

A friend suggested that I keep a coin taped over my baby's umbilical hernia. Will that help it?

No, because the great majority of umbilical hernias will close spontaneously between the ages of one and two years. On the other hand, the coin or the tape may irritate the baby's skin and cause the growth of bacteria that produce a skin infection that could be serious in small babies.

ORESTES S. VALDES, M.D., F.A.A.P
Crevecoeur, Missouri

One of my newborn's eyes continuously drains. Is this something that I should be concerned about?

Frequently, a newborn's eyes may be "mattery" the first one to three days of life as a result of the application of silver nitrate, a slightly irritating chemical placed in the eyes of most newborn babies in this country to prevent eye infections. If one or both of a baby's eyes drain for more than three days, or if during the first three days the drainage seems to be increasing rather than decreasing, this may represent an infection and you should certainly consult the baby's physician. At any time, if you should notice marked redness of the eyes, or eyelids with profuse pus formation, you should obviously call the doctor. Most eye infections in babies are minor and easily treated, but some are quite serious, and the child's doctor needs to decide. Some babies seem to have recurrent or persistent draining eyes. These babies may also seem to have excessive tearing on one or both sides of the eyes. This is generally caused by plugged or partially plugged tear ducts. Tears are normally made in a gland located above and lateral to the eye itself. The tears wash from the outside across the eye towards the nose and then drain from the inside corner of the eye (the puncta) down through the tear duct and into the nose. This is why your nose runs when you cry. If the duct that conducts the tears from the puncta to the nose is obstructed or partially obstructed, then the tears back up in the duct into the eye. This causes the eye to tear excessively and also these stagnant tears tend to get infected. These infections are generally mild and can be treated or not treated at the discretion of the baby's pediatrician. Some feel that massaging along and just below the inner corner of the eye may help to clear the tear ducts. This condition generally clears spontaneously by six to twelve months of age, but a baby who is having more frequent or more serious infections, or one whose tear ducts do not clear spontaneously, may need to have the ducts probed by an ophthalmologist.

BRUCE S. STRIMLING, M.D.
Eugene, Oregon

How should I clean my baby's ears?

Your baby's ears should be cleaned as gently as possible, with water and occasionally a very mild soap. It is important to avoid probing your baby's external ear canals, since a rapid movement could result in damage to the external canal or to the eardrum. Usually, earwax is not harmful, although your health care practitioner may occasionally suggest the careful application of a substance to facilitate its removal in order to have an unobstructed view of your child's eardrums.

JOHN S. O'SHEA, M.D.
Providence, Rhode Island

Is it safe to clean my newborn's nostrils with cotton swabs?

The cotton swab, which appears very innocent, can be extremely dangerous when used improperly by an unsuspecting parent or caregiver. The swab is generally intended to clean *external* surfaces of the body. When inserted into an opening (notably the nose and ears), much damage can be done to delicate structures and tissues inside. Babies are characteristically uncooperative when it comes to cleaning these areas. A sudden movement or jump can cause the swab to penetrate too deeply.

Using a washcloth to clean the baby's nose carries much less risk of unintentional injury than does the cotton swab. If the swabs are used, they should clean only external surfaces and not be inserted into any opening. Debris in the nose will usually cause the baby to sneeze, which is the best (and natural) way to keep the nose clean.

STEPHEN H. SHELDON, D.O., F.A.A.P.
Chicago, Illinois

My newborn seems to hold his head to one side most of the day. Is this normal?

Positional head tilting is usually a result of an infant's developing a favorite position of the head after being left on its back most of the time. You can usually easily correct this by turning your child's head in the opposite direction several times daily and by leaving the infant on his stomach so that, in raising his head, there will be active stretching of the neck muscles. Occasionally, a hematoma, or knot, will form in one of the neck muscles, thereby shortening the muscle and requiring more aggressive exercises. Because of this and the rare possibility of an underlying abnormality of the bones in the neck, which can cause a head tilt, any infant whose head stays in one position most of the time should be seen by his or her physician.

ROBERT E. GLENN, M.D.
Little Rock, Arkansas

My newborn has an extra finger. When should I have it removed?

Extra fingers (or toes) are termed polydactyly. These extra digits most commonly occur on the little finger side of the hand, but may also occur on the thumb side. Duplications of the thumb generally occur in isolated incidents in babies with no family history of extra digits. The cause of this type of polydactyly is unknown, but it is usually not a hereditary problem. Duplications of the fingers on the little finger side of the hand are usually encountered as isolated incidents in babies from families whose members, usually one of the parents, have also had extra fingers. This type of polydactyly is hereditary, with each affected individual having a 50 percent chance of passing the condition on to each potential offspring.

Some families with many members who have extra fingers or toes do not look upon polydactyly as a problem and therefore opt not to have them removed. (In most cases, removal of extra fingers is for cosmetic and not for functional reasons.) If parents wish to have their baby's extra finger removed, the timing of the removal will depend on the anatomy of the extra finger. If the extra digit is attached to the side of the hand by a small skin tag with no bony connection, it can be "tied off" by the pediatrician with a suture shortly after birth. If, however, there are bony connections between the extra finger and the hand, removal should be carried out by a plastic or hand surgeon. Most surgeons prefer to perform such cosmetic surgery when children are older, usually of preschool age.

H. EUGENE HOYME, M.D.
Burlington, Vermont

Why does my jaundiced newborn need to be under a fluorescent light?

It is a fortunate property of bilirubin that it can be changed by exposure to certain rays of visible light into forms that are not dangerous to the brain and are rapidly excreted from the body.

This form of treatment of jaundice of the newborn is called phototherapy, whereby the body of a jaundiced infant is irradiated by fluorescent lights that contain rays of the blue part of the spectrum. It is this wavelength band of light that alters bilirubin. It will penetrate the skin sufficiently to change the pigment discoloring the skin and circulating in the fine blood vessels in the skin layers.

Phototherapy, if maintained for a sufficient length of time—usually two or three days, but sometimes longer—will prevent the dangerous accumulation of bilirubin, will thereby prevent brain damage, and will cause the jaundice to disappear.

THOMAS R. C. SISSON, M.D., F.A.A.P.
Perth Amboy, New Jersey

Why do I have to wait until my baby weighs five pounds before I can take him home?

There is nothing magic about five pounds. The baby should go home after he has started to gain weight; when the family has demonstrated an ability to care for the baby adequately; and when necessary support systems such as a visiting nurse are enlisted.

D. H. CORSER, M.D.
La Crosse, Wisconsin

My newborn's skin is turning a yellowish tinge. Should I be concerned? What should I do?

Yes, you should be concerned. Although about 40 percent to 50 percent of newborn infants develop some yellow coloring of the skin, a condition called jaundice of the newborn, about 10 percent require some form of treatment.

Jaundice in newborns is either physiologic and self-limited or due to underlying conditions that themselves may be serious, such as an incompatibility of the mother's and baby's blood types, infection, poor fluid intake, prematurity, or a number of other conditions.

A pediatrician should be consulted promptly since it may not be enough merely to treat the jaundice; a primary cause should be treated as well.

THOMAS R. C. SISSON, M.D., F.A.A.P.
Perth Amboy, New Jersey

Why does my premature baby need to be in an incubator?

Incubators are primarily designed to provide heat. The smaller a baby is, the more difficulty it has in conserving heat and therefore maintaining body temperature. Furthermore, cooling can cause problems with the infant's breathing and lessen the chance of survival. Finally, by having to use more energy for maintaining temperature, the child has less left for growth.

Prematures often have problems with breathing and require additional oxygen. By enclosing the baby in an incubator, higher oxygen levels can be provided if necessary. The incubator also serves to prevent contamination of the environment with infectious agents, provided that good care is taken washing the hands and keeping supplies clean. Because they are made of transparent materials, incubators allow good visibility of the baby, so that very careful watch can be maintained by the nurses and doctors. Since the incubator is warm, no clothing is needed, permitting observation of the entire body.

JOHN P. GRAUSZ, M.D.
Milwaukee, Wisconsin

My newborn has a heart murmur. Is this serious?

Not necessarily so. When a baby is born, it has to adjust to a new type of circulation, and in this changeover from intrauterine to extrauterine channels of blood flow, murmurs may be heard transiently and disappear rather fast. However, if the murmur persists, the baby should be examined more frequently than the usual monthly checkups at least for the first several months. Symptoms of respiratory distress, fatigue on sucking, turning blue, failure to gain weight or excessive gain in weight, and excessive sweating are some of the signs and symptoms that may accompany a more serious heart condition. The mere presence of a murmur does not mean serious heart disease. Your pediatrician can guide you accurately in the assessment of the murmur and the need for a consultation by a pediatric cardiologist.

MILTON PRYSTOWSKY, M.D., F.A.A.P., F.A.C.C.
Nutley, New Jersey

My newborn's cuticles look red and are a little swollen. Is this normal?

Yes, this problem is very normal and very common not only in the newborn period but also in young infants between one and four months of age. Many times the very soft tissue that surrounds nail beds is slightly swollen and can be inflamed by the very sharp, thin nail that tends to bore itself in this soft, swollen tissue. Most older children and adults are able to trim their nails appropriately to avoid this complication. However, the newborn infant has nails that are not easily manicured. Although the cuticles look red and inflamed, it is rarely a major problem, and usually careful cleansing with soap and water and the topical application of an over-the-counter triple antibiotic ointment will keep the tissue healthy until the nail bed has matured enough for careful manicuring. On rare occasions this superficial infection will form a small abscess that will produce a small boil. Should this be the case, your physician should examine the infant for more vigorous treatment.

JAMES C. KELLY, M.D., F.A.A.P.
Springfield, Missouri

My nine-day-old baby has a few yellowish blisters on his neck and groin. Is this normal?

These blisters may be normal but should be watched carefully. They may be the beginning of an infection of the skin. You should soak the areas with a moist washcloth for five minutes three times a day. Keep a close watch on the blisters. If they seem to be enlarging or spreading, contact your baby's physician.

THEODORE S. TAPPER, M.D.
Philadelphia, Pennsylvania

My newborn has the hiccups a lot. What can I do for him? Are the hiccups serious?

Hiccups are not serious. Although we do not know the exact cause of them, they are usually associated with some regurgitation of the stomach contents to the esophagus (the food pipe leading to the stomach). The best approach is to refeed your infant a small amount. That should take care of most situations. If hiccups persist in spite of feeding you should discuss this with your pediatrician. This is not considered a medical emergency.

BENJAMIN SIEGEL, M.D.
Boston, Massachusetts

My newborn has been unable to come home with me because he has jaundice. What causes this?

Jaundice is very common in newborn infants. It is caused by the accumulation of bilirubin in the tissues and blood. Bilirubin is derived from the breakdown of hemoglobin and is a pigmented substance. As it is deposited in the skin in greater and greater amounts the skin turns yellow. This is jaundice.

At the same time, the amount of bilirubin in the blood increases. When the levels in blood are low there is no harm, but above moderate levels there is danger of bilirubin entering the brain and causing permanent damage to the cells of the central nervous system.

In some cases, jaundice in newborn infants continues to increase at the time a mother is ready to go home from the hospital. Her infant, however, should remain in the nursery until the elevated bilirubin levels are treated, or they are found to subside naturally, thereby assuring the baby's safety.

THOMAS R. C. SISSON, M.D., F.A.A.P.
Perth Amboy, New Jersey

What is an infant's normal body temperature?

An infant's normal body temperature, taken rectally, is between 98° and 100° Fahrenheit.

MERRITT B. LOW, M.D., F.A.A.P.
Ashfield, Massachusetts

My baby's circumcision site is bleeding slightly. Is this all right? Should I do anything?

There should be no persistent bleeding after a circumcision. If it lasts longer than four to six hours, please call your doctor.

AVRUM L. KATCHER, M.D., F.A.A.P.
Flemington, New Jersey

What temperature should our newborn's room be?

When advising parents on climatic guidelines for helping to keep their newborn healthy, several factors must be considered. The mean temperature and usual humidity of the areas where the infant will spend most of its time are the most important.

In nurseries for newborns, room temperatures are maintained between 72° and 74°, and infants are wrapped well, but not tightly. This is because the newborn's temperature control mechanisms are often unstable for their first few days of life. After three to four weeks of age, wrapping should be loose.

Humidity cannot be judged as accurately as room temperatures. However, it should be understood that the hotter the air, the drier it becomes. Air that is too dry can be counterproductive, as it reduces the natural moisture in the infant's nose and throat and often dries the skin. A controllable cool-mist vaporizer or humidifier can be of value, if used judiciously.

Most parents tend to overdress their infants and overheat their homes. One indication of overdressing or overheating an infant is a heat rash. This usually appears on the forehead, nose, and neck as small, skin-colored raised areas.

Be certain your child does not perspire when dressed for outside cold weather. Clothing and coverings for inside use should be of mostly cotton material. Keep in mind that most babies are overheated.

ALBERT L. GASKINS, M.D.
Philadelphia, Pennsylvania

Is it harmful to my newborn to have plants growing in her room?

Plants in the nursery can certainly add to a warm, cheery environment, and inherently they pose no danger. When you choose plants for the nursery, you should keep in mind the most common problems associated with household plants: allergic reaction, contact dermatitis, and poisoning.

Flowering plants will cause an allergic reaction if the baby should be sensitive to pollens. Plants also tend to be dust-catchers and can thereby aggravate a child who is sensitive to mites. Flowering plants should be kept out of the nursery, and if there is a strong family history of allergies, the wisest choice would be to have no plants at all.

Plants that are known to attract bugs and plants with a propensity to disease are poor choices for the nursery. Never treat plants for insects or disease in the baby's room.

Contact dermatitis and poisoning from ingestion occur only if the baby comes in direct contact with the plant. It would definitely be in the best interest of the baby and the plant to ensure that all household plants be kept out of reach.

ROBERT J. PARR, M.D.
Buffalo Grove, Illinois

Do you recommend bumper pads for cribs?

Bumper pads are helpful in preventing children from hitting their heads against the bed and also prevent the possibility of getting their heads wedged between the mattress and the rail of the bed.

FERNANDO J. deCASTRO, M.D.
St. Louis, Missouri

When my newborn breathes, both her abdomen and chest rise and fall simultaneously. Is she having difficulty breathing?

No. Normal breathing in infants involves the use of two sets of muscles: the intercostals (muscles attached to the ribs) and the diaphragms (muscles that separate the chest and lungs from the abdomen). The diaphragms are even more important for breathing in newborns because their chest walls are more pliable than are those of older children. Thus, when an infant takes in a breath, the chest will expand and the upper abdomen in particular will rise at the same time because the diaphragm lowers to allow a full breath to enter the chest.

ANNE B. FLETCHER, M.D.
Washington, D.C.

How should I bathe my baby before the cord stump falls off?

The umbilical stump dries up and falls off about one week after delivery. It is important to keep the area as clean and dry as possible to prevent infection in the skin around the umbilicus. Many physicians recommend applying rubbing alcohol on a cotton ball several times each day to the cord stump until it does fall off. Oozing of blood from the umbilicus for a day or two is normal after the stump is gone. A washcloth and water should be used to carefully wash around the cord area. When the cord is off and the bleeding has stopped, the child can then be washed in a bathtub.

ALAN R. RUSHTON, M.D., Ph.D.
Flemington, New Jersey

My infant's soft spot is sunken and it pulsates. Is this normal?

Yes. The spot is particularly sunken when the baby is being held with its head up. The pulsation is, of course, due to the blood coming to the brain at each heartbeat. The soft spot will fill up and bulge as the baby cries or strains at stool.

M. E. SYMONDS, M.D.
Mountainside, New Jersey

Why is my newborn's skin peeling? What can I do?

Newborn babies are covered with a white, fatty lubricating material called vernix. During the first week after delivery, the vernix begins to dry and form thin flakes. The outer layer of a newborn's skin also begins to dry and peel during this time. This combination of events often produces dry, flaky skin with cracks that may appear somewhat reddened. Occasionally, the skin cracks will actually bleed. In the vast majority of cases, the process of peeling is not uncomfortable for the baby, although it may look ugly to the parents. No treatment is needed since this is a normal occurrence. If the cracks are deep and bleeding, or if the child appears to be uncomfortable when the skin is touched, an application of a moisturizing cream such as Eucerin, Nivea, Alpha-Keri, or Lubriderm several times each day will soothe the sore areas and allow the normal peeling process to proceed. By seven to ten days after delivery, the baby's skin has usually completely adapted to life outside of the mother, and the baby has soft, smooth skin without any peeling, cracking, or blisters. The physician should be consulted if the parents are still concerned about the appearance of the baby's skin at this time.

ALAN R. RUSHTON, M.D., Ph.D.
Flemington, New Jersey

My infant is ten days old, and his cord stump hasn't fallen off yet. Is this all right?

Some cord stumps remain for two weeks or so. If there is no surrounding redness or purulent drainage, and the baby is acting all right, you need not worry.

MERRITT B. LOW, M.D., F.A.A.P.
Ashfield, Massachusetts

What is the average length and weight of a newborn?

There is only a slight difference in size between male and female newborns. They are not quite the same, but the average weight is seven pounds, and the average length is approximately nineteen to twenty inches. Babies born closer to sea level tend to be larger, and they are smaller if born at higher elevations. Babies are also smaller at birth if they are born early, if the mother is a cigarette smoker, or if she abuses alcohol or other drugs.

AVRUM L. KATCHER, M.D., F.A.A.P.
Flemington, New Jersey

My newborn's scrotal sac looks as though it has fluid in it. Is this abnormal? Will it take care of itself?

The presence of fluid in the scrotal sac is common in newborn baby boys. It is not harmful or painful to the baby and in most cases will gradually disappear in several weeks. Occasionally, the fluid collection (called a hydrocele) will persist and, if so, it is usually associated with a congenital hernia on the same side. If this is the case, it can be corrected by a simple surgical procedure. Your pediatrician will check the baby's scrotum during his regular checkups and will advise you if he or she feels that a consultation with a surgeon is necessary.

MARY B. McMURRAY, M.D.
Worcester, Massachusetts

Can I paint the inside of the house with a newborn present? Would the fumes harm the baby or cause breathing problems?

Paint fumes are potentially toxic, but with adequate ventilation of fresh air there should be no problem to a newborn or infant from fresh paint inside a house.

Paints are available in a variety of types and are composed of complex mixtures of solid compounds and liquid solvents. Only the solvent may be a problem in regard to this particular question, because the paint is not actually eaten. Hydrocarbons are often the solvents and may represent 75 percent or more of the mixture. Aromatic hydrocarbons are especially volatile and therefore easily vaporize into the air, where toxic fumes may accumulate in closed spaces. When these toxic fumes are breathed by a human being, they are rapidly transported to the brain where they may cause poisonous effects such as headache, nausea, euphoria, dizziness, irritability, weakness, or fatigue. The fumes can cause excitement, abdominal pains, vomiting, nonspecific psychological reactions, coma, seizures (convulsions, fits), and even death. Hydrocarbons also may be irritating to the skin of the eyes, nose, throat, and lungs. Infants with pulmonary (lung) problems such as asthma, bronchiolitis, pneumonia, chronic lung disease, croup, and so forth, may be especially susceptible to the irritating hydrocarbons and their chest problems may become aggravated. Some individuals are particularly bothered by the odor or smell of chemicals even though there is no toxic hazard; these hypersensitive people may experience nausea, dizziness, headache, weakness, or fatigue.

First aid or immediate treatment for any of these problems caused by the fumes of fresh paint is to have the victim breathe fresh air (or oxygen by mask, if available).

To play it safe when painting a house, open the windows and doors to aerate the room(s) for an hour or two, thereby dispersing any toxic fumes that may collect.

GARY S. WASSERMAN, D.O.
Kansas City, Missouri

My newborn is not circumcised. How do I wash his genital area to prevent infection?

Most physicians now feel that overtreatment of a noncircumcised penis does more harm than good. Overly energetic attempts to retract the foreskin can cause irritation and even scarring. Leave it alone. Wash the end gently, as you would any other part of the body. If the very end looks sore, put a dab of Vaseline on it once or twice a day. If there is swelling, call the doctor. Even then, there's no cause for alarm.

MERRITT B. LOW, M.D., F.A.A.P.
Ashfield, Massachusetts

Will being in a cigarette-smoke-filled room be unhealthy for my newborn?

Yes. It has been proven that a nonsmoker who inhales smoke faces as much harm as the smoker. It should also be remembered that smoking by the mother during pregnancy as well as afterward may be detrimental to the baby's health.

STEPHEN E. WALLACE, M.D., F.A.A.P.
Springfield, Illinois

How should I wash my newborn's hair, and how often?

Washing a newborn's hair is necessary only when you see foreign material on the scalp. This material is usually old cells from the lining of the skin of the top of the head, which a gentle baby shampoo will take care of adequately. A condition resembling cradle cap (a very thick, crusted appearance to the scalp) must be treated with special shampoo or medications, and it is a good idea to contact your doctor about this.

DAVID J. TEPPER, M.D.
Chattanooga, Tennessee

My newborn has a yellowish discharge from both eyes. Is this normal?

Discharge from the eyes is a common occurrence in newborn infants and may be caused by a number of different agents. Such a discharge is never normal. It is a sign of inflammation of the eye in the same way that redness around a cut is a sign of inflammation.

The discharge might be the sign of an infection of the *conjunctiva,* or surface of the eye. Such infections can usually be treated by means of antibiotics given orally or with eye drops. Most of these infections are not serious, and the baby's vision is usually not in danger, but there are some types of infection, such as gonorrhea, that can be quite serious and may even require hospitalization for treatment.

The discharge could be a reaction to a foreign material on the surface of the eyes. Most states require by law that all newborn infants receive eye medication at birth in order to prevent a gonorrheal infection. Such medication, especially silver nitrate, may cause a discharge that persists for a few days after birth, but this does not require treatment.

An eye discharge might also result from a disorder of the tear-producing system. Tears are the natural means by which foreign materials are washed from the surface of the eye. Disorders involving tear production may require a minor surgical procedure to correct.

There are a number of other very unusual conditions that can cause eye discharge. Any baby with eye drainage that persists for more than a day or two, or whose drainage progressively worsens, should be seen by a physician. Swelling or redness of the eyelids can be the sign of a more serious condition, and a physician should be consulted as soon as possible.

Yellow drainage is more commonly associated with an infection that requires treatment, while white drainage is usually associated with a reaction to foreign material on the eye's surface.

MICHAEL B. SHEEHAN, M.D.
Kansas City, Missouri

What exactly causes sudden infant death?

We do not know the cause of sudden infant death, but we have many theories. The theory that has most evidence to support it is that the immature brain sometimes has reduced sensitivity to the buildup of carbon dioxide. Carbon dioxide is a strong stimulus to drawing the next breath, but occasionally in infancy the brain center is slow to respond during deep sleep, and the infant will experience cardiopulmonary arrest. There appears to be a familial tendency toward this.

M. E. SYMONDS, M.D.
Mountainside, New Jersey

What type of clothing is appropriate for the newborn?

Cotton is the best material for clothing that comes in contact with the newborn infant's skin. The following items are useful for day and night use: a cotton knit wrap-around (not over-the-head) undershirt that has short sleeves and that is fastened with tape or snaps; cotton socks for cold days or nights; a long cotton knit robe, kimono-style; a jacket of cotton or of a mixture of wool and cotton for colder weather; a cotton receiving blanket about 30" square, to wrap the infant snugly (most infants sleep better when quite firmly bundled); a cotton knit cap (a lot of heat is lost through the head).

M. E. SYMONDS, M.D.
Mountainside, New Jersey

What is the best and safest way to carry my newborn?

Actually, newborns are very sturdy and can sometimes withstand accidents better than older children or adults do. But, unlike older people, young babies have not developed enough muscle tone to provide basic body support for the head, and they do not anticipate events in order to brace themselves ahead of time. This is why special attention must be given to the manner in which the child is held.

A child's head, neck, and buttocks should be supported whenever he or she is carried, whether by a parent or in a seat. Special attention must be given when the baby is in an upright position, such as over the shoulder. Young babies will generally move their heads on their own and may suddenly lose control. A hand should be kept behind the head as a gentle support while the baby is being carried this way. Infant seats must be appropriate to the child's age—a seat well-designed for a two-year-old would be inadequate for a two-week-old child.

Perhaps the most important time to be concerned about how you carry your child is when you are riding in a car. The major cause of death among children after the first week of life is automobile accidents. The only safe way for any child to be transported in a car is to be secured in a car seat designed for his or her age. Sitting on a parent's lap, unstrapped in a car seat, or in a car seat designed for a child of a different age can all lead to serious injury or death.

The final point about carrying a newborn is to try to place the child in a position where he or she can see your face. A newborn will selectively look at the parent's face over all other options. This interaction facilitates the baby's intellectual and physical growth. Eye contact should be promoted when safety and reason permit.

H. PATRICK STERN, M.D.
Little Rock, Arkansas

Can my baby use a small pillow?

There is no reason for a baby to need or use a small pillow.

MERRITT B. LOW, M.D., F.A.A.P.
Ashfield, Massachusetts

What is PKU?

PKU is phenylketonuria. Phenylketonuria is an inherited disease of the metabolism of a certain amino acid, phenylalanine, that is present in protein found in such foods as meat and milk. When a child who has PKU eats meat or drinks milk, the amino acid phenylalanine does not get utilized by the body effectively and accumulates as phenylketones. Phenylketones come out in the urine as phenylketonuria or can accumulate in the brain, producing mental retardation.

FERNANDO J. deCASTRO, M.D.
St. Louis, Missouri

Is the tendency to sudden infant death syndrome hereditary? Is it more common in some families than others?

No, it is not usually thought to be hereditary. However, sudden infant death syndrome has been found to occur in some families more than once, but no hereditary nature has ever been attributed to it.

JEANNE M. EULBERG, M.D.
Kansas City, Kansas

What is the usual age range for sudden infant death?

Sudden infant death syndrome, also called crib death, occurs mainly in the youngest age group of four weeks to four months of age in apparently healthy infants. It is also sometimes seen in a slightly older group up to two and one-half years of age. Some of these may have been treated for minor upper respiratory infections such as the common cold or flu.

Much study is going on into the background of crib death infants, especially those who are disadvantaged, ill, weak, small or handicapped. Monitors and sensors are being used to stimulate those infants thought to be at risk because of previous suspected episodes or as indicated by the experience of the researchers. One of the most important aspects of these tragedies is the emotional support necessary to help the affected families deal with unwarranted feelings of guilt because of suspected neglect or carelessness on the part of a parent.

At present, there is no way of accurately predicting the occurrence of this syndrome; there is also no sure preventative, and there is no cure.

Fortunately, the incidence of crib death is rare in the infant population, and a pediatrician may see only one in several years of a busy practice.

GEORGE B. RICHARDSON, M.D.
Charleston, South Carolina

My newborn's breathing is very rapid. Is this normal?

Newborn babies normally breathe about thirty to forty times per minute, about twice as fast as adults. A baby's breathing may quicken to around sixty times a minute when he or she is excited or stimulated, but it should slow down when the stimulation ceases.

Persistent rapid breathing might be a sign of serious illness and should never be ignored. Particularly worrisome signs include persistent rapid breathing while sleeping, interruptions of nursing so that the infant may catch his or her breath, changes in skin color to blue or gray, or an increase in paleness. Rapid breathing may accompany other symptoms, such as increased lethargy or sleepiness, decreased interest in sucking and eating, choking and gagging, and noisy breathing.

Because of the serious nature of many of the illnesses that cause rapid breathing, a physician should be consulted if this condition causes concern.

MICHAEL B. SHEEHAN, M.D.
Kansas City, Missouri

I found my baby limp, but after I shook her she began to breathe again. Was this an aborted sudden infant death?

The concept of an "aborted" sudden infant death is difficult to define, even for a pediatrician. Many experts on the sudden infant death syndrome don't believe that the terms "aborted" or "near miss" can apply to sudden infant deaths. Until the exact cause or causes of sudden infant death are found, the medical profession will not be able to tell when such a death has "almost" occurred.

Nevertheless, any infant who experiences an episode of limpness and cessation of breathing should be examined by a physician. Serious infections of the bloodstream or nervous system, or the possibility of epileptic convulsions or other central nervous system disturbances, deserve medical consideration and evaluation.

PAUL DUNCAN, M.D.
Oklahoma City, Oklahoma

My newborn had a full head of hair. Now he is going bald. Is this normal? Is this caused by a vitamin deficiency?

Your newborn is losing normal, temporary hair, which will be replaced in a natural, physiologic way. This is not related to any disease such as a vitamin deficiency. The baby's initial complement of hair is sometimes lost rapidly, leaving the baby rather bald, or it can be lost gradually while the new hair is growing in. This process is part of normal newborn maturation. The appearance is often exaggerated by the hair color—very blond hair is not as readily visible as dark hair, and causes a more bald but still normal appearance.

ROBERT FOMALONT, M.D.
Princeton, New Jersey

My baby was premature. Why did this happen? Will any of my future children be premature?

There are many causes of prematurity, such as the mother's health, nutrition, and age; the baby's position and health when in the womb; family history; bleeding late in pregnancy; multiple birth; or stress. Sometimes the cause is completely unknown. Pinning down the exact cause usually will give insight into future prospects for recurrence of the problem.

MERRITT B. LOW, M.D., F.A.A.P.
Ashfield, Massachusetts

While my baby is in the hospital, why can't he come to me for feedings even if I have a slight fever? I feel fine.

Your doctor has to make the decision, and if he or she thinks you may have a transmissible infection, he or she may want to keep you and your baby apart, even if you do feel fine yourself. The separation may be temporarily necessary pending an exact diagnosis. Doctors usually understand the problem and are as liberal as is safe.

MERRITT B. LOW, M.D., F.A.A.P.
Ashfield, Massachusetts

CHAPTER 22

Poison Ivy

My toddler has poison ivy around his eyes. Will the poison ivy damage his eyes if it gets into them?

Poison ivy will affect the tissue around the eyes, but it will not affect the eyes themselves. The skin around the eye is attached loosely and will swell easily, closing the eye. All of this is external to the eyeball, and treatment is directed to this area, not to the eye itself. Of course, rubbing the itching skin only irritates the area. Cool compresses and antipruritic (anti-itch) medication will alleviate some of the symptoms.

ROBERT FOMALONT, M.D.
Princeton, New Jersey

My child has poison ivy on his legs, and it is very itchy. What can I use on it?

The itching is caused by a resinous oil from the plant. A similar oil is found on poison oak and poison sumac, and the effects of all three plants are similar and the treatment is the same. First of all, any clothing that had been worn in the wooded area where the child contacted the plant should be laundered to prevent further contact with the offending oil. If the itchy area is weeping or oozing, it will be necessary to use an astringent soak to dry and soothe the area. Burow's solution is ideal for this purpose, and it can be obtained from a pharmacy without a prescription under the brand name of Domeboro or BuroSol powder. Mix a packet of the powder with a pint to a quart of water, soak some strips of cotton cloth with the solution, then apply the strips to the moist area, changing them frequently, for about fifteen minutes three times daily until the skin is no longer weeping. If the skin is not weeping or oozing, soak the legs in warm water or wrap them in hot, moist towels for about fifteen minutes as often as necessary. The legs may itch even more when the heat is first applied, but will itch much less for about an hour or two afterward. Mild hydrocortisone lotion is also available without prescription and may be applied to dry skin between soaks for relief from itching. If these measures do not relieve the itching, it may be necessary to consult your doctor for something stronger.

RONALD G. PALMER, M.D., F.A.A.P.
Carson City, Nevada

My toddler's hands are covered with big blisters from poison ivy. How can I take care of them?

Large blisters from poison ivy indicate a fairly severe reaction and may mean that your child will need to see his or her pediatrician.

The child should have a good bath and shampoo as soon as you suspect a poison ivy reaction. Any clothes he or she was wearing should be washed well. This will remove the oil of the poison ivy and reduce the chance of more reaction. Use rubber gloves to handle soiled clothes if you are sensitive to poison ivy. The area around the blisters and the blisters themselves should be gently cleaned with soap and water and wiped with alcohol. Manicure scissors that have been similarly cleaned can be used to remove as much of the blister top as possible.

The raw areas under the blister should be soaked with wet packs. Make a solution of one packet or one tablet of Domeboro in one pint of cool water. Soak a clean cotton muslin (like a tea towel) in this solution and lay it on the raw area for twenty minutes three times a day, until the area dries up, usually within three or four days.

If the child is old enough to leave the area alone, leave it open to the air. If he or she picks at it or sucks it, it would be best to cover it with dry gauze between soakings. If the area becomes more red or swollen consult your pediatrician.

RUSSELL D. ETZENHOUSER, M.D.
Overland Park, Kansas

Can scratching areas covered by poison ivy cause it to spread?

Rashes from contact with poison ivy, poison oak, and poison sumac are very common in the United States. They are caused by a reaction to an oil in these plants.

The oil can get onto the skin by direct contact with the plant or, indirectly, by contact with the furs of pets or from clothing, or from the smoke of burning leaves. Once the oil is on the skin, it often gets onto the fingers and can be transmitted to other parts of the body. Washing with soap and water removes the oil.

Except in very sensitive people, the rash usually doesn't break out until one to three days after exposure to the oil. The rash, including fluid from any blisters, is *not* contagious so long as the oil has been washed off. Therefore, oil on the fingers can cause the rash to occur on various parts of the body. However, after the oil has been removed, scratching the affected areas will not spread the rash.

ALAN COX, M.D.
Oklahoma City, Oklahoma

CHAPTER 23

Poisons

At what age is it safe for my child to use ipecac?

Syrup of ipecac, available in pharmacies in one-ounce bottles without a prescription, is a drug that makes almost all infants and children vomit. It is used especially to produce vomiting in children who have ingested poisonous substances, something that young children, particularly toddlers, are likely to do during the course of normal development. All parents should have ipecac in the home.

Ingestions are common during the late infancy and toddler years; fortunately, most things small children put in their mouths are relatively nontoxic. Some commonly used drugs, such as aspirin, acetaminophen (Tylenol), or vitamins, especially with iron, are safe when used according to instructions. But when snacked upon in large amounts by curious toddlers, they may be very poisonous, and urgent treatment will be needed to prevent harm to the child. This is usually when ipecac is recommended because, if given shortly after the ingestion, usually within the hour, a good portion of this poison will be vomited up instead of being absorbed into the body, where it will cause harm. It is very effective and frequently eliminates any harmful effect of the poison.

A main question is: when to use ipecac? Although most ingestions by children do not cause lasting harm, when you discover that your child has ingested something that is possibly poisonous it is best to call upon an expert to get advice on what to do. The best source of information would be, of course, your pediatrician. In many communities, however, there is a poison control center where you can telephone and speak to a specialist who will ask you questions about the substances the child has ingested and then give you advice on the next thing to do. As a rule, it is always best to contact your physician or poison control center before giving ipecac to any child, so always make sure your physician's phone number and that of the poison control center near you are readily available.

If you are unable to reach either your pediatrician or the center, it will probably be all right to give ipecac to a child suspected of ingesting a poison, *except in the following situations:*

(1) If the child is sleepy, unable to be aroused, or extremely agitated

(2) When petroleum products, such as furniture polish, paint thinner, nail polish remover, or corrosives, such as crystal drain cleaners, liquid drain cleaners, or acids, are suspected of having been ingested

If these conditions do not exist or those particular substances have not been ingested, give ipecac according to the following dosage schedule:

1 month to 6 months: 1 teaspoonful by mouth (5 ml)

6 months to 1 year: 2 teaspoonfuls by mouth (10 ml)

Over 1 year: 3 teaspoonfuls by mouth (15 ml)

A second dose, but no more, may be given if specifically directed.

Give 4 ozs. to 12 ozs. of water after the dose. Usually within fifteen to twenty minutes the child will vomit and may continue doing so for the next fifteen to twenty minutes. Stay with the child during this time and when he or she begins to vomit take care to position his or her head so there is no chance of his or her accidentally inhaling the vomit. The child may be permitted to get up and walk around if he or she chooses. After you have given the ipecac you should continue to try to contact the physician or the poison control center because in certain cases other treatments may be needed.

Remember that most childhood poisonings have an excellent outcome if treatment is given promptly. Of course, it is better to prevent such happenings by removing those items which are most likely to be available and ingested by a child or, if they are absolutely needed, by placing them in a locked container. The wonderful curiosity and enthusiasm for exploration of infants and toddlers allows them to discover even the most secret hiding places, and the only way to prevent them from getting into potential poisons is not to have such poisons in the house, or have them locked up.

Ipecac is an important drug for everyone to have in their homes, and it should be used under the guidance of a physician or a poison control center. A reasonable amount of preventive effort by parents can make the need for this drug unnecessary.

EDWARD W. COLLINS, M.D.
Providence, Rhode Island

What is the best way to make my child vomit if she has swallowed something poisonous?

Before doing anything, you should immediately contact your physician or your local poison control center to determine if inducing emesis (vomiting) is indicated for the particular poison ingested. Although emesis is usually indicated for most poisonings, there are those for which it is not. Caustics such as lye or acid and some petroleum products are such poisons.

If emesis is to be induced, the safest and most effective emetic is syrup of ipecac, which when given orally usually induces vomiting within ten to twenty minutes. It is more effective if water or another liquid is given immediately after the ipecac. If no vomiting occurs within twenty minutes, the ipecac can be repeated. But, you should consult with your physician, since ipecac itself can be toxic if too much is given and absorbed. You can purchase syrup of ipecac from your pharmacy without a prescription, and most pediatricians encourage parents to keep (in a safe place) a bottle at home in case it is needed. Other agents, such as salt water or dirty dish water, or even inserting a finger down the child's throat, that have been used in the past to induce vomiting are to be condemned as they are generally ineffective and often dangerous.

C. WARREN DERRICK JR., M.D.
Columbia, South Carolina

What should I keep on hand in case my child eats or drinks something poisonous?

Although prevention is the best treatment for poisoning, it seems that there is always one child in every family who is able to overcome all obstacles in order to take something that is poisonous. Because such accidents are totally unpredictable, it's very important for every family with young children to have the phone number of a pediatrician (because he or she is well trained to deal with most poison emergencies), and that of the local or regional poison control center. Most of these centers are also well equipped to answer parents' specific questions about the possible harm that might come to a child who has swallowed a poison or other drug.

A one-ounce bottle of syrup of ipecac should be at hand. This medicine is very inexpensive and is available at most pharmacies without a prescription. Syrup of ipecac does one thing: when an adequate amount, usually a tablespoonful, is taken by mouth and is followed by a glass of water, it causes the child to vomit, usually within twenty minutes. This empties the stomach of poison and, therefore, prevents serious damage to the child. The dose may be repeated once, usually on the way to the doctor's office or emergency room.

Phone numbers and the syrup of ipecac should be placed together because it's important to get some advice before using this medicine. In the case of some poisonings, it would be more harmful to have the child vomit than not, and at times, a child's condition also makes vomiting a bad idea. Some keep an ipecac label by their doctor's phone number near the telephone; others write the number on the bottle of ipecac so that the two are always associated in their minds when their child has a poisoning accident.

JOSEPH ZANGA, M.D.
Richmond, Virginia

CHAPTER 24

Respiratory Problems

Is there any medication to prevent my baby from getting croup?

No, there is no medication known to be effective in preventing croup.

ALLAN G. FREEMAN, M.D.
Keene, New Hampshire

My toddler woke with a barky cough last night and had some problems breathing because of it. Is there anything I can give him when this happens?

The most common cause of a barky cough is an illness called croup, which is usually caused by a virus and therefore will not respond to treatment with an antibiotic. The virus causes irritation and swelling of the tissues in the upper trachea (windpipe). A child will go to sleep feeling fine and wake up during the night with a barky cough. It is usually better in the morning but may recur the following evening, generally in a milder form.

There are no specific treatments, but you may use steam, which is best produced by turning on the shower in a closed bathroom. When the child has improved, a humidifier (cold air is preferable) may be used the rest of the night and again the following evening. Some children will improve with exposure to the outside night air. The illness may have fever, for which your favorite fever remedy may be used.

Because the symptoms are caused by swelling of the mucous membranes and the production of secretions, some physicians advise the use of a decongestant-expectorant preparation. You should consult your physician for his preferences for future cases, but for a sudden episode you may give any of the standard cough preparations.

The illness is self-limiting and you do not have to be overly concerned with this noisy, frightening cough if your child will sit comfortably on your lap and be put at ease by watching television or by listening to stories, or by other, similar mild distractions.

A more serious problem can be developing if your toddler shows signs of drooling with difficulty in respiration, an inability to swallow liquids, or if he has signs of "air hunger" so that he is restless and unable to be put at ease with simple distractions. Should these symptoms develop, you should contact your physician immediately.

ROBERT F. MILLHOUSE, M.D.
Canoga Park, California

My toddler has been coughing for the past few days and now she's sweating profusely and having difficulty breathing. Is she wheezing? What should I do to help her?

Wheezing is usually audible, especially if you put your ear close to the child's chest. The breathing sounds squeaky. This problem usually requires medical help. Sometimes, if the condition is not truly asthmatic, steam or cool mist can help the child breathe. Talk with your doctor as soon as possible.

MERRITT B. LOW, M.D., F.A.A.P.
Ashfield, Massachusetts

How does the shower help when my baby has croup?

Croup, or laryngotracheobronchitis, is most commonly caused by viral agents that cause swelling of the tissue immediately below the vocal cords. This swelling, along with the production of mucus, causes narrowing of the infant's airway. This narrowing results in hoarseness, rapid and somewhat labored breathing, and a characteristic barking cough. It has been a common observation that infants who have mild forms of croup often improve dramatically when taken out into the cold night air on the way to the emergency room. It is clear that humidified air, such as that produced in a bathroom by a running shower, often improves the symptoms of the mild form of the disease. No one is entirely certain why this is so, although there are many hypotheses. Whether the cool mist shrinks the inflamed tissue, or loosens secretions so that they may be more effectively removed, the shower often seems to do the trick. Although the majority of children recover spontaneously, one must not overlook the potential seriousness of this illness. If the infant does not improve, appears to become extremely restless, or runs a high fever, the parents should immediately consult their physician.

GERALD B. HICKSON, M.D.
Nashville, Tennessee

My baby is very stuffed up and cannot nurse. What can I do for him?

A newborn baby breathes through his nose and has to learn to breathe through his mouth. Thus, a baby with a stuffy nose may have difficulty feeding. One of the most effective methods of clearing an infant's stuffy nose is to use saline (saltwater) nose drops. Commercial preparations of this are available at any pharmacy, but you can make a similar solution at home by adding one-quarter teaspoon of table salt to one cup of boiled water. Then, before each feeding, if the baby is stuffed up, simply use a soft pliable dropper (please do not use glass eyedroppers), and add about three or four drops of the saline solution into each of the baby's nostrils. Wait fifteen seconds and draw out the mucus from the nose with a bulb syringe. This procedure can be repeated once, if needed, before starting to nurse. Use the bulb syringe gently, because the baby's nose can become irritated. If the mucus becomes green- or yellow-colored and quite profuse, you should call your pediatrician. If the baby's room is quite dry, you might want to run a humidifier in the room while he sleeps. Decongestants or medicated nose drops are seldom necessary for this problem in young infants.

LINDA C. LONEY, M.D.
St. Louis, Missouri

My baby-sitter's son has bronchitis. Is there any danger to my infant?

A quick answer to your question is that if your baby-sitter is not ill herself, and if your baby will not be brought into contact with the sitter's son, your infant is in no danger.

Bronchitis is a virus infection of the respiratory tract. Although it is contagious by direct contact with the individual who is sick, it is not transmitted by a healthy third person. For this reason, if your baby remains in your home, and only the baby-sitter (not her son also) visits your house, there is no problem. It is possible, though, that the baby-sitter may have caught the illness from her son, and may be in the early stages of the disease. Therefore, it would be wise to inquire about her state of health before she comes to you. Minor symptoms such as a sore throat, tiredness, or just "not feeling well" may be the only complaints, but they may signal the onset of the disease.

Often people refer to a persistent severe cough, or a cough due to bronchial asthma or an allergy as bronchitis. These conditions are not contagious and are not to be confused with the question we have discussed.

BERNARD M. CURTIS, M.D.
Wantagh, New York

Is a humidifier as good as a vaporizer?

A humidifier is an important item and it should not be confused with a vaporizer. The humidifier is generally placed in a room to give off low levels of humidity continuously. It is especially useful in the wintertime, when forced-air furnaces cause the level of humidity in a house to become quite low. The device makes the room more comfortable and breathing somewhat easier for a sick child. However, a humidifier will not accomplish the important job that is accomplished by a vaporizer. A vaporizer delivers a more concentrated humidity and does so over a much smaller area. Unfortunately, a vaporizer is often used incorrectly, that is, it is simply put in the middle of a room and used as a humidifier, increasing the relative humidity slightly, but not sufficiently to do much for the child's respiratory problem. To be used correctly, the vaporizer should provide intense humidity over a very small area and be applied more or less directly to the child's bronchial tree. When children are hospitalized for respiratory problems, they are often put into a steam tent, which is a plastic tent into which some type of vaporizer is run. Something similar can be set up at home. In the past, it was not advisable to use a tent at home with a vaporizer in it, because hot steam vaporizers were used and there was a great possibility of the child's being burned by the intense heat in a closed space. Now, however, more cold steam vaporizers are being used, and these instruments can be run directly into a tent. A cold steam vaporizer may be less dangerous to the child. You may build a tent around the child's bed, or, in the case of an older child, during the daytime build a tent over some chairs and permit the child to play in that environment. The tent can be built very easily by stretching a sheet over the bed or by stretching a sheet between chairs and then running the vaporizer directly into this homemade croup tent. When used in this fashion, a vaporizer can be very helpful in freeing irritations and infections of the upper bronchial tree. A vaporizer is not, however, helpful in the treatment of lower tract illnesses such as pneumonia or bronchitis.

RICHARD A. GUTHRIE, M.D.
Wichita, Kansas

My baby has a cough that is constant, and lately he has coughed so hard that he vomits. What can I do for him?

You should be aware that coughing is one of the body's defenses. When mucus accumulates faster than it can be removed or when foreign materials, such as smoke or dust, are aspirated, special sensors in the trachea and lungs set off coughing. This is to help remove the offending matter.

In the colder months, there is the greatest likelihood that your child will have increased amounts of mucus that will cause him not only to cough but to gag and vomit. He must be examined to be sure other common causes of a persistent cough, such as asthma or a swallowed foreign body, aren't present.

JAMES L. HUGHES, M.D.
Greenville, North Carolina

My infant coughs only at night and has no other signs of a cold. Should I use a humidifier?

Yes, the use of a humidifier is an excellent idea under the circumstances. It would be practical to get a vaporizer that has a removable top so that it could be used as either a humidifier or vaporizer. Cold steam humidifiers are recommended because they are significantly safer than the hot steam vaporizers. What is important to remember is that in wintertime, especially in cold climates, dry heat in homes tends to dry out the mucous membranes and aggravate a dry cough.

JEROME E. KWAKO, M.D.
Duluth, Minnesota

What is the best way to give medicine to my infant son?

Carefully follow instructions given by your doctor about the medicine. You need to know the name of the medicine, the amount to be given, how often the medicine is to be given, and how long the baby is to receive the medicine. This information is on the bottle of the medicine. Keep all medicine out of reach of other children.

Ask your doctor or pharmacist if the medicine should be given before, with, or between feedings. The timing may have an effect on the absorption of the medicine. You should know why you are giving your baby the medicine. It is also important to know about any of its side effects. Your doctor or pharmacist will tell you what to watch for and observe. Call your doctor if any rash or itching occurs while your baby is taking the medicine.

You must be careful about measuring the amount of medicine. Follow the instructions given on the bottle. An ordinary household teaspoon can vary in size. Use a standard measuring spoon such as one used in cooking. A syringe can also be used as a measuring device.

Be patient when giving medicine to an infant. Hold the baby in your arms with his head up slightly or in a feeding position. When using a syringe or a dropper, gently and slowly drop the medicine toward the back center portion of the baby's mouth, gently stroking the baby's cheek to encourage sucking. You can also place the medicine in an empty nipple and place it in the baby's mouth to encourage sucking. If a large amount of medicine is to be given, the baby might need burping. Take your time when giving any medicine. If the baby fusses a lot and cries, stop, let him rest, and then continue. Be persistent; even if the baby doesn't like the taste of the medicine, he needs it. Always hold and cuddle him after he takes the medicine.

If your baby starts to gag, stop, allow him to rest, comfort him, and then continue with smaller amounts of the medicine. If he vomits, turn his head sideways, pat him gently on the back and clear his mouth. Try to estimate the amount of medicine vomited and ask your doctor if the dose should be repeated. Try not to give any medicine on a full stomach.

You can put the medicine in a small amount of food if the infant is on baby food. A tablet can be crushed and mixed in applesauce. Do not mix medicine with formula as it is difficult to determine how much medicine the baby has taken when it is mixed with formula. Some medicines are not absorbed well with milk or food.

LYDIA A. CHAPMAN, M.D.
Washington, D.C.

What is asthma? What is the cause?

Asthma is a lung disease that is characterized by episodes of shortness of breath, coughing, and wheezing. These symptoms are caused by obstruction of air flow in and out of the air passages in the lung, called bronchial tubes or bronchioles. Three abnormalities obstruct the air flow: spasm of the muscle surrounding the bronchioles, inflammation and swelling of the lining of the bronchioles, and production of excessive amounts of sticky mucus, which is difficult to cough up and which forms plugs.

The basic defect causing these abnormalities, and therefore the symptoms, is an excessive irritability, whose cause is still unknown, of the bronchioles. An asthma attack may vary considerably among individual asthmatics. One person may wheeze all year if around cats, another may wheeze only during ragweed season and have associated hay fever. Triggering factors common to many asthmatics include viral infections, such as the common cold or influenza, exercise, and irritants such as smoke, dust, or air pollutants.

Although asthma may occur at any age, it usually develops before the age of ten, with the vast majority before age eight and half before age three.

There is a tendency for asthma to begin at an earlier age in children who also have eczema and hay fever. There is an increased chance of later development of asthma in infants and children with "wheezy bronchitis" or wheezing associated with respiratory infections.

Several studies have shown that an improvement or remission in asthmatic symptoms may occur during adolescence, leading to the conclusion that one can outgrow asthma. However, severe asthma and asthma that begins when a child is younger than three years of age tend to persist.

Children may inherit a predisposition to developing eczema, hay fever (allergic rhinitis), or asthma either singly or in combination. There is a high correlation between childhood asthma and the incidence of hay fever and eczema among close relatives, and there is a significantly greater incidence of asthma in identical twins as compared to fraternal twins or non-twin siblings. The correlation is far from absolute, though, and in many cases no family history of respiratory and/or allergic disease will be elicited.

Asthma makes its first appearance in several different ways. In infants and young children it usually first occurs with a viral respiratory infection, a severe chest cold with accompanying wheezing, a high-pitched whistling sound, and/or a tight hacking or rattling cough. The infant may breathe rapidly with a marked see-saw movement of the chest wall indicating difficult breathing. All of these symptoms are similar to croup or bronchiolitis, a severe respiratory infection fairly common in infancy and difficult, if not impossible, to distinguish from asthma when it first occurs. Fever may or may not be present. A chest X ray may show an abnormal collection of fluid, which may be attributed to a viral pneumonia, but which may also be caused by a mucous plug, as is frequently seen in asthma. In an infant, it may be only after two or three such episodes that it is possible to diagnose asthma.

Indeed, since it is so often a viral respiratory infection that triggers the initial asthma attack, it is impossible to draw a line between infection and asthma. Persistent wheezing, lasting several weeks, even after the discomfort of the acute illness subsides, is a clue. Some infants are cheerful, have good appetites, and grow and develop normally in spite of chronic wheezing and coughing. Others are fretful, eat and sleep poorly, and have poor weight gain. Obviously the latter group needs to be evaluated and treated, as does the former group, if only to counsel the parents about future episodes of more acute wheezing.

Other problems such as food and foreign objects aspirated into the airways and subtle anatomical malformations of the windpipe and airways, cystic fibrosis, and other rare lung and heart problems need to be ruled out before asthma may be diagnosed.

One should always strive to eliminate irritants such as smoke, dust, air pollution, and chemical irritants from an asthmatic's environment. Removal of furry pets from the home is often emotionally traumatic, and perhaps should be undertaken only after there is evidence to suggest that their presence exacerbates the child's respiratory problems. Prevention of viral infections is nearly impossible without isolating the child from parents, caregivers, siblings and other children.

The elimination of so-called allergenic foods, such as milk, eggs, corn, and wheat, has been recommended by many physicians for infants from families with histories of allergies. There is no evidence, however, that blanket elimination without specific indication is beneficial. If the infant is truly allergic to a food, symptoms will usually be obvious and fairly immediate, within minutes to several hours, and will include wheezing, vomiting, diarrhea, or skin rash. In this case, after consultation with a physician, the food should be eliminated and the nutritional balance of the diet should be assessed and appropriate substitutions made, if necessary. The role of breast-feeding in preventing subsequent asthma in infants with a family history of asthma and/or allergic disease is controversial. The beneficial effects of breast-feeding a child with or without asthma and allergic disease are convincing and breast-feeding is recommended. Whether breast-feeding as a sole method of feeding and its duration for a given length of time prevent subsequent development of asthma remain to be proven conclusively and need to be discussed individually with the child's physician.

Most childhood asthma has a good prognosis if diagnosed early and treated properly, with medications if necessary. Parents should be aware of the possibility of asthma in an infant who has recurrent respiratory problems, and discuss it with the child's physician.

ANNE MANON BRENNER, M.D.
Denver, Colorado

When I put my hand on my baby's chest, I can feel a rattling. Should that be there?

There may be many reasons for rattling in a baby's chest. It may be the result of an abnormality of the conducting airways, such as the pharynx, trachea, bronchi, and bronchioles, that creates signs and symptoms of obstruction. In very young infants, a rattling in the chest may be caused by a pooling of saliva. The rattling may be accompanied by other signs of obstruction of the airways, such as inspiratory stridor (a whistling sound during breathing), rhonchus (a rattling in the throat), wheezing, or prolonged expiratory or inspiratory time. These signs may also be seen when use of the chest muscles results in the pulling in of the spaces between the ribs and abdomen.

Causes of compression of the airways are many, including infections, congenital anomalies, enlarged thymus gland, allergy, aspiration of a foreign body, and tumors.

By and large, an obstruction in intrathoracic airways results in greater difficulty in breathing in than in breathing out.

When there is difficulty in breathing, rattling or poor feeding are usually present, and this warrants immediate medical attention.

SABURO HARA, M.D.
Nashville, Tennessee

My baby sounds congested when he coughs but I can't tell if the congestion is in his throat or in his chest. What should I do?

Any cough, especially if it is accompanied by a fever and/or rapid breathing, should be evaluated by a doctor. When the cough sounds like a barking dog or a seal, then the trouble is probably due to a problem in the throat or in the voice box (larynx). When this happens, you may notice that the child is also having some difficulty breathing *in.*

If the cough sounds worse when the child breathes *out,* and particularly if he also wheezes, then the problem is in the chest. Sometimes there is very little coughing, but the child is breathing rapidly; this could be caused by congestion deep in the chest.

In most cases (with the exception of asthma), a humidifier, which makes a cool mist, is very helpful when placed by the bed. It's also important to keep the child's nose unblocked by using a nose syringe and some saline nose drops.

JOHN HOWARD STRIMAS, M.D.
Johnson City, Tennessee

Can I give cough medicine to my baby?

Cough medicines in general should not be given to small babies without a doctor's specific permission. Many of these medications contain drugs that should not be given to children under two years of age.

DAVID J. TEPPER, M.D.
Chattanooga, Tennessee

What is croup? What causes it?

Croup encompasses a number of problems, usually of an acute infectious nature, in the upper airway in children. It is characterized by a brassy, "barky" cough, which may be accompanied by hoarseness and respiratory difficulties. However, a croupy cough can also be related to other upper airway problems, such as aspiration of a foreign body.

The upper airway in children is like the neck of a bottle, with the lungs representing the lower portion of the bottle. Any degree of obstruction, such as from inflammation or a foreign body, may cause a severe narrowing of the airway. As little as one millimeter of swelling in a child's upper airway can reduce the breathing area by as much as one-half to two-thirds of its normal size.

There can be many causes, including bacteria and viruses, for infectious croup. Some of these are common and mild, whereas others may be uncommon and severe. The common form of croup, acute laryngotracheal bronchitis, is caused primarily by viruses. It is most common in children younger than three years of age and occurs most often at around twenty-one months of age. Most children have an upper airway tract infection for several days before they develop the brassy cough of croup. The course of the illness usually waxes and wanes and is usually worse at night. The respiratory distress is usually mild. In some instances, however, respiratory distress may develop rapidly as the infection progresses down the bronchial tree.

The outcome of infectious croup depends on the severity of the infection and the age of the child. Obviously, younger children with smaller airways have more difficulty than older children. A very mild case may require only a cool-mist vaporizer, cool night air, or the moisture from a steaming shower. Most afebrile children with mild croup can be safely and effectively managed at home. However, any child with croup who has a fever or any signs of respiratory difficulty must be seen immediately by a physician. Complications, although uncommon, do arise, and they can be life-threatening. Any upper respiratory infection that causes only a runny nose or conjunctivitis in other family members may cause significant problems in the young child.

DON C. VAN DYKE, M.D.
Atlantic City, New Jersey

My baby has a dry cough and is hoarse when she cries. Could she have a sore throat?

Yes, but hoarseness is usually due to inflammation in the larynx, or voice box. This is a common illness in children, and in its more severe form it is known as croup. Croup is usually caused by a viral infection; it is a minor, self-limiting disease. Croup may respond to simple measures such as increasing the humidity in the baby's environment by using a vaporizer. If the baby has acute difficulty with her breathing, you should consult your pediatrician.

STEPHEN E. WALLACE, M.D., F.A.A.P.
Springfield, Illinois

Does having a bad asthma attack mean that my child will have to be hospitalized?

Young children who suffer from asthma may have episodes of wheezing that will warrant consultation with a physician. Mild wheezing in an asthmatic is not uncommon and may regularly respond to home treatment and a medication regimen as outlined by your physician. Moderate wheezing will usually necessitate a visit to physician's office or to the hospital emergency room. Again, response is variable, but many children can return home with a specific treatment plan, including periodic visits to the doctor.

Severe episodes of wheezing are usually associated with some degree of breathing difficulty and may necessitate a more comprehensive treatment plan that may include hospitalization. Generally, wheezing in itself does not determine whether the child will need hospitalization, but if a child has wheezing in addition to difficulty in breathing, restlessness, vomiting, poor feeding, or high fever, hospitalization will probably be required.

RALPH E. CAPRIO, M.D.
New York, New York

CHAPTER 25

Skin

What is the cause of prickly heat? What is the best way to care for it?

Prickly heat is caused by a plugging of the pores and sweat ducts of the skin with keratin, which is one of the substances that constitutes the skin. This condition is most often seen in hot, humid weather but may also be encountered when a child has a high fever. Overdressing a child or covering the skin with a dressing such as petroleum, which clogs the pores, aggravates prickly heat. The best way to care for this disorder is to keep the skin clean and dry and to keep the patient in a cool area as much as possible.

KATHERINE M. KNIGHT, M.D.
New Orleans, Louisiana

How do I care for my baby's scalp to clear up cradle cap? Will he get it again?

Cradle cap is a form of seborrheic dermatitis. It is a chronic condition that usually starts in the first two weeks of life and is characterized by reddened areas with yellow scales or crusts. Cradle cap can spread to other parts of the body such as the eyebrows, around the mouth, the navel, the armpits, or groin. It has the tendency to be a recurring problem.

The treatment of cradle cap consists basically of using an antiseborrheic shampoo such as Selsun or Sebulex on a daily basis. After improvement, shampoo two or three times a week. Following the shampooing, use a moderately stiff brush to help remove the scales. An alternative treatment that is frequently effective is the use of a coal tar ointment containing 1 percent salicylic acid, 3 percent sulfur, and 1 percent hydrocortisone in a water-miscible base. If the cradle cap is very mild, sometimes just the use of a topical corticosteroid preparation three or four times daily is sufficient; or soften the scales by applying petroleum jelly the night before the shampoo. It is important to treat the cradle cap vigorously and to be aware that it can recur.

WALTER B. WATSON, M.D., F.A.A.P.
Casper, Wyoming

My son has a raised red birthmark on his back. Can that be removed? Will it increase in size?

Birthmarks of the type you describe are common in babies and are made up of a thick network of blood vessels that rise above the surface of the skin. They look like strawberries and in fact are called by that name. They may become larger in the first year or two, causing some parents to fear needlessly that they are malignant. In the majority of cases no treatment is required, as these birthmarks can be expected to disappear by five or six years of age, leaving only a small scar.

ROBERT L. GUY, M.D.
New Orleans, Louisiana

Is there any chance that a birthmark could turn cancerous?

The hemangioma type of birthmark, which is red and is present at birth or appears during the first few months of life, very rarely develops a malignant growth, so that treatment depends upon other considerations.

However, the back nevi that are present at birth may later develop into cancers. The larger they are the more likely it is that this may occur. The pediatrician who is following the child for routine care can best decide if and when they should be removed to prevent this, and also to aid in the child's appearance.

E. B. ALPERN, M.D.
Detroit, Michigan

Is it dangerous if a birthmark is scratched?

Most birthmarks are made up of normal skin cells and organs, such as sweat glands. The normal skin cells are merely concentrated to a greater degree in birthmarks. For example, the typical mole is an area of skin where those cells which give color to all areas of skin are present in greater than normal numbers, thus imparting the usual deep-brown color to a mole. Therefore, when birthmarks are scratched, they heal in the same fashion as the rest of the skin and should not be cause for concern.

A situation that should be evaluated is one in which there is chronic or recurrent injury to a birthmark. Certain types of birthmarks, when subject to continuous injury, such as that caused by tight clothing, can undergo serious changes. If a parent is aware of this, the birthmark should be checked by a doctor.

MICHAEL KILCULLEN, M.D.
Woodstock, Vermont

My baby has a mole on her face. Should this be removed? When is the best time?

Whether a mole on the face should be removed or not depends on several factors, including size of the mole, its appearance, and its presence or absence at birth.

If the mole is large and dark and was present at birth (a pigmented giant nevus), removal prior to two years of age is preferred. This type of mole is considered precancerous.

If the mole was not present at birth and is not very large, the risk of cancerous change prior to adolescence is very, very small. Such a mole is sometimes removed for cosmetic purposes. This removal is best delayed until your baby is at least of school age to obtain the best cosmetic result.

You should consult with your baby's doctor if any of the following changes occur in any mole: sudden change in size or shape; change in color, especially if red or blue; ulceration or bleeding; or the mole becomes lumpy or crusted. These changes may be an indication of early cancerous change.

DAVID KESSEL, M.D.
Arvada, Colorado

Can my whole family catch eczema from my toddler?

No. Eczema is a skin condition that occurs in approximately 3 percent of all infants. We often see a familial tendency for susceptibility to eczema as well as to other conditions such as hay fever and asthma. It would therefore not be unusual for more than one child in a family to have this type of dermatitis at the same time. However, it is not spread from one individual to another. Sometimes, when a patch of eczema becomes cracked or scratched, a secondary bacterial infection like an impetigo can develop. This infection can then be passed on to others by direct contact.

MARY B. McMURRAY, M.D.
Worcester, Massachusetts

Is ringworm contagious? For how long? How could my child have caught it?

Ringworm is a fungal infection that affects chiefly the scalp or the skin. The infection may be passed from other children or from animals, particularly puppies and kittens. It can be contagious, and treatment should be continued for at least two or three weeks.

JOSEPH L. KLOSS, M.D.
Akron, Ohio

My child is losing hair in patches on his head. Could ringworm be causing this?

Certainly ringworm could cause hair loss in patches. However, this could also be due to alopecia areata or to trichotillomania. Usually when the child has a fungus infection, or ringworm, there is inflammation of the scalp and there is sick-looking hair that, when pulled from the scalp, comes out easily in numbers greater than ten to twenty. When this happens, the child most likely has ringworm. This can be confirmed by a culture of a shaving of the scalp. In alopecia areata, which is a psychological condition, the child has bald patches with no irritation of the scalp, and when one pulls the hair around a patch, usually no hair comes out. The child could have trichotillomania, which means that the child is pulling the hair again, for psychological reasons. In trichotillomania the child may also swallow the hair and develop a bezoar, a hard mass in the stomach or intestines. When the child has a bezoar, he frequently develops severe anemia because the hair irritates the stomach and the child loses blood and iron from the gastro-intestinal tract.

FERNANDO J. deCASTRO, M.D.
St. Louis, Missouri

What is the treatment for ringworm? How long should I use the medication on the affected areas?

Ringworm refers to a variety of fungal infections of the skin, scalp, and/or nails. For simple localized areas of infection, usually a topical fungicidal cream or lotion, such as Lotrimin (Clotrimazole) or Halotex (Haloprogen), applied twice daily for two to three weeks will eradicate the infection. Rarely, more severe involvement, especially of the nails, will require systematic medication (such as griseofulvin) for one to three months or longer, depending on clinical response.

WARREN SWEBERG, M.D., F.A.A.P.
East Brunswick, New Jersey

What is impetigo and what does it look like?

Impetigo is an infection of the skin caused by the staphylococcus (staph) and streptococcus (strep) bacteria. This disease starts as a small blister, often near the mouth, which quickly enlarges, bursts, and is replaced by a wet, oozing, honey-colored patch. The patch tends to dry first in the middle, leaving a ring of infection around it, which can be mistaken for ringworm, a fungal infection.

The germ is spread by scratching the infected area and then touching other parts of the body, such as the face, arms, legs, or vagina. It can be passed from child to child. Impetigo is highly contagious; it should be diagnosed by a physician and is usually treated with antibiotics.

Parents must resist the temptation to pick at the crusts or to clean them vigorously, as both of these practices may spread the infection.

OWEN MATHIEU, M.D.
Boston, Massachusetts

Is impetigo contagious? How is it passed from one person to another?

Yes, impetigo is contagious. The oozing material beneath the crusts on the ruptured pustules is loaded with bacteria, usually of the streptococcal and staphylococcal varieties. The disease can be transmitted if a person who may have minor breaks in the skin touches the infected areas or contaminated clothing of someone who has impetigo.

KATHERINE M. KNIGHT, M.D.
New Orleans, Louisiana

My toddler seems to have athlete's foot ever since walking in a public bathroom at the beach. What should I use for it?

Athlete's foot, which is a fungus infection that usually involves the toe webs and the subdigital crevices, is rare in toddlers. In this age group, the rash is more likely to be either simple maceration and peeling of the interdigital spaces, or contact dermatitis caused by footwear. Initial treatment should include perforated, less restrictive shoes; wearing only socks and/or slippers in the house; cotton socks only (synthetic materials do not absorb perspiration); thorough cleansing and drying of feet each morning and evening; an antifungal powder during the day; and an antifungal, antibacterial, anti-inflammatory cream at night (by prescription). If no improvement is noticed in seven to ten days, an office visit should be scheduled for further evaluation and possible culture.

FURMAN T. UPDIKE, M.D.
York, Pennsylvania

What causes thrush? Is thrush contagious?

Thrush is the common name for a frequently encountered oral infection in babies. It is caused by the same fungus that causes some vaginal infections in women. It is usually indicated by the presence of white patches in the mouth and may cause minor feeding problems. The fungus is normally acquired during the birth process. It is not usually contagious except between infants who share the same pacifiers, nipples, or toys.

STEPHEN E. WALLACE, M.D., F.A.A.P.
Springfield, Illinois

My infant was with another child who developed roseola yesterday. Is roseola contagious? What is its incubation period?

Roseola is not ordinarily considered to be contagious, but there have been cases reported of apparent spreading from child to child, especially in institutions. The incubation period is probably around fourteen days, possibly a little less.

MERRITT B. LOW, M.D., F.A.A.P.
Ashfield, Massachusetts

What is eczema? How did my toddler get it? Is there a topical ointment I can use to clear it up?

Eczema is an inflammatory reaction of the skin caused by allergy. The allergy may be due to substances eaten or inhaled by the child. Sometimes no such external substance can be identified, but the child develops eczema as a spontaneous tissue reaction. In either case, there is usually a strong familial predisposition to the condition. Coal tar ointments are helpful, but messy. Steroid creams are effective, but must be used carefully and only with medical guidance.

M. E. SYMONDS, M.D.
Mountainside, New Jersey

My infant had a high fever for a few days and now it is gone. He now has a rash all over his body. What caused it?

The most likely cause for your child's fever is a condition commonly called baby measles or Roseola Infantum or Exanthem Subitum. This illness typically begins in a healthy infant between the ages of three and eighteen months with the onset of a fever of between 102° and 104°. The fever is usually responsive to medications such as aspirin and cool baths. The child does not act ill when the fever is treated. The fever breaks after two to three days, and the child erupts with a fine rash over the chest, back, arms, and legs, but seems perfectly healthy. The rash may last from a few hours to one or two days. This illness acts like a viral illness (although a virus has never been isolated in any cases to this time) in that it is contagious and has an incubation period of seven to ten days. It is not felt to be a dangerous illness and is not known to cause any problems in unborn infants. The only danger in roseola are the occasional convulsions that may occur due to the rapid onset of high fever.

DAVID L. WRIGHT, M.D., Ph.D.
Franklin, Pennsylvania

My newborn's tongue is coated with a patchy white substance, and he seems to be having trouble nursing because of it. What is wrong?

A patchy white substance coating the tongue and the inside of the cheeks on a young baby is almost always caused by infection from the monilia fungus. This is commonly called thrush. Children with this condition will often have difficulty nursing because the mouth is somewhat tender. Treatment consists of either a purple dye, which is painted in the mouth with a Q-tip, or a medication prescribed by the doctor and given to the baby with a dropper. Thrush is sometimes very difficult to cure, and you must be very diligent in using the medication as prescribed. It is also important that the mother's breasts be kept very clean, and nipples and pacifiers be sterilized very thoroughly until the infection is completely cleared.

DAVID J. TEPPER, M.D.
Chattanooga, Tennessee

My toddler's playmate has scabies. Should my child have any treatment?

It would depend on how intimate the relationship is between your child and the playmate. If this was a regular, day-in, day-out type of relationship, it would be wise for the child to get treated. If the contact was a casual, infrequent one, treatment would probably not be required.

This recommendation is based on the current understanding that if scabies is found in one member of a family, the other members are infected. Even though symptoms may not be evident, they should be treated. It is known that it takes about six weeks after infection by the scabies mite before the clinical disease appears.

T. F. MCNAIR SCOTT, M.D.
Philadelphia, Pennsylvania

My infant has thrush and is nursing. Will my breasts become infected?

Thrush is caused by yeast. It is considered an opportunistic infection, which means that normally it causes no problems even when it is present. Because of their immature infection-fighting system, normal newborns pick up some opportunistic infections that would invariably occur in older children or adults in conjunction with other health problems. Thrush is one of these types of infection. Although treatment is recommended for the baby, this infection usually goes away by itself, although not as quickly. The yeast itself will often stay around after the infection has gone and the baby shows no more symptoms.

A woman with normal breasts would not develop any problem if yeast were applied directly to them. However, many nursing mothers develop some irritation and cracking on and around the nipples, and this could allow an opportunistic organism like yeast to set up an infection that would not otherwise occur. Thus, when yeast from the baby's mouth comes in contact with the irritated breast, it becomes possible for an infection to start.

You probably need not stop nursing if your child develops thrush. In fact, because breast milk contains infection-fighting substances, it is a good idea

233

to continue nursing. You should take more careful care of your breasts to minimize the chance that irritation will allow the infection to start. Yeast needs moisture to grow, so cleansing with a mild soap and warm water, followed by careful drying after each feeding, would be necessary. Even if a yeast infection does occur on your breast, nursing can still continue. This depends on the severity of the infection, the persistence of the infection in the face of nursing, and the type of treatment needed. Consult your doctor for guidance in each case.

H. PATRICK STERN, M.D.
Little Rock, Arkansas

My toddler broke out in hives. Can this mean she is allergic to the antibiotic she is now taking?

Yes, but hives may be due to a multitude of causes, one of which is drug allergy. Other causes are food allergies, viral infections, chemicals in the environment, emotional upset, and stress. In at least half of the cases, no definite cause is ever identified.

STEPHEN E. WALLACE, M.D., F.A.A.P.
Springfield, Illinois

What is cradle cap and what is the cause of it? Is cradle cap contagious?

Cradle cap is a relatively common condition that affects the scalp of newborn infants during their first, second, and, sometimes, third week of life. The affected scalp loses its normally smooth appearance and develops adherent, yellow, greasy scales or crusted patches. Extensive cradle cap spreads beyond the parts with hair to areas adjacent to the ears, to the eyelid margins, and even to the forehead. The condition may last three to six weeks or longer, during which time, however, the child remains quite healthy.

Although a source of worry for parents, true cradle cap clears up without blemishes or any consequences to the child's health. It should be pointed out, however, that this scalp skin inflammation (dermatitis) is occasionally the forerunner of a generalized abnormal reaction of the skin of the entire body, which becomes full-blown by two to four months of age. In such a case the child is sick and shows other symptoms of illness. Simple cradle cap is very effectively treated with specially formulated shampoos.

A definite cause of cradle cap is not known, although some doctors believe that it is a member of a family of reactive skin conditions (dermatitis) that are transmitted genetically. Cradle cap is not contagious.

ANTOINE K. FOMUFOD, M.D., M.P.H., F.A.A.P.
Washington, D.C.

My infant has a fine, red rash over his body. Could this be measles?

A fine, red rash can mean measles, but regular measles always has other signs and symptoms—cough, fever, red eyes. German measles (rubella) can be associated with almost no other signs except a rash, as is the case with mild scarlet fever or other febrile illness. Allergies can cause red rashes, as can irritants to the skin, such as soaps and detergents. Be prepared to give a meaningful description of the rash when you call your doctor. Such an account should include mention of areas particularly affected, areas not affected, signs of general upset or illness, anything in the mouth or eyes, itching or lack of itching, signs of roughness or "pebbliness," size and shape of individual spots (unless it all runs together), and color (pink, red, very dark, very light, or any spots that look bloody).

MERRITT B. LOW, M.D., F.A.A.P.
Ashfield, Massachusetts

What do I do to care for impetigo? How long does it take for the affected areas to clear up?

Impetigo is a superficial infection of the skin most commonly due to the same streptococcal bacteria that cause strep throat. Yellow, crusted, weeping skin lesions or blisters may be first noted on the face, especially beneath the nose, on the cheeks, or around the ear lobes. Fever is unusual, but lymph nodes may be swollen near the affected areas.

Impetigo is contagious and can be spread by contact with the weeping skin lesions. Affected areas should be washed with soap, and fingernails should be trimmed to help reduce scratching and prevent spread of infection to other parts of the body, other family members, and playmates. Antibiotic therapy, usually penicillin by mouth or by injection, is needed to eradicate the skin infection and prevent possible later complications involving the kidneys. Antibiotic ointments are usually ineffective and may cause an allergic response in the skin. Affected areas will begin to clear in three to five days, but ten days of oral antibiotic therapy should be completed, even if the skin has cleared completely.

JOHN W. KULIG, M.D., F.A.A.P.
Boston, Massachusetts

CHAPTER 26

Social Development and Safety

When can my newborn go outside?

There are many different opinions on this. While there is no absolute answer to this question, it is generally felt that newborn infants should not be exposed to crowds, either at home or outside. Under usual circumstances, it is best for the infant to remain at home until ten days of age. In the event a trip outside the home is necessary, the baby should be dressed appropriately for the outside climate. If the baby is appropriately dressed and not exposed to crowds, it is entirely safe to take the baby outside.

ROBERT SPIERER, M.D.
Edison, New Jersey

When can my infant be taken to the beach?

An infant should not be taken to the beach before six months of age. From six to twelve months of age, time at the beach should be limited to thirty to sixty minutes a day in the early morning or late afternoon. The child should be protected from sunlight with a brimmed hat and a light cotton top with sleeves to protect the shoulders from sunburn.

From twelve to twenty-four months of age, the child can spend one to two hours at the beach with the following precautions: The child should be exposed to sunlight gradually, starting with ten minutes a day and doubling the time each day as long as no excessive reddening of the skin occurs; the child should wear a brimmed hat and a light cotton top after the first hour;

and, if it is a hot day, juice should be given to the child. The time at the beach should be before 11 A.M. or after 3 P.M. to avoid the time of maximum intensity of the sun's rays. An umbrella does not protect the child from sunburn.

If the child is fair-skinned or sensitive to sunlight, a sunscreen applied to the skin may be helpful, and exposure to sunlight should be brief.

CONCETTA M. RENKUN, M.D.
Haddonfield, New Jersey

When can my infant go camping with us and sleep out in a tent?

Young babies usually travel very well. Many fall asleep very quickly in a car seat and will rest for several hours until they are ready to eat. Camping with a baby should not present any particular problems for the family. Babies do have sensitive skin and should be protected from direct sunshine and biting insects. Proper nutrition is very important regardless of the baby's location. Breast-feeding is convenient while traveling because no special preparations are required for the mother or the child. When infant formula is used, it is important to boil the local water for fifteen minutes before mixing it with the formula concentrate or powder. Newborns and young infants are particularly susceptible to intestinal infections from contaminated water.

For the most part, infants adjust very well to new schedules and enjoy seeing new people and places.

ALAN R. RUSHTON, M.D., Ph.D.
Flemington, New Jersey

Can I enroll my baby in a Water Babies program?

The answer depends on what your expectations are of Water Babies or Infant Water Adjustment and Swimming programs.

If you want your infant to share and participate in an enjoyable situation that conceivably might help in his or her neuromuscular development, the answer would be a qualified yes. You must be certain that your infant will be supervised continuously on a one-to-one basis during the entire program. The program should be carefully structured with adequate staff and well-maintained facilities. Check with your pediatrician before enrolling your child if he or she has a medical problem.

If, on the other hand, you want to enroll your infant in such a program in order to make him or her "water ready," *beware*! Accidental drownings or near drownings occur just as frequently among young children who have graduated from such programs as among those who have never been formally trained. In April 1980, the American Academy of Pediatrics issued a statement concerning swimming instructions for infants:

> Although it might be possible to teach young infants to [swim], infants cannot be expected to learn the elements of water safety or to react appropriately in emergencies. No young child, particularly those who are pre-school aged, can ever be considered "water safe." Parents may develop a false sense of security if they feel their young child can "swim" a few strokes.*

Furthermore, the Academy recommends that parents be instructed in methods that have been proven effective in reducing the number of drownings in children. These include constant supervision by adults, flotation jackets, and adequate enclosures to effectively prevent access to pools, excavations, and so forth.

HECTOR L. HIDALGO, M.D.
Oklahoma City, Oklahoma

*Committee on Pediatric Aspects of Physical Fitness, Recreation and Sports, American Academy of Pediatrics, "Swimming Instructions for Infants," *Pediatrics* 65, no. 4 (April 1980): 847.

Are bug repellents safe to use around my infant son?

Adults can fight off bugs, unless they are totally outnumbered, or they can cover themselves or spray themselves with a mildly obnoxiously smelling bug repellent. But your child can't do any of these things by himself. A two-year-old will watch a fly on his nose until he's cross-eyed, and a mosquito unhindered from any baby will drink until its stomach is full (and its poison is emptied into the wound). You can keep the baby inside in the summer (that means you stay there, too), or let him be outside but keep him covered up (and invite heat rash itches, too), or cover his carriage with netting (not practical after five months of age). Or you can spray the environment or him with a variety of insect repellents. There certainly is no question that various insecticides used in the past have been shown to have adverse effects upon the environment on some occasions. However, there do not seem to be any currently used bug repellents that have been proven to be injurious to humans with ordinary usage. Some children have been driven nearly mad with mosquito bites and chiggers, and overseas children have had their eyes disfigured and blinded by trachoma from flies crawling over them. And the most prevalent disease in the world is still malaria—spread by mosquitoes. Not one child's life should be jeopardized by an insect repellent, but thousands of lives have been spared, and much suffering has been avoided through the judicious use of insect repellents.

ROBERT EASTON, M.D.
Peoria, Illinois

Is our toddler too young to learn a second language?

A toddler who has made good progress with his or her mother tongue should have no difficulty learning a second language from, for example, a grandmother or baby-sitter, and should be able to keep the two languages separate and to know when to use which language.

If, on the other hand, there is for any reason delayed or otherwise abnormal development of the primary language, the toddler should not be confused by being exposed to a second language.

M. E. SYMONDS, M.D.
Mountainside, New Jersey

My one-year-old is content to play by himself and is not interested in other infants. Is this appropriate for his age?

A one-year-old child does not socially interact with other infants in a manner that reveals a distinct interest in or fascination with another infant, or even a new toy within his reach. His motor skills allow him to explore, pick up, and manipulate objects, and his curiosity is the expression of his development level at this age. He must be reassured by his mother's voice or nearby presence; this shows his social dependency on her. As he approaches his second birthday, he will not only be more aware of the presence of a playmate, but will be more interested in what another child is doing, and he will establish a social relationship such as imitating play or engaging in combat.

G. EARL TREVATHAN JR., M.D.
Greenville, North Carolina

My eighteen-month-old cries when visiting children play with her toys. How should I handle this?

Don't be surprised at your daughter's behavior. Although toddlers enjoy friends, they frequently do not play well with them. They are more apt to play by themselves, stopping occasionally to argue over the possession of a toy. They are willing to let others play with their toys only if they do not want them at the moment. Taking turns and sharing with friends can require several years to learn.

You can help your child become more generous. As she becomes older, suggest that she share a toy. However, do not force her to give it up if she strongly objects. When she is willing to relinquish a toy to a friend, see that she gets it back soon. Your daughter gradually will learn that two people can stack blocks or roll a ball, and that it is fun to share with others.

JERRY G. JONES, M.D.
Little Rock, Arkansas

My toddler can climb out of her car seat. What should I do?

The toddler should be introduced to the car seat in a calm, matter-of-fact manner and should be allowed to look it over. Parents and older children should set an example for toddlers by wearing safety belts.

Praise your child often for *acceptable* behaviors and try to make rides a pleasant experience, with appropriate conversation and simple games. Engage the child in conversation about the sights seen during the car ride.

Let her know who the boss is and help her understand that you will not drive the car unless everyone is belted in. If she begins to release the seat belt or climb out of the car seat, immediately say "no" in a firm voice, stopping the car if necessary. A firm slap on the hand if the child repeatedly disobeys may help you enforce the rule. Be sure to investigate well the use of any child restraint system before you buy it to try to avoid any potential difficulty when you use it.

SHARON POHORECKI, R.N., C.P.N.P.
Toledo, Ohio

When should I start my toddler in a play group or nursery school?

There is no definite answer to this question. It varies with the child and family circumstances. A substantial number, perhaps a majority of children will already have been cared for in a day-care center or a home with other children present during the first year because the mother works. In effect, this is the child's first play group or nursery school.

Ideally, a toddler is ready for a play group or nursery school when he or she is able to walk, say a few words, make needs known, and play simple games. If a child shows an unusual degree of anxiety and dependency when separated from mother and home, the parents should consult their pediatrician about whether or not to delay starting the child in a nursery school.

MICHAEL PARRINO, M.D.
Columbia, South Carolina

What kind of car seat is best for an infant?

More than 1,000 children under the age of five die in car accidents every year. In addition, more than 100,000 children in the same age group are injured, often permanently. The proper use of car seats would substantially reduce the number of these deaths and injuries. Parents should become familiarized with any laws their state has enacted regarding mandatory use of car seats.

Most car seats are adaptable for both an infant and a toddler. In order to be acceptable, a car seat must have passed simulated crash test standards *and* be used according to manufacturer recommendations. Thus a car seat for which tethering is recommended must be truly tethered in order to be safe (this can be done in an auto garage). Car seats that have been rated highly and can be used for infants and toddlers include:

Bobby-Mac Deluxe II	Safe-T-Shield 81-A
Bobby-Mac Champion	Astroseat 9100
Bobby-Mac Super	Hi-Rider
Century 100	Care Seat
Century 200	One Step
Century 300	Wee Care #597-A
Safe-T-Seat 78-A	Wee Care #599-A
Safe 'N Easy Recliner 313-A	Travel Tot #369

Parents should also be aware of any laws enacted in their state pertaining to car safety.

KATHERINE C. TEETS-GRIMM, M.D.
New York, New York

Can my toddler just keep the lap seat belt on that is already in the car? I can pull it very snug.

No. Automobile seat belts should not be used for toddlers. Toddlers are too active and will squirm free, slip out from the belt, loosen the belt by playing with the buckle, or, if they remained restrained, will receive severe intra-abdominal or spinal cord injuries. Remember, children are inquisitive and can open anything. Do not trust a simple seat belt catch.

The child should be in a seat appropriate to his or her size. The abdominal belt as well as the shoulder harness restraining both shoulders should be used routinely. A seat belt and shoulder harness should also be worn by the driver and adult passengers. Children must weigh at least forty pounds to be strapped with an adult seat belt, and they should never wear a shoulder harness if they are under four and one-half feet tall.

JOSEPH A. DAVIES III, M.D.
Freehold, New Jersey

Why can't a passenger in a car just hold a baby instead of putting the baby in a car seat?

It has been demonstrated by crash testing that even a strong man's arms are not strong enough to hold a baby securely at the force levels in many automobile crashes. The baby may be torn from the person's arms and will fly freely, striking the inside of the car and receiving serious injury. The only safe way to travel with a baby in an automobile is to strap the baby carefully into a safety seat that has been tested and demonstrated to be adequate for child restraint. *Consumer's Guide* publishes lists of tested and approved restraints for infants and young children.

AVRUM L. KATCHER, M.D., F.A.A.P.
Flemington, New Jersey

When can my infant go in a plane?

A baby may ride in an airplane anytime after he or she has been examined and determined a healthy newborn.

SIDNEY W. COREN, M.D.
Virginia Beach, Virginia

Are "umbrella" carriages safe?

"Umbrella" and folding carriages are usually safe if they are made by reputable manufacturers and are used as directed. Occasional freak accidents have been reported and usually are followed by withdrawal from the market for satisfactory modifications of the carriage in question.

MERRITT B. LOW, M.D., F.A.A.P.
Ashfield, Massachusetts

Can my baby go in an airplane if she has a cold?

Yes, she can. This is true even though the irregular changes in barometric pressures that occur even in well-pressurized airplane cabins can cause changes in pressures in the middle ear, which in turn cause some children to have earaches. Crying and nursing or bottle-feeding help little infants regulate their ear pressures. Older children can do the same by blowing balloons, yawning, swallowing, chewing gum, or sucking candy.

These changes in ear pressure in a child who has a cold and who is known to be prone to ear infections may predispose her to a new ear infection, or may aggravate a latent one. These considerations should not prevent you from taking your child on a planned or necessary flight. The risks are low, and your physician may prescribe some effective preventive measures.

ELIAS S. SROUJI, M.D., M.P.H.
Oklahoma City, Oklahoma

CHAPTER 27

Stings, Lice, and Ticks

How can I tell if my child is allergic to stings?

If your child has been stung by an insect and develops a local reaction of swelling and itching at the site of the sting, or a systemic reaction of generalized swelling, a rash, hoarseness, wheezing, and, at times, shock, then he or she is obviously allergic to stings. If no local or systemic reaction occurs after being stung, then all one can say is that the child is not allergic to that particular insect, but may be to others. If your child has a history of allergy, then he or she is more likely to be allergic to stings than are children without an allergic history. If he or she is allergic to stings, it may be advisable always to carry a kit containing adrenaline and syringe, antihistamine, tourniquet, and so forth. Your pediatrician can advise you best on this and may well seek the consultation of a pediatric allergist with regard to diagnosis and management, including skin tests and desensitization.

MILTON PRYSTOWSKY, M.D., F.A.A.P., F.A.C.C.
Nutley, New Jersey

My child was stung this morning by a bee and now he has a low-grade fever. Is this a result of the sting?

The usual reaction to the sting of a bee, wasp, hornet, or yellow jacket is immediate pain that subsides within a few minutes but is followed by local redness, swelling, and itching. Numerous stings sustained within a short period of time can cause vomiting, diarrhea, fainting, headache, generalized swelling, and fever, but single stings do not cause fever except when they cause a rare type of allergic reaction known as serum sickness. Symptoms of serum sickness include swelling of lymph glands, malaise, headache, generalized hives, and painful joints as well as fever, but these symptoms usually begin only ten to fourteen days after the sting.

The common allergic symptoms that follow bee stings include sneezing, generalized itching or flushing with a sensation of warmth but no fever, difficulty with breathing, and loss of consciousness. There may be generalized hives and, occasionally, abdominal pain, vomiting, or diarrhea. Any of these symptoms may occur alone or in combination. The most severe reactions occur within seconds or minutes after the sting; less severe reactions may begin several hours later. Immediate treatment must be sought at a hospital emergency room if there are severe reactions.

Wasp, yellow jacket, and hornet stings often transmit bacteria, which can cause a local infection of the skin at the site of the sting with more extensive swelling, redness, and tenderness as well as fever within a few hours or days. The presence of tenderness instead of itching helps to differentiate the infected sting from the normal reaction to a bee sting.

Fever that has begun several hours after a single sting and without other signs or symptoms is probably unrelated to the sting.

R. MICHAEL SLY, M.D.
Washington, D.C.

The area where my toddler was stung by a bee is red and hard, and there is a little knot under the skin. Is this normal?

This reaction is a normal inflammatory response. When bees, yellow jackets, hornets, or wasps sting, they not only puncture the skin but they also inject some venom. This substance causes the body to respond by mounting a typical local inflammatory response. This consists of redness, heat, swelling, and pain. The purpose of inflammation in this instance is to aid in the destruction and removal of the injurious material. Although this reaction is normal initially, it can be considered abnormal if it persists for several days, indicating a possible infection, which should then be treated by a physician. A dangerous allergic reaction usually takes place in the first thirty minutes following a sting. An allergic reaction at this age is extremely rare, especially if it is the first sting, and so is usually not a consideration.

247

But if the redness or swelling is so large as to cross two joints or is associated with other generalized body reactions, such as hives or difficulty in breathing, a physician should be contacted.

ARTHUR J. TORRE, M.D., F.A.A.P., A.F.A.C.A.
Little Falls, New Jersey

My toddler was just stung by a bee. The area that was stung is very swollen and hot. What should I do?

Many children will have an acute allergic reaction to bee venom within minutes after a bee sting. The first thing to do is apply an ice pack to the site of the sting. This decreases blood flow to the area, reduces local redness and puffiness, and slows the spread of venom in the local circulation. Occasionally, a massive allergic reaction may occur, causing swelling of an entire arm or leg, difficulty in breathing or swallowing, or actual loss of consciousness. Such cases should be seen by a physician immediately.

The bee's stinger may also carry bacteria through the skin surface and set up a local infection, so it should be removed. If the sting area is still red and tender several hours after ice is applied, an infection may be developing. In this case, the child should also be evaluated by a physician.

ALAN R. RUSHTON, M.D., Ph.D.
Flemington, New Jersey

Is it important to remove a bee's stinger from the skin? What happens if I cannot get it out?

When a bee stings, its stinger is anchored by two barbed lancets, which are difficult to remove. The area stung should be scraped with a sharp knife and cleansed with soap and water. Repeated pulling and manipulation will further disrupt the poison sac and cause more venom to be squeezed into the tissue.

A physician should be consulted if the stinger cannot be removed at home, if the child has a reaction of body hives, tightness of the throat, shortness of breath, or difficulty in swallowing, or if the child has had previous allergic reactions.

Conservative home treatment consists of applying ice packs to decrease the swelling, elevating the stung area, and putting calamine lotion or a mixture of meat tenderizer and water on the affected area to help relieve the discomfort.

STEPHANIE W. PERRY, M.D.
Nashville, Tennessee

I removed a tick from my child two days ago, and now the area is red and puffy. Is this normal?

Yes. This is normal because generally what occurs is the reaction of the skin and surrounding area to either the bite of the tick or part of the tick's head remaining in the skin. What needs to be considered now is that the area involved could become worse, and if this does occur, then you may need to consider further treatment of this area. It is rather common that these areas tend to get a secondary infection and may need to be treated with warm soaks and antibiotic ointment, and occasionally even an injection of antibiotics. What is important now is to continue observing this area. If the swelling continues to increase in size and severity and becomes more red and puffy, you should contact your doctor.

JEROME E. KWAKO, M.D.
Duluth, Minnesota

Can a tick cause any illnesses in my child?

Ticks can transmit a number of diseases to humans. Rocky Mountain spotted fever and tick typhus have been reported throughout the United States, with most cases occurring along the East Coast. Symptoms of high fever, headache, rash, and muscle and joint pain may develop two to fourteen days after a bite by an infected tick. These infections can be quite serious, and the physician should be consulted immediately.

The best approach to management of tick-borne infections is the prevention of tick bites. Ticks are most active during the spring and summer.

They may be contracted while a child is playing outside or with a dog that has been outside. In areas where ticks are found, parents should inspect their children and pets two or three times each day to detect ticks. Imbedded ticks should not be pulled out. They should be touched with a hot matchtip or covered with rubbing alcohol. The tick will be irritated and will release its hold on the skin. Then it can be removed easily.

ALAN R. RUSHTON, M.D., Ph.D.
Flemington, New Jersey

I was told that a tick can cause Rocky Mountain spotted fever. Is this true?

A dog tick, Dermacentor variabilis, in the eastern United States, and a wood tick, Dermacentor andersoni, in the western United States, carry the infectious agent Rickettsia rickettsie, which causes Rocky Mountain spotted fever. The tick itself, or its bite, does not cause this disease. However, the bacteria-like agent that causes the disease can be transmitted by a tick bite.

As a parent, you should know that Rocky Mountain spotted fever is a very severe disease that occurs in late spring and summer. If an infected tick bites an individual, within three to ten days that person may have nausea, loss of appetite, headache, high fever, chills, and a rash that starts on the third or fourth day of illness. The rash is first seen on the arms and legs and then on the chest and abdomen. It looks like small, red, raised bumps, which can become larger and resemble small bleeding spots.

Should you see these signs or symptoms in a family member, please call your doctor promptly. If you suspect Rocky Mountain spotted fever, say so. Communication of your suspicions is always helpful in administering medical care. Early diagnosis and therapy offer the best opportunity for a rapid return to health from this infection.

It is wise to employ good rodent control year round in your home. Tick infections should always be treated in your pets. A tick repellent should be applied whenever you go into woodland. After an outing always thoroughly inspect your family and pets for ticks.

PETER C. FREIS, M.D.
Metuchen, New Jersey

My child has lice. Should I do anything to the hats and combs he has been using lately?

Yes. The eggs from the lice are likely to be left in hats, combs, and brushes and can reinfest your child or others. The items of clothing should be either dry-cleaned or washed in very hot or boiling water. Similarly, the combs and brushes that you have used on your child should be thoroughly cleansed to rid them of the lice eggs. These items could be washed thoroughly with the same treatment shampoo, such as Kwell, that you used on your child, leaving them to soak in Kwell for several hours before rinsing them and using them again.

FRANK M. SHEPARD, M.D.
Johnson City, Tennessee

Can lice be living in my furniture, and if so, what can I do?

Head lice are very common, especially in schools, and can be very difficult to eradicate. The first thing to do, of course, is to kill the small animals that are living in the scalp with one of several preparations. It is also a good idea to spray furniture with some type of insecticide that will kill the insects. You can also purchase a commercial fumigating bomb for the entire house.

DAVID J. TEPPER, M.D.
Chattanooga, Tennessee

What are the symptoms of Rocky Mountain spotted fever?

Rocky Mountain spotted fever is caused by a germ called rickettsia, which may be spread through the bite of an infected tick.

Symptoms of this illness appear a few days after exposure to the tick and initially are similar to the symptoms of many other infectious illnesses. They include loss of appetite, aches and pains, headache, and low-grade fever. Later, the flat, red rash that is very characteristic of the illness develops. It usually appears first on the hands and feet and spreads to the rest of the body. The fever may become much higher, and puffiness may occur. Symptoms of a cold are usually not present. The illness itself is very variable and the symptoms may be either mild or very severe.

There are specific tests your doctor may do to confirm the diagnosis. There are also antibiotics your doctor can prescribe to effectively treat the illness.

Rocky Mountain spotted fever is more prevalent in some areas (it may commonly occur in places far from the Rocky Mountains) and at certain times of the year (it is most common during the summer). It is an unusual illness in infants because they rarely have access to tick-infested areas.

THOMAS L. KENNEDY III, M.D.
Farmington, Connecticut

My toddler has been reinfested with lice for the third time. Is it still safe to use Kwell?

Kwell is widely used and very effective for the treatment of scabies and lice. It is available by prescription only in three forms—cream, lotion, and shampoo. The manufacturer's recommendation for treatment of head lice is to shampoo for four minutes and then rinse thoroughly. This may be repeated in twenty-four hours if necessary. This treatment will not, however, remove the nits that adhere to the hair. These must be carefully removed with a fine-tooth comb. Sometimes they can be loosened with a solution of one part vinegar and one part water.

Kwell has been associated with some complications in small children when it has been used excessively. Experimental studies have shown that Kwell can be absorbed through the skin. Convulsions occur in animals after ingestion or even absorption of large amounts through the skin. Convulsions have now been reported in children after Kwell has been applied to the skin. In most cases, however, the application was excessive or prolonged. It is probably safe to use Kwell as prescribed by your doctor.

It should not be used more than once in twenty-four hours. If repeated reinfestations of lice occur, consult your pediatrician. There are other medicines that are effective in treating lice, and your doctor may want to use something other than Kwell, especially in younger children with repeated reinfestations, because of the possibility of convulsions.

If a child is having repeated infestations of lice, it is important to determine the source of the lice. Lice can be spread by means of combs, brushes, and clothing, and by human contact. All sheets, towels, and clothing should be washed in very hot water or dry-cleaned, and all combs and brushes discarded. All persons who have been in contact with an infested person should be treated.

JAMIE HEWELL, M.D.
St. Louis, Missouri

What would happen if I were unable to remove the whole tick from my child?

Although tick bites are usually harmless, they may occasionally cause Rocky Mountain spotted fever or tick paralysis. Both of these are potentially extremely harmful diseases. The former is manifested by fever and rash and frequently by headache and muscle pain. Tick paralysis probably occurs less frequently than Rocky Mountain spotted fever and consists of generalized weakness that usually progresses until the tick is removed. Ticks can also cause red and itchy reactions at the site of the bite.

To minimize the chance of any after-effects, it is best to try to detach the entire tick from a child's skin as soon as possible. Petrolatum, or petroleum jelly, is effective and safe. If these are unavailable, heat should be applied very carefully to the tick.

JOHN S. O'SHEA, M.D.
Providence, Rhode Island

CHAPTER 28

Stitches and Burns

My toddler pulled out one of her stitches. Should it be replaced?

Stitches are used to hold gaping edges of skin together. They are best left in for five to ten days. Sometimes some come out early by themselves or as a result of pulling or licking. If they stay in for two or three days, that is usually enough time to hold the edges of skin together. So, if one comes out, check to see if the skin edges are still staying together. Sometimes a sterile tape strip or so-called butterfly tape will do enough reinforcing to hold the skin together. If "gaping" is marked, the doctor may have to restitch the wound. You can help judge the situation by seeing how large the "gaping" is—and then call the doctor for a decision on what needs to be done.

MERRITT B. LOW, M.D., F.A.A.P.
Ashfield, Massachusetts

The scar left from the stitches on my toddler's knee is raised and bumpy. Will that eventually go away?

Whenever the skin is cut, a scar, or permanent mark, will result. Luckily, the healing process starts as soon as the wound has occurred. The purpose of stitches is to aid in healing, by bringing the edges of the cut together and thus lessening the amount of scarring. As you watch this entire process, you will see the wound progress from a depressed red line to a slightly wider, usually elevated, red mark. This mark will gradually become less evident, and will fade in color and decrease in size. Ultimately, the final scar will be near normal skin color and will not be raised. Some individuals have a tendency, however, to develop larger scars, or keloids, but this is not usually serious and can be easily diagnosed by your doctor. In any case, the healing process can be delayed by infection or repeated injury to the area. Also, the healing time may vary, usually taking six to twelve months or longer, depending on the area of the body injured. In most instances, if a scar is red and bumpy, you can expect more resolution, or softening and disappearance of swelling. The fact that your child's cut was on the knee, an area subject to frequent movement and trauma, may delay the process slightly, but one would expect the scar to become smoother and less apparent in time.

NANCY W. DeTORA, M.D.
Worcester, Massachusetts

The area around the stitches on my toddler's knee is very red and warm. Is that all right?

In the normal healing process of any wound, granulation tissue (small, rounded masses of tissue) forms. This tissue is much pinker and warmer than the surrounding tissue as a result of increased blood flow. If the stitches are several days old and ready to be removed, this may be normal. However, infection also appears in this way, and if there is much tenderness or drainage associated with the lesion the child may need additional therapy.

KATHERINE M. KNIGHT, M.D.
New Orleans, Louisiana

Is sunburn harmful to my infant's skin?

Sunburn is potentially very harmful to your baby's skin. It is caused by ultraviolet rays that are emitted from the sun. The primary effect produced by these rays is a redness of the skin, which occurs approximately six to twelve hours after the initial exposure. This redness reaches its peak within twenty-four hours. Redness, exquisite tenderness, pain, edema, and blistering are the primary effects of sunburn seen in children. There is also an increase in thickness of some of the layers of the skin and an increased deepening of the skin color (tanning). It must be remembered that sunburn is actually a burn and should be treated as if your child had touched a hot object. The area of the burn should be covered with cool, wet compresses and mild analgesics such as aspirin or acetaminophen. Over-the-counter preparations are relatively ineffective and can cause potentially harmful side effects due to a skin rash that sometimes results from these preparations. The most effective way to avoid sunburn is to take preventive measures. The best topical sunscreen is paraminobenzoic acid (PABA), which, when applied to the skin, absorbs the harmful sun rays. Long-term lesions from a severe or moderate sunburn are not often seen in children, but the known consequences in older people are premature aging of the skin, some skin cancers, and probably melanomas. These all occur with increased frequency in sun-damaged skin. The labels on sunscreen preparations that are on the market indicate the amount of protection that each has to offer. It is recommended that all children be protected by the use of the sunscreens, especially those children who are fair and who are potentially most susceptible to the sun's rays.

JEANNE M. EULBERG, M.D.
Kansas City, Kansas

Will the bright sun hurt my infant son's eyes?

The bright sun is uncomfortable for the baby's eyes, but does not cause any damage. This is because the baby automatically protects himself, depending on how bright the sun is. His pupils get smaller to let in less light, and the baby may actually close his eyes and turn his head away from the sun. Because infants prefer dim light, they would be more comfortable in the shade or wearing a small hat.

DEBORAH L. MADAUSKY, M.D.
Worcester, Massachusetts

How can I tell if a blister is infected?

A blister is a manifestation of local skin irritation. It looks like a localized collection of fluid under the skin. Cleanliness and protection are the only care required for the simple blister. Infections by bacteria, on the other hand, result in some combination of redness, warmth, tenderness, and swelling. Parents may suspect a secondary infection of a blister if there is gradual redness, diffuse swelling, and so forth, particularly in the presence of fever.

The spontaneous appearance of several blisters, however, may herald the onset of a bacterial skin infection called impetigo. It is advisable to contact a medical provider in this situation because impetigo is relatively infectious.

PATRICK H. CASEY, M.D.
Little Rock, Arkansas

My infant got sunburned on her arms, and there is slight blistering. What can I do for this?

If the area around the sunburn gets reddened, if pus-like matter begins to discharge from it, or if the child has fever or acts sick, call the doctor.

It is recommended that infants spend some time in the sun, but a suntan is not a particular sign of health. The sun only ages the skin and increases dryness and the frequency of skin tumors.

AVRUM L. KATCHER, M.D., F.A.A.P.
Flemington, New Jersey

What can I use as a sunscreen for my infant?

Don't overexpose your infant to sun in any case, especially if he or she is fair-complexioned. There are many commercial sunscreens available in drugstores, some of them graded in terms of their filtering powers. You have to find out for yourself what works best, starting cautiously with only a few minutes of exposure a day. Sun is beneficial to the skin in optimal amounts, but a heavy tan is not really the sign of good health, and as people get older too much sun can be dangerous and can cause skin cancer. Too much filtering, however, can remove the sun's benefits, such as vitamin D.

MERRITT B. LOW, M.D., F.A.A.P.
Ashfield, Massachusetts

My toddler has a cut in his knee that was stitched. When he bent his leg, one of the stitches came apart and the cut opened. Can and should that be restitched?

When your toddler's knee was cut, the first bleeding helped to wash away some of the bacteria that can cause infection. Now the cut is healing from within and it should not be closed off with a new stitch because bacteria are on the surface of and inside the cut. It is wise to call your doctor or the surgeon who sewed the wound, who will probably recommend that the open area be covered with a clean dressing until it heals. An antibiotic salve or powder may also be recommended for local application to shorten the healing time.

STANLEY ZIPSER, M.D.
New York, New York

The area where my toddler had second-degree burns is completely healed. Should I protect this area from the sun?

In second-degree burns the part of the skin that reconstructs itself is not lost. During the process of healing, new skin forms and this skin, not unlike the skin of a new infant, may be more sensitive to exposure to direct sunlight. When you may allow your child to be in the direct sunlight would depend on how much time has lapsed since the burn, on whether the skin appears completely normal and has no unusual pinkness, and on the usual pigmentation of his or her skin. In general, you should be cautious about exposing any toddler to too much direct sun for long periods of time.

KATHERINE M. KNIGHT, M.D.
New Orleans, Louisiana

My toddler burned his finger on the stove. The finger has now blistered and is very red. What should I do? Should I break the blister?

Whenever a child has a *small* burn, you should first cool it under cold water. This will cool any grease or material still on the skin and make the burn feel better. Don't put anything else on it until you and/or your pediatrician decide what to do about it. If the burn extends to more than a couple of fingers or has gray-white areas, cover the burned area with a clean cloth and call your pediatrician.

It sounds as if your child has only a small blister on one finger and some redness around it. Do not break the blister. It provides a covering for the burned area. Wash the burn gently with soap and water and then cover it with a sterile piece of gauze to protect it. Some doctors like to put an antibiotic ointment under the dressing. Gently wash the burned area once a day with soap and water and keep it covered with a clean dressing. Small blisters and redness usually heal quickly.

ELIZABETH M. SPECHT, M.D.
Akron, Ohio

Is it all right for recently put in stitches to get wet?

It is safe for recently put in sutures to get wet. The sutured area may be bathed or cleaned as long as it is dried well afterward. We routinely recommend cleansing sutures at least daily with hydrogen peroxide, to reduce crusting, and then drying well.

MARTIN L. COHEN, M.D.
Morristown, New Jersey

CHAPTER 29

Swallowing Substances

My toddler swallowed a small amount of perfume. Will that hurt her? Should I make her vomit?

Most perfumes contain essential oils (which affect the body like turpentine) and alcohol. The danger of these chemicals is proportional to the amount swallowed. It is estimated that an adult would have to drink an ounce or more of perfume to be in danger of dying.

If the perfume came in the usual small bottle with a tiny opening, you should observe her for signs of chemical pneumonia. These signs would include coughing, fever, and labored breathing. If she drank a large volume of perfume it might be useful to have her stomach pumped, but this decision would best be made by her physician, who would weigh the risk of the procedure against the risk of retaining the chemical. You should not make her vomit.

CHARLES A. KECK, M.D.
Olympia, Washington

I have just discovered that my toddler may have been eating the paint off an old paperweight. Can she get lead poisoning from this?

Depending on the age of the paperweight and the type of paint that was used on it, it is possible that your child may have eaten some lead-based paint. Before the 1950s, most indoor and outdoor paint in the United States contained enough lead to cause poisoning if chips of paint were eaten by a child. By law, the amount of lead in paints made in the United States is now so low that lead poisoning is not possible. Painted items and pieces of pottery that are imported, however, are potential sources of lead poisoning because it is possible that the amount of lead in paints in foreign countries is not controlled.

Even if the paint on the paperweight contained lead, the chance of poisoning depends on how much paint your child ate and how much lead the paint contained. The symptoms of lead poisoning are pallor, poor appetite, listlessness, vomiting, and abdominal pain. Convulsions and difficulties in balance occur in severe cases. Your physician or local health department should be able to do a screening test for lead poisoning from a blood sample. Of course you'll want to put the paperweight and all other old, painted items out of reach of your toddler. Strip the paint off old toys and furniture such as the crib if you're not sure of the lead content. And continue to keep careful watch that your child doesn't put other potentially harmful objects in her mouth.

CAROLE A. STASHWICK, M.D.
Hanover, New Hampshire

My toddler swallowed a closed safety pin. Will it harm her if it starts to rust before it comes out in her stools? How long will it take to work its way out?

An X ray should be taken to determine if the pin was swallowed and, if so, where it is. If the pin sticks in the esophagus, or swallowing tube, it will require removal with a special instrument. If the pin reaches the stomach it almost always will pass through the intestinal tract within one week, often within forty-eight hours, and will cause no harm. If the pin is not retrieved by careful examination of the stool, another X ray in one week usually shows it is gone. Rarely, the pin may remain in the stomach for weeks and, if so, can usually be removed with a special instrument called a gastroscope. Surprisingly, these facts are usually true whether the safety pin is open or closed.

RICHARD K. DANIS, M.D.
St. Louis, Missouri

Can a swallowed small metal object puncture anything or cause a blockage somewhere? How can I tell?

Ingestion of a small object such as a penny is usually not a serious problem. If the child has any difficulty in swallowing or breathing, or if there is a cough, there may be blockage in the trachea or upper airway.

If these difficulties are not evident, then all the stools should be strained. Only in this way will the object be found. Most often the object will be passed in the stools within several days.

If after a week it is not passed, an X ray should be taken. In many cases it may be that the parents erred and the child did not really swallow the object. An X ray is a precaution to be sure the object is not trapped somewhere in the intestinal tract.

GERALD N. IZZO, M.D., F.A.A.P., P.C.
Rockville Centre, New York

My twenty-month-old just ate some dirt from our backyard. Will this hurt her?

In general, several mouthfuls of dirt will not create any problems unless fertilizer, insecticide, and so forth, were added to the dirt. On the other hand, a child who consistently eats dirt and other unusual items, such as paint, is demonstrating a problem known as pica. This habit should be discussed with your pediatrician; with proper guidance, it can be corrected.

BETTY A. LOWE, M.D.
Little Rock, Arkansas

My toddler just ate a cigarette butt. Will that hurt her?

The answer is yes. If a child were to absorb all the nicotine contained within a cigarette butt, he or she could become toxic. Agitation, vomiting, diarrhea, weakness, confusion, and possibly seizures may result. Usually, however, nicotine absorbed from a cigarette butt produces vomiting and therefore prevents further absorption of the butt. If a child swallows one or more cigarette butts and does not vomit ten to twenty minutes later, syrup of ipecac should be administered to induce vomiting, but under the guidance of a pediatrician or poison control center.

SUMAN WASON, M.D.
Boston, Massachusetts

My toddler seems to have swallowed some water while in a chlorinated pool. Will this harm him?

Chlorine is added to swimming pools to inhibit the growth of certain bacteria and other microorganisms. When used in the proper concentrations, it is usually harmless, even if swallowed. Nothing need be done to treat children who have ingested pool water. Undiluted chlorine and other pool chemicals, on the other hand, are extremely hazardous if taken internally. The ingestion of a large amount of pool water might result in vomiting, but there are no serious reactions. The most common problem encountered in chlorinated pools is eye irritation.

The greatest danger to the child is breathing the pool water into the lungs. This can result in drowning, near-drowning, or severe pneumonia. A large amount of water need not be inhaled. Severe problems can occur even with a small amount. The added presence of chlorine can be extremely irritating to the lungs. Drownings can be easily prevented by providing constant adult supervision whenever the child goes swimming, playing, or walking in or near swimming pools or bodies of water.

STEPHEN H. SHELDON, D.O., F.A.A.P.
Chicago, Illinois

My baby was playing with the contents of his diaper. I'm not sure if he got any in his mouth. Will it hurt him if he did?

No. It is admittedly very unpleasant to observe this investigative behavior, but it is reassuring to know that the contents of the stool will be handled by and passed through the child's digestive system in the same manner that food is. Although there are bacteria in the stool, they are part of the normal makeup of the colon or bowel and would not cause the child illness, as would outside bacteria. If this is a one-time incident, certainly it can be ignored. If the child continues to do this after gentle guidance and the replacement of this activity for another, more acceptable behavior, one could worry that the child may be developing pica, which is the eating of unnatural, nonfood objects beyond the range of normal curiosity. This would cause serious concern if the child ate noxious or poisonous substances. However, most babies develop a taste for food and usually prefer it to nonfood products, the eating of which usually occurs when a child is hungry. You should be alerted to this fact and take care that the child does not become too hungry before food is again served to him.

EVELYN BAUGH, M.D.
Toledo, Ohio

CHAPTER 30

Talking

When do children say their first words?

The production of human language requires the coordinated action of the palate, tongue, lips, jaws, and vocal cords. Each of these organs is controlled by different nerve centers in the brain. The child's ability first to produce noises, then specific sounds, and finally real words in the first year of life reflects the maturation of these complex body parts.

Most babies begin to coo during the first two months of life. Laughing and squealing begin at around three to four months of age. By nine months, most babies have begun to say "Mama" or "Dada," although they do not relate these to particular people. Imitation of adult speech sounds begins at around the same time. By the first birthday, most babies have begun to associate "Mama" and "Dada" with the appropriate person and may have begun to say other simple words such as "hi," "bye," "kitty," or "woof woof." An enormous amount of language develops rapidly after twelve months of age. Babies say new words, learn to combine them into short phrases, and start to understand directions from other people by the second birthday.

The process of language formation begins when babies imitate the speech sounds they hear. Even a small hearing deficit can hinder the distinction between similar sounds and impede the normal process of learning speech. If there is any question about a child's ability to hear well, a careful testing program should be performed as soon as possible to determine whether he or she can hear accurately.

ALAN R. RUSHTON, M.D., Ph.D.
Flemington, New Jersey

By the end of a child's first year, how large a vocabulary is normal? What about the end of the second year?

The twelve-month-old infant usually has found that at least one sound or combination of sounds such as "Mama" produces a desired end, generally attention or food. Between the ages of one and two, children learn that other sounds also produce desired results and their vocabulary grows. They begin to combine various sounds into complex but unintelligible sequences. At twenty-four months of age, this meaningless jargon usually has given way to a few two- and three-word phrases, such as "want cookie" and "go bye-bye." At this time, a parent or another adult close to the child should be able to interpret about half of a child's words and phrases.

JERRY G. JONES, M.D.
Little Rock, Arkansas

My eighteen-month-old son still doesn't talk, not even to say "Mama" or "Dada." Is this normal?

No. By eighteen months of age a child should be saying three or four words spontaneously and repeating many more. If a child isn't doing this, the parents should make certain that the child hears normally, that other developmental skills are at an eighteen-month level, and that the child's social development is normal. If your eighteen-month-old child isn't talking, he should be evaluated by his physician and a speech pathologist.

G. DEAN TIMMONS, M.D.
Akron, Ohio

The nursery intern said my baby is tongue-tied. What does that mean? Will it interfere with his speech development?

Normally there is a thin web of tissue that extends from the underside of the tongue to the floor of the mouth. If this web of tissue connects to the very tip of the tongue and is short enough to restrict the movement of the tongue, the child is often said to be tongue-tied. Such a condition rarely results in problems, as the web of tissue stretches, and the tongue becomes more mobile as the child grows. If sufficient mobility is not achieved and there is risk of speech impairment, a minor surgical procedure will correct the problem. This procedure is best carried out at about one year of age. When performed earlier, particularly in the newborn period, the need for it cannot be accurately assessed and the risk of infection or hemorrhage is much higher.

KENNETH L. WIBLE, M.D.
Morgantown, West Virginia

My toddler lisps. Will this condition correct itself as she grows older?

Lisping in the toddler years is not uncommon, and usually nothing needs to be done other than to try not to imitate the child and think that what she is doing is funny. The child should be talked to in an adult fashion; and without correcting the child, one should expect her to answer back correctly. If there is no improvement within a reasonable time, i.e., six to nine months, it is a good idea to have her sent to a speech therapist to correct her speech.

FERNANDO J. deCASTRO, M.D.
St. Louis, Missouri

CHAPTER 31

Teeth
and Teething

Some of my toddler's teeth are decayed. Should I have these taken care of?

Absolutely, yes. Primary teeth form the foundation for the development of the child's entire mouth, speech, and eating, and damage to these teeth can severely affect the development of the child's permanent teeth at a later date. Any child, regardless of his or her age, may be treated successfully by a trained pediatric dentist. In dentistry, more than in almost any other area of medicine, an ounce of prevention is worth a pound of cure.

RICHARD HOLSTEIN, D.M.D.
Princeton, New Jersey

My neighbor's toddler is to have his teeth capped. Is this necessary, since he will lose these teeth in a few years?

Capping the teeth is necessary when the decay has spread so far in the tooth that other types of filling materials cannot be used. Caps are also used when a considerable part of the tooth is lost due to fracture and when the teeth have defective formation, producing a rough surface that can readily allow decay to start. When decay attacks the tooth and is not stopped, it will reach the nerve of the tooth and cause an abscess infection. This may be associated with toothaches before and during the infection. If the abscess is not treated, it can cause defective formation in the permanent tooth or teeth below the infected primary (baby) tooth. These defects in the permanent teeth can be white spots, yellow areas, or pitted surfaces on the teeth. These areas are quite susceptible to decay and cause a poor appearance.

Therefore, it is important to maintain the primary teeth in good condition to allow proper development of the permanent teeth. It is worthwhile to point out that the upper front baby teeth are normally lost between the ages of six and eight. If these baby teeth are extracted rather than capped (as sometimes is necessary), the child may be without front teeth from four to six years. This may produce psychological problems because of teasing by playmates and the fact that the child is different from his friends. Replacement teeth can be made, but very young children do not tend to be receptive to them; the natural teeth are always better.

ALLEN W. ANDERSON, D.D.S., M.S.
Chicago, Illinois

When should I expect my baby's first teeth to begin to break through?

It is important to remember that every baby is different, and so are the *exact* times that the first teeth erupt. Usually, your baby's first teeth break through at about six months of age in the front part of the mouth. Most babies will have first teeth by ten to twelve months of age at the latest.

STERLING L. RONK, D.D.S.
Gainesville, Florida

When should my child first visit the dentist?

Normally, a young child need not see a dentist until he or she is around twenty-four months of age. By this time most of the primary teeth have erupted and a comprehensive preventive program can be initiated. Any early dental decay or dental developmental problems can be detected at this time and treated in a conservative manner. There are, however, special instances when a child may need to see a dentist at an earlier age. One of these is when a toddler receives a traumatic blow to one or more of his or her anterior teeth. Another is the use of a nighttime nursing bottle past twelve months of age. This can cause a rapidly destructive form of dental decay.

FRANK J. COURTS, M.D.
Gainesville, Florida

My infant is teething and has an area of black and blue on his gum near the new tooth. Is this anything to worry about?

An area of bluish purple swelling of the gum tissue associated with an erupting tooth is commonly called an eruption hematoma. The bluish color is due to slight bleeding into the tissues during the eruption process. This area develops prior to the actual eruption of the primary tooth, and treatment is usually unnecessary. Once the erupting tooth breaks through the tissue, the hematoma will subside.

R. G. JERRELL, D.D.S.
Gainesville, Florida

My toddler has buck teeth from sucking her thumb. Will this affect the position of her permanent teeth?

The position of the baby teeth may be due to the thumb-sucking but it could also be due to the growth pattern of the upper and lower jaws. If the position of the baby teeth is due to the growth pattern, the thumb-sucking will tend to exaggerate the situation. Since the thumb-sucking alone could cause the buck teeth, the teeth will usually return to their normal position when the thumb-sucking stops. Approximately 80 percent of children stop sucking their thumbs by the age of four. This allows plenty of time for the teeth to return to normal position before the permanent teeth start erupting at about seven years of age. Usually the permanent teeth position will not be affected by thumb-sucking if the habit stops by the age of five.

There are many reasons for thumb-sucking. Evaluation by the dentist will determine the best approach toward breaking the thumb-sucking habit. Generally, parents are advised not to draw attention to the thumb-sucking at any age because it may strengthen the habit. It is perfectly normal for children to suck their thumbs, fingers, or pacifiers until age three or four. If the habit does not show signs of reduction by the age of four-and-one-half, the dentist may wish to begin treatment aimed at discontinuing the habit before the permanent teeth erupt.

ALLEN W. ANDERSON, D.D.S., M.S.
Chicago, Illinois

My toddler just fell off a low bench and completely knocked out his two front teeth. What should I do?

First, see if your child has any other injuries besides the two lost teeth. Check for cuts and bleeding elsewhere about the head. See if he can walk and if he appears dizzy. If none of these conditions, which would need the attention of a physician immediately, is apparent, collect the two teeth if you can find them. If they cannot be found, a chest X ray should be taken to rule out the possibility of aspiration or swallowing of the teeth. Take the child and the teeth to a dentist for examination. Do not be overly concerned about any bleeding from the gum area. This will stop shortly. Of course, the whole situation appears much worse than it actually is. If the accident occurred in a dirty area (in the basement or outdoors), the pediatrician should be contacted about a booster to prevent tetanus.

The dentist should examine the child's mouth for other injuries such as lip or tongue cuts and other loose teeth. An X ray of the area should be taken to check for bone fractures, tooth fragments if the teeth were fractured, and the position of the developing permanent teeth.

Although it is tempting to replant the lost teeth in their original position, this is not usually recommended for baby teeth because of the high frequency of failure for such teeth. The problems associated with replanted baby teeth may very well require the extraction of these teeth several months later.

ALLEN W. ANDERSON, D.D.S., M.S.
Chicago, Illinois

Which is less harmful to the position of a child's teeth—a pacifier or thumb-sucking?

A pacifier is much less harmful to the eventual position of a child's teeth than is thumb-sucking. The reason for this is the fact that thumb-sucking puts a certain amount of forward pressure on the child's front teeth, thus possibly leading to orthodontic problems when the child is older. A pacifier seems not to lead to orthodontic problems as much as thumb-sucking because there isn't as much forward pressure involved, especially if one uses one of the newer pacifiers designed by orthodontists. As annoying as both these habits appear to be to parents, the odds are that little adverse effect will come from them, even from thumb-sucking, if the habit doesn't persist past early childhood. If thumb-sucking persists in the older child, for example, one older than six, the odds are that significant orthodontic problems will arise, and the child may need dental braces.

RICHARD G. GRECO, M.D.
Providence, Rhode Island

When should I start brushing my baby's teeth?

You should begin to clean your infant's teeth as soon as he or she has any. Use a small, very soft brush, which you can get from your dentist. It is also important to try to train the child with teeth from a bottle as soon as possible because many caries, or cavities, are caused by milk that remains in the mouth for long periods of time.

KATHERINE M. KNIGHT, M.D.
New Orleans, Louisiana

My sixteen-month-old fell and hit his mouth. I can see now that one of his teeth is loose. Should I be concerned about this?

Yes, because there could be some treatment needed immediately and there may be complications later on. Whenever a tooth is hit, it is possible that the nerve of the tooth has been injured or severed. If this injury is severe, the nerve may die and become infected. This infection may occur within a week or two or perhaps as long as a year later. If diagnosed early, it can usually be treated by the dentist, who may not have to extract the tooth. It is important to point out that it is quite likely that the teeth next to the loose tooth were also injured and could develop the same infection as the loose tooth.

The possibility of a fracture of the root of the tooth must be considered if a tooth is loose. An X ray of the area is needed to make this determination. Although this possibility as well as the possibility of bone fracture are not likely in very young children, the X ray is also useful to examine the tooth root surface, the position of the baby tooth in relation to the developing permanent tooth near it, and as a base line to compare changes that could occur with nerve infection. Some teeth with root fractures will need to be extracted.

In some situations where the tooth is quite loose, there may be a need for the dentist to stabilize the loose tooth with some type of splint. Also, in some patients, the tooth may be lost early because of accelerated root resorption (dissolving of the root). Thus, it is important that regular routine checkups include assessment of the condition of the injured teeth.

ALLEN W. ANDERSON, D.D.S., M.S.
Chicago, Illinois

Should I stop my toddler from sucking her thumb?

Most pediatricians feel that thumb-sucking is a natural and harmless childhood habit. It is known that babies suck their thumbs before birth and many babies appear to derive comfort from this activity during the early years of life. There is no good evidence that it is harmful, and some very good studies have shown it doesn't harm the teeth. Many parents are alarmed when their baby starts thumb-sucking but only because they have heard it may be harmful. In general, the less attention paid to the habit the sooner it will stop.

JOHN M. THOMAS, M.D.
Omaha, Nebraska

My baby is having a rough time teething. Is this usual? What can I do to ease the pain?

It's easy to assume that a baby of teething age is having problems caused by teething. Disorders such as fever, rash, convulsions, diarrhea, and vomiting are often blamed on the "teething monster"—none of it true! All of these, plus marked irritability, are more often signs of a real illness and should be investigated. Fever virtually always means that an infection is present somewhere—look for it! Find the underlying disease instead of incriminating a normal growth process such as teething. As a general rule, sprouting the twenty teeth that appear by the age of two produces no discomfort at all, or sometimes a small amount of "itchy" gums, easily relieved by massage with a teething ring, or a bit of tough food such as toast, or even a parent's bare finger. The teething lotions sold in drugstores may taste good and spicy and may numb the gums slightly, but their real effect has been debated.

ARTHUR A. STAMLER, M.D.
Carrollton, Alabama

My toddler fell yesterday, striking his two front teeth. Today the teeth are black. What should I do?

It is very unusual to have such drastic color change so rapidly following an injury to the teeth. In any event, the child should be examined by a dentist, and his teeth should be X-rayed. A change in color in the teeth following injury may occur. The color changes can be a more yellow or a pink tooth, or the tooth may become more gray or brown. Each of these color changes should be monitored by the dentist. The gray or darkening color change may accompany the death of the nerve of the tooth and carry with it the possibility of infection. If infection were to occur, nerve treatment would be required.

Sometimes the color change will disappear or improve, but this should not be expected. Although it is possible to bleach the discoloration, this is not generally recommended for baby teeth. In general, it is best to leave the tooth alone unless the dentist finds some definite complication that needs treatment.

ALLEN W. ANDERSON, D.D.S., M.S.
Chicago, Illinois

My toddler has a callus on his thumb from sucking it. Is there anything I can do for it?

Callus formation as a result of thumb-sucking is a protective mechanism, and nothing should be done to remove the callus. Often, instead of a build-up of skin, the opposite occurs, namely redness and a breakdown of the skin layer due to the recurrent moisture and irritation. As for thumb-sucking itself, it is a common habit in infancy and does not cause permanent tooth damage provided the habit stops prior to age four or five. Toddlers tend to suck the thumb when they are tired or sad. Thumb-sucking readily disappears when the infant is busy or preoccupied.

ELLIOT A. MILGRAM, M.D., F.A.A.P.
Succasunna, New Jersey

Will drinking milk at night in bed be as harmful to my toddler's teeth as drinking juices?

Teeth decayed by excessive use of nursing bottles are seen in some infants who use bottles past the usual period of weaning. This decay can also be seen in infants who use a pacifier or sweetened fruit juice taken from a bottle. Milk or sweetened juices drunk at naptime or bedtime in bed are equally harmful to the infant's teeth. The lower teeth are protected by the tongue, whereas the other teeth are bathed by the bottle's contents.

The cause of this decay is the presence of a fermentable carbohydrate that is acted upon by oral bacteria to produce acids capable of dissolving the teeth enamel. Whenever the infant goes to sleep with a bottle, the liquid, whether it is milk or sweetened fruit juice, pools and collects around the necks of teeth, causing decalcification. Milk is less conducive to teeth decay, but neither milk nor sweetened fruit juices should be given to the infant at naptime or bedtime with the bottle left in the mouth.

G. W. ERICKSON, M.D.
South Bend, Indiana

In what order will my infant's teeth come?

The first teeth your infant will have are the central incisors, the two teeth in the very front part of the jaw. A few months later the lateral incisors will erupt (come through the gum tissue). These teeth are next to and behind the central incisors. A space will appear as the next teeth come through because the first molars erupt before the cuspids (eye teeth), which are then followed by the second molars. The lower teeth usually erupt before the upper teeth.

CARROLL G. BENNETT, D.D.S.
Gainesville, Florida

CHAPTER 32

Toddler

Our twenty-month-old son will not stay in bed at night. He stays in bed for only ten minutes and then he gets out. We put him back in bed and he continues to get up. We often find him between us in our bed during the night. What can we do to stop this?

There is not so much concern about the amount of sleep your youngster is getting as the lack of sleep, calm, and quiet you are getting. Parents need some quiet time to themselves. Also, children seem to do better when they get used to some routines and rules. Reasoning with a twenty-month-old about going to bed and staying there seldom accomplishes anything. Neither do coaxing, begging, or bargaining.

The best way to get a youngster to go to bed and stay there is to set some rules about bedtime right now and then stick to them. Decide when you want him to go to bed. Then set up a pattern of several things that happen every night when you put him to bed. Bedtime should be a happy time, when parents have some precious private moments with their kids.

For example, a bedtime ritual might start with a bath and putting on pajamas. Then perhaps you will want to include a "good-night drink," which may be a tiny bit in the bottom of a cup—just enough to wet the whistle and not enough to fill up the bladder.

Next, you may want to have story time in the youngster's bedroom. You may want to hold him on your lap in a rocking chair or on the edge of his bed. The important thing is to be comfortable and relaxed and happy—and to read happy, non-scary stories.

Then spend a few minutes telling him what a great boy he is. Let him know he is special. Remind him about everything he did well that day. This positive-thinking approach will help him be the boy you want him to be. It's also calming and fun. You may want to say prayers with him, or sing a song, or turn on some quiet music. Then, after some big hugs, let him know lovingly and firmly that the day is over.

That's it. Period. No more good-night drinks. He has had one. Good night. I love you.

If he does get up, put him back to bed swiftly—immediately. Pick him up and whisk him off to bed instantly—no snacks, no drinks, no games or other rewards for getting up. If you do this consistently, every time he gets up, he will realize the game is over. He might get up six or eight times, or maybe twenty-six or twenty-eight times, but every time he does, put him back in his bed without hesitation or delays.

It is important that no one deviate from this plan. If anyone—mom, dad, an older youngster, grandmother, Aunt Mabel, or a baby-sitter—rewards him in any way for getting up, you have to start all over.

Tonight's the night. Make bedtime a happy time, and then insist he stay in bed, no matter what. It's worth it.

GLEN C. GRIFFIN, M.D.
Bountiful, Utah

My toddler's knees and ankles look swollen, and he has a fever. What could this be?

There are many causes of joint-swelling in children, all of which cases require medical attention. Causes of joint-swelling include trauma, juvenile rheumatoid arthritis, rheumatic fever, collagen vascular disease, and infectious arthritis. *All* children with fever and swelling of a joint should be seen immediately by their physician.

Your toddler could possibly have juvenile rheumatoid arthritis, which may occur in what is called a polyarticular variety, where more than one joint is simultaneously involved. Unfortunately, joint-swelling may not be appreciated by the parents and what they may observe is a refusal by the child to use the swollen joint. The overriding principle should be that any child with fever or fever and a limp and who fails to use a limb or joint should immediately be seen by his or her physician.

GERALD B. HICKSON, M.D.
Nashville, Tennessee

My toddler sounds very hoarse, but she doesn't have any cold symptoms. What can I do?

A hoarse sound to the voice may be the first sign of what is called croup, and it must be watched very closely. Croup is a form of infection in the windpipe and voice box that causes swelling and leads to a barking sound. One of the first things to do when this symptom develops is to run a cool-mist humidifier in your child's room and encourage her to drink as many fluids as possible. However, if the child develops any respiratory distress, she should be taken to the doctor as soon as possible.

DAVID J. TEPPER, M.D.
Chattanooga, Tennessee

My child gets the hiccups quite often. What can I do for them?

Hiccups commonly occur in infants and are totally benign. They may start spontaneously or be associated with feedings. They stop on their own, but warm, sweetened water or tea may hasten their disappearance. The dose should be 4 ozs. of tea or 4 ozs. of water to ½ teaspoon of table sugar.

With toddlers, hiccups usually have no meaning and will spontaneously disappear within five to fifteen minutes. If they last more than one hour without interruption, you should contact your child's pediatrician.

ROBERT T. STONE, M.D., F.A.A.P., F.A.C.G.
Akron, Ohio

My toddler is having a nosebleed. How do I stop It?

Nosebleeds (epistaxes) are frequent and benign occurrences in childhood. It is important that the parent keep calm and reassuring, because if the child is apprehensive and crying, the nosebleed can be aggravated.

A nosebleed usually stops spontaneously without treatment within ten minutes, and the amount of blood lost is almost always very small. It can be controlled effectively by having the child sit up with the head slightly forward so that blood isn't swallowed. While instructing the child to breathe quietly through the mouth, firmly pinch both nostrils closed with your thumb and index finger. Do this for ten minutes. If the bleeding doesn't stop, you are probably pressing on the wrong spot, so try it one more time. Some doctors advise packing with cotton or tissue in the lower part of the bleeding side. Leaning the head backward or applying ice packs to the nose and upper lip are ineffective methods of stopping a nosebleed.

Epistaxis is usually bleeding from one nostril, and occasionally both nostrils, due to the rupture of tiny blood vessels located near the front part of the center wall (septum) of the nose. It is almost always caused by picking at or rubbing the nose, especially during the cold season and at nighttime, when the humidity is lowest. Good ways to prevent frequent nosebleeds are: keep fingernails short and smooth; use a humidifier or vaporizer during the cold season; and apply a small amount of petroleum jelly to the inside of each nostril.

Call your pediatrician if the bleeding doesn't stop after two ten-minute periods of direct application of pressure, if your child feels dizzy and looks pale when he or she gets up, if your child looks ill, if the bleeding episodes are frequent enough to bother you, and if the child is younger than nine months of age.

HECTOR L. HIDALGO, M.D.
Oklahoma City, Oklahoma

My twenty-month-old son is not very gentle with my newborn. What can I do?

Some older children show various emotional reactions at the arrival of a new baby in the house. When a mother has little time or energy to devote to the toddler after she brings home a new baby, the older child may think that he has been neglected and is no longer being loved. He starts feeling that his mother no longer belongs to him all the time, and that someone else who has priority over him gets all the attention. This big change in his home environment is not easy for him to accept, and he expresses his anxiety in various ways. The one seen very commonly is the feeling of jealousy for the new infant. He shows his anger toward the baby and tries to hurt him physically. He just does not like him and wants to get rid of him. The infant can get hurt if the problem is not promptly recognized. Other expressions of his anxiety are temper tantrums, bed-wetting, more demanding behavior, mealtime problems, and other behavior disturbances. In other words, he is showing a revolt against the baby.

The child usually overcomes this anxiety in time if he is handled properly. When the baby arrives home, he should be encouraged to participate in its care so that he does not feel left out. The child's emotional needs should be recognized and fulfilled. He does need individual attention. This can be provided by the mother when the baby is asleep and in the interim by the father. Fortunately, most of the time this problem does not last long, and there is no evidence that this will affect his future development or personality.

SUDESH KATARIA, M.D.
Greenville, North Carolina

My toddler bites when he is reprimanded. What should I do to stop this?

Biting is aggressive behavior. Aggression is a part of normal development and of psychosocial disturbance as well. Aggressive behavior such as biting is an attempt to attract attention or an act of hostility whose major motivation is to inflict physical or psychological pain. Biting as an aggressive behavior is seen more often in children two years of age and older. Biting may be a part of a spectrum of aggressive outbursts that include temper tantrums, screaming, and kicking. Usually, such behavior in a two-year-old is directed toward the parent in response to demands or in response to the frustration of desires that were not met. It is usually only in the older child that such behavior is more likely to be directed to siblings or peers. The solution to aggressive behavior such as biting is linked to its cause. When a child is showing such behavior, it should be determined whether the problem exists solely with the child, or is only the symptom of other problems in the family.

In an older child, biting is learned behavior. If a child is biting, he or she has obviously received some sort of subtle message that this is acceptable behavior. If it is not acceptable behavior, it is, at the very least, very effective behavior. In managing a biting child, the questions, then, are "How is the child getting the message that biting is acceptable behavior?"

and "Why is such behavior perceived as being so effective?"

Unfortunately, most parents meet such behavior with very negative responses. The negative responses may at times be somewhat inappropriate and are more often signs of parental anger and displeasure than setting limits for the child. Often, such behavioral management ends with such negative reinforcement that no effort is made to find the major factors contributing to the behavior.

Biting in children should be looked upon not as a minor annoyance but as a major sign of concern to be discussed with the family physician or pediatrician. If major problems are identified, then additional help or counseling may be needed.

DON C. VAN DYKE, M.D.
Atlantic City, New Jersey

At what temperature should we keep our toddler's room?

The temperature comfort zone for toddlers should be similar to that of their parents. For example, during the winter, when the thermostat might be set at 60°–65°, the toddler will be comfortable if appropriately dressed and blanketed. If the parents require two blankets, a similar number should be considered for their child. Toddlers who are likely to toss and turn and crawl out from under their blankets should be dressed in a warm blanket-sleeper. However, there is no need to keep the toddler any warmer than his parents.

In summary, toddlers need no special consideration for determining house temperature, as long as they, like their parents, are dressed appropriately for the temperature chosen.

MAX BURGDORF, M.D.
St. Louis, Missouri

My toddler's tonsils are often very large. When should he have them removed?

Doctors' thinking regarding the removal of tonsils has changed over the last twenty years. Large tonsils, without associated problems, are not considered reason enough for removal. The specific situations in which parents' judgment contributes to the decision to remove tonsils are when tonsils are large enough to obstruct breathing or the swallowing of food, or when recurrent tonsil infections result in multiple school absences. Doctors are normally already involved in the ongoing care of the child at the time large tonsils are causing a problem, and they will likely suggest tonsillectomy if they feel it appropriate. Reasons for tonsillectomy include the formation of an abscess around the tonsils and recurrent ear infections.

Tonsillectomy is not an insignificant operation, and the decision to remove tonsils is not one to be taken lightly. Parents should always be in communication with their pediatrician or ear-nose-throat specialist in this decision-making process.

PATRICK H. CASEY, M.D.
Little Rock, Arkansas

My toddler has been vomiting all night. What should I do?

Vomiting is usually the result of a mild viral infection, requires no specific medication, and lasts a day or less. If your child has a high fever, is not responding well, or is not urinating, there may be a more serious illness present, and an examination may be necessary. Diarrhea often accompanies vomiting and may also need attention. The first thing to do for your vomiting child is to stop solid feedings, offer only tiny sips of clear liquids, such as sugar-water, tea, cola or other carbonated beverages (which have been stirred to flatten their carbonation), or apple juice. Offer teaspoonfuls of clear liquids every five to ten minutes while your child is awake, and increase the amounts slowly as tolerated. After the liquids are retained without further vomiting, you can offer Jell-O, crackers, toast, and dry cereal before returning to a normal diet. Oral medication and rectal suppositories are usually not helpful and are not recommended.

Since this condition is usually mild and short-lived, be careful to watch for other more important developments such as rash, increasing lethargy, excessive drowsiness, sunken eyes, dry parched lips, heavy breathing, watery diarrhea, and lack of urination. These symptoms should be reported to your doctor at once.

ARTHUR MARON, M.D.
West Orange, New Jersey

My twenty-two-month-old holds his breath when I scold him. How should I handle these episodes? Can he hold his breath so long as to pass out?

He can hold his breath for some length of time and may then pass out. Fortunately, at this point automatic mechanisms usually take over, and he will begin breathing again. These episodes are, however, upsetting to everyone, so it would be better if they could be avoided.

If, as you indicate, these spells occur only when you scold him, the answer is probably not with him. It is doubtful that he has any disease. Why do you feel it is necessary to scold him? At twenty-two months of age, he is only beginning to develop acceptable behavior. He needs your guidance in a very positive way, not the negative way shown in scolding.

ROBERT H. TRIMBY, M.D.
East Lansing, Michigan

How can I stop my toddler from biting his nails?

Do not nag him, but divert him and give him plenty to do. For an older toddler, you may apply bitter substances to the nails if you have tried more conservative approaches and feel you must do something more. Sometimes an analysis of daily routines will give helpful hints for relief of this symptom of stress and strain.

MERRITT B. LOW, M.D., F.A.A.P.
Ashfield, Massachusetts

My toddler seems to have an infected nail. What can I do for this?

The most common cause of infected nails is aggressive nail trimming. The best way to trim the nail is *not* to curve the edges at the corners because this damages the groove, where infection usually sets in. Then trauma frequently allows the area to become infected. Using nail clippers rather than pointed scissors makes the nail quite straight across the end. Once a nail appears infected, using soaks of an antiseptic solution or a simple, saturated salt solution seems to help. The way to soak a toddler's hand is to wrap it in a washcloth saturated with the solution while the child is preoccupied with something like watching television. Some youngsters will tolerate an absorbent dressing soaked in the solution for fifteen to twenty minutes. This should be repeated two or three times a day. If loose skin is seen, trim it away. If red streaking should occur or the child develops a fever, he or she should be taken to the doctor.

GAIL H. GALLEMORE, M.D.
Johnson City, Tennessee

My toddler will be undergoing minor surgery soon. Should I stay overnight in the hospital with her?

Separation from the parent appears to be most upsetting to children between the ages of six months and four years. Separation of the neonate from its mother may interfere with normal "bonding" and lead to childhood anxiety and other adverse emotional changes. Parents should spend as much time as possible with the child and, if possible, stay with the child when he or she has to stay overnight in the hospital. Many operations on infants and children are now performed in an outpatient setting. The children are quickly returned to their parents following surgery and discharged home without requiring a stay in the hospital. This is the ideal way to prevent anxiety in the child who is to undergo surgery.

CONRAD WESSELHOEFT JR., M.D.
Providence, Rhode Island

Is there any harm in letting my little girl take bubble baths?

Bubble bath is a detergent solution or powder that makes lots of suds. Detergents are drying to the skin and mucous membranes anywhere on the body because they remove all the oils from the surface. In addition, little girls have a very short tube (urethra) from their bladder to the exterior so that bath water easily washes into the bladder and vagina all the time. The addition of bubble bath to the water can then wash the detergent into the bladder and vagina and irritate the linings. If a little girl takes bubble baths regularly, she may develop a chemical irritation that causes painful urination, just as if she had an infection. An occasional bubble bath would not be harmful, but regular use should be avoided.

LOIS A. POUNDS, M.D.
Pittsburgh, Pennsylvania

My toddler has a small stone in his nostril. How do I get it out?

It depends greatly on the following conditions. First, you must be able to see the stone clearly. Second, you will need an instrument, such as a pair of blunt tweezers or forceps, that can grasp the stone firmly without slipping, and safely, so as not to injure the nostril. Third, you will need an extra pair of hands to hold the little guy absolutely still—in other words, another very *strong* person. If these conditions cannot be met, forget about doing it yourself. You may cause more harm than good.

With one person holding the infant firmly in an *upright* position, the second person tries to extricate the stone gently with the instrument. If you fail to get a good grip on the stone, do not persist. It is better to call the doctor or take the child to the emergency room. Above all, avoid pushing the stone in further and making it more difficult for even the doctor to get it out.

C. H. EDWIN LEE, M.D.
Bridgewater, New Jersey

My toddler was just discovered to have a heart murmur. Will he outgrow it?

When doctors hear a heart murmur in a toddler, they may hear either a functional, or innocent, heart murmur or a murmur caused by a heart abnormality (organic heart disease).

Many children are found to have what is known as an innocent, or functional, heart murmur. It is not unusual for the murmur to be first heard when the child is a toddler. The murmur may be heard on some, but not necessarily all examinations. It is not unusual for the murmur to be absent for a number of years and then to be heard again when the child is an adolescent. The murmur is not of any significance and is not associated with heart disease. The child's activities should not be changed. He should not be limited in any way because he has the murmur.

If a sophisticated enough test is done, a murmur actually can be found in virtually every child. It is relatively easy to hear a murmur in about 30 percent of all children, but if a phonocardiogram is performed, some noise representing a murmur can be picked up in virtually all children.

Very infrequently a new murmur that represents organic heart disease will be found in a toddler. By examining the child over the course of time, the doctor can distinguish this type of an organic murmur from the typical innocent murmur and determine what appropriate further tests can be done.

PAUL SIMONS, M.D.
St. Louis, Missouri

My toddler has bad breath. I just started noticing it this past week. What could cause this?

In a child two years of age or younger, the two most common causes of bad breath would be acute stomatitis and acute pharyngitis caused by bacteria or viruses. These are normally, but not always, accompanied by fever and other signs of infection, for example, loss of appetite and enlarged lymph nodes in the neck.

In a child who has bad breath, but is otherwise well, chronic mouth-breathing, thumb-sucking, or blanket-sucking may be the cause. These all lead to drying of the oral secretions and production of odor by bacteria in plaque and debris around the teeth, tongue, gums, and tonsils. Rarely, a foreign body such as a pea playfully pushed up a nostril and then stuck there and left to decay may be the cause.

If all these possibilities are eliminated, then you must consult your pediatrician about a rare cause such as an esophageal diverticulum, gastric bezoar, bronchiectasis, or lung abscess. These last, however, are fortunately very rare occurrences.

MICHAEL PARRINO, M.D.
Columbia, South Carolina

My two-year-old has a fever and diarrhea and doesn't want to walk. What could be wrong with him?

A two-year-old who has fever and diarrhea and who doesn't want to walk may be suffering from a mild disinclination to walk just because he doesn't feel well. On the other hand, he may be severely dehydrated and too weak and ill to walk. Diarrhea that lasts for more than twenty-four hours, is accompanied by fever, or is bloody should be reported at once to your doctor.

ROBERT FOMALONT, M.D.
Princeton, New Jersey

What should I do for the chafing and dry skin that my toddler seems to get each winter?

Winter dry skin is fairly common. Make sure there is moisture in the air in your home. Bathe the child less frequently and use a petrolatum lotion or cream on his or her skin. If the condition is worse in creases or on the cheeks, it may be eczema and may need analysis and stronger creams. You should seek professional help for such a condition.

MERRITT B. LOW, M.D., F.A.A.P.
Ashfield, Massachusetts

CHAPTER 33

Toilet Training

How do I go about toilet training my child?

Wait until your child is ready to be trained. You can tell children are ready when they can walk freely about the house and are capable of getting on and off the potty chair easily; they can easily lower and raise their pants by themselves; they know many of the necessary words such as "wet," "dry," "potty," "BM," and know what the words mean; they can follow simple instructions from their parents without being negative or requiring threats or nagging; they empty their bladder completely, several times each day, rather than dribbling throughout the day.

Because most children are not "ready" until they are at least two years of age, and because there is frequently pressure to train them before that age, several pretraining steps should be considered. When you are changing your child's diaper, work on teaching the vocabulary that goes along with toilet training. Have the child actually feel the fresh diaper and explain that it is dry and feel a wet diaper and explain that it is wet. When either parent is going to the toilet, he or she can tell the child, for example, "Mommy is going pee-pee in the potty." When the child has a bowel movement in his or her diaper, he or she can be present when the diaper is emptied into the toilet. You can tell the youngster very briefly that that is where Mommy and Daddy have their BMs. During regular dressing and undressing times, the child should be encouraged to help as much as possible, particularly with raising and lowering the pants. When you go on shopping trips, your child can be taken into public rest rooms—this serves the purpose of telling the child that it is all right to go to the toilet in public rest rooms. The parent should avoid the temptation to wait always until they get home to go to the toilet, because toddlers simply don't have either the capacity or the control to wait that long.

In preparation for actually beginning the toilet training, the parent needs to make sure that the child has an easily accessible potty chair or that there is a small step in front of the regular toilet. Children cannot be expected to balance on the toilet while also attempting to urinate. The child should have many pairs of training pants, probably ten or so. This will allow for many accidents before the laundry needs to be done again. Also, it is more economical to do a full load of wash than to do only two or three pairs of training pants. If the parent is using a commercial laundromat, this is even more important. The child's training pants should be big enough to let them slip easily over the child's hips and bottom but small enough so that they won't fall down.

The parents need to be sure when they are ready to begin the toilet training. Times that should specifically be avoided are: two months before the expected due date or the adoption of a new baby; two months before a move, regardless of whether it is local or long-distance; when either parent or the child or a sibling isn't feeling well. If the child gets the flu, for example, in the midst of toilet training, it may be necessary to put him or her back into diapers. A reasonable period of time to wait after a new baby or a move is one to three months. After an illness, only a day or two is usually necessary.

When the toilet training actually begins, all of the preparations discussed above pays off because the child is now capable of being trained. Regardless of how the child is actually trained, several things must occur: The parent must be free to drop everything when the child's need to use the toilet arises. The child can be encouraged to use the toilet more by being allowed an unrestricted intake of fluids. (Avoid any juices that tend to give the child loose stools or diarrhea!) Once the toilet training begins, the parents should help the child to learn what is actually expected by explaining that he or she can *hear* Mommy or Daddy going to the toilet, and then having the youngster listen while the parent urinates in the toilet. This exercise helps to get away from teaching the child that just sitting on the potty chair is the same as going pee-pee in the potty.

Boys should initially be taught to urinate sitting down—not standing up. If they begin to urinate standing up, and hear a noise or are startled, they will usually urinate all over the bathroom. Also, if you are using a potty chair with a plastic deflector on the front for your son, you may want to shorten the point and round it off with scissors before your son sits down on the deflector.

Independent of the method of toilet training, expect an occasional accident for about six months after your training is completed. Many children still have a couple of accidents a year until they are six or seven years old. Wetting at night or bed wetting (enuresis) has little or nothing to do with toilet training and should be expected in children under the age of three. Most professionals do not consider bed wetting a problem before at least five years of age. Children do not intentionally wet their beds, so they should *never* be punished for bed wetting.

Most toddlers cannot wipe themselves very well after a bowel movement, particularly if it is soft or loose. Many children are four years old before they can wipe themselves properly. If your child has hard or dry bowel movements, or ever complains that his or her bottom hurts after having a BM, you should consider a more balanced diet, including more natural fiber or roughage in the daily diet. Nothing will produce more of a setback in your toilet training efforts than a painful bowel movement. If your child has frequent bouts with constipation or hard stools, you should consult your child's doctor before attempting toilet training.

EDWARD R. CHRISTOPHERSON, Ph.D.
Kansas City, Kansas

Should I expect my toddler's bowels to be trained at the same time as his bladder?

No. The mechanisms for training the bladder and the bowels are comparable in that there is a need for the brain to comprehend the concept of control of the time to stimulate or inhibit the release of the contents of the bowel and bladder by influencing the muscles that control these organs. However, these are two separate organ systems, and the nerve control is separate for each. The bowels are part of the gastrointestinal tract. In a newborn baby, the gastrointestinal tract works as a straight tube in the sense that, when the baby drinks formula, he or she automatically has a bowel movement. As the baby matures, the bladder and bowel mechanisms separate, and the large bowels "learn" to hold the stool and to pass the contents only once a day. This is all done without conscious control. As we toilet train a child, the child develops the concept of having the bowel movement in the toilet instead of in the diaper.

The urinary tract, including the kidney and bladder, is another system of the body and is not under the same nervous system control as the bowels. It is not directly related to eating and involves an entirely different aspect of toilet training. The unconscious emptying of the bladder, which makes the diaper wet, usually seems to be the best trigger to suggest to the child that this is what the parents are talking about when they say to "use the toilet." Then, of course, the urge to urinate becomes a much different sensation for the child than the urge to defecate. Both of these conscious controls of elimination seem to occur around the same time, but we do see persistence of poor urinary control for a much longer period of time in a large majority of children.

EVELYN BAUGH, M.D.
Toldeo, Ohio

Now that my toddler is toilet trained, he is having accidents. What could be the cause of this?

A toddler who is toilet trained and is having accidents is demonstrating very normal behavior. The period of maturation from not being trained to being trained is usually a gradual one and although the child may seem fully trained, his nervous system has not yet sufficiently developed to permit him to be always completely trained.

Apart from a physical maturation requirement for complete training, there is an emotional factor. The toddler is still emotionally immature and will be easily distracted by play or other activities. This distraction leads to accidents.

JOSEPH C. SABELLA, M.D., F.A.A.P.
Ridgewood, New Jersey

When should I consider toilet training my child?

Toilet training is quite often seen in terms of a parent's pride in a major developmental milestone or as an end to the inconvenience of cleaning a mess. The child's developmental and physiological readiness should dictate the time for toilet training.

Most children are generally started on toilet training between eighteen and twenty-four months of age. Prior to this time, it is useful to have parents trained to anticipate the child's bathroom needs. Girls are generally easier to train than boys and appear to be ready earlier. Nevertheless, each child should be individually evaluated, based on his or her maturity, and on the development of motor skills. It is unfair to compare the child with siblings or other children.

Parents usually hear about early toilet training successes, and not about the child who is toilet trained at three and one-half years of age. Regardless of age, toilet training should be a positive experience for the child. Training should, at the beginning, last only a few minutes and proceed at a relaxed pace. A child should never be kept on the potty for any length of time. Your expressions of pride and happiness with success and your acceptance of failure are important at this time. Special consideration is needed for children who were premature babies, who are mentally or physically handicapped, who have a chronic or prolonged illness, or who have undergone surgery, especially in the genital or rectal area. Parents generally are more demanding of the first child and less demanding of subsequent children. They are usually more willing to let a subsequent child take longer to be toilet trained.

A separate, smaller adapter seat placed over the regular toilet seat provides more comfort, and the child can then use the toilet without supervision. Watching siblings or peers use the toilet is sometimes of help to the child.

Nighttime accidents are common among preschool children. They also occur with illness, emotional or physical stress, and with the arrival of a new sibling.

YOSHIO G. MIYAZAKI, M.D.
Omaha, Nebraska

Is there any harm in toilet training my son too early?

Yes, indeed. The harm occurs in varying degrees, usually in the area of emotional problems, depending upon how this subject is approached.

There are few areas of child care and guidance about which so much misunderstanding and faulty information exist. Toilet training is, after all, a training technique and, as in other areas of human training, requires time, patience, a reasonable goal, cooperation, and reward.

We will discuss some basics in obtaining cooperation and especially in helping you to begin with a relaxed attitude. You must not feel driven to accomplish this training in any particular set time because children vary in their response to training techniques, making it useless and even harmful to be too strict.

Remember that physically your child needs to be able to sit up and to have a reasonably predictable bowel movement time, often after a meal in the morning. These two abilities do not usually appear *together* until about fifteen to eighteen months of age. Starting the training before that time is very unlikely to lead to success, only to frustration on everybody's part. Also, by fifteen to eighteen months of age your child will have had time to learn other cooperative acts with you, such as feeding, dressing, and cleaning before toilet training is begun.

Thus you can see that how you have handled your child in the first year will have a direct bearing on how successful toilet training will be later.

Let us hope that your fifteen- to eighteen-month-old child will have no fear or "taboo" about the bathroom and its fixtures, having watched you many times doing everything without guilt and doing it properly. This will help your child mimic you, having first learned to trust you.

The child may use either his potty, which rests on the floor beside the regular toilet, or the regular toilet fitted with a child's seat. Be reassuring, gentle, and encouraging. Place the child on the seat and give a few words of praise and a smile, to let him see that he has done something good just by being there. Letting the child hold a favorite toy may help relax him. Give him some idea of what is expected, such as pointing to the stomach and making a grunting sound yourself as a kind of demonstration. Repetition of this at a time when the child is ready to have a movement is usually successful, and after wiping comes the praise—a hug and a play period will do just fine.

Attention span is short at this age so don't try too long. Ten minutes or less is enough, and if it did not work, let the child down and say something like, "That's O.K., don't worry, we'll do it better next time." There should be no bodily punishment, no put-down.

Now you can see that if you start this training too early and are too demanding, the child cannot possibly cope with it and therefore becomes badly frightened and even resentful of the parents who ask too much too soon. That kind of fear may last a long time. Patience is so important here.

Remember, it is cooperation you want, and actually it is true that most children in stable homes will train themselves by three years of age, provided that they are simply encouraged and have no fear of the bathroom.

This is because children really want to do what their parents or other children are doing and constantly mimic us. Younger children learn mostly by example, so give them good ones to follow.

E. W. EBERLING, M.D.
Tucson, Arizona

My child is bed-wetting. What can I do?

Many children wet the bed until after they start to school. A simple office examination and urinalysis should rule out serious diseases or congenital deformities.

The causes of bed-wetting are usually simple. A child's bladder is not large enough to hold eight hours of urine, and the child sleeps so soundly that a full bladder will not wake him or her. Therefore, there are wet sheets each morning.

Two exercises may help. Get the child to hold his or her urine as long as possible during the day. This stretches the bladder and allows it to hold more urine. Also, starting and stopping the stream of urine may increase muscle control.

Most pediatricians are opposed to drug therapy for this common problem.

ROBERT S. CAUSEY, JR., M.D.
Marietta, Georgia

CHAPTER 34

Vitamins and Fluoride

How long will my child need to take vitamin supplements?

Vitamin supplements are usually given at least until a child is of school age. They are vastly overused, and some physicians do not use them much, if at all. They may help—and they are not harmful—in prescribed quantities. There are, however, more and more toxic situations arising from indiscriminate use in these days of super vitamins and megavitamins.

MERRITT B. LOW, M.D., F.A.A.P.
Ashfield, Massachusetts

My toddler doesn't eat well. Should I start him on multiple vitamins?

When small children begin to eat independently, their rate of growth begins to slow down, and their need for a large intake of calories is somewhat less than during the first year of life. Many toddlers show their newly found independence, as well as their need for relatively fewer calories, by developing unpredictable eating habits. It would be unusual for a normal toddler, offered a balanced diet in normal amounts, to eat so little that normal growth and development would stop. If your child is growing and developing normally, you need not worry that he is being underfed. If your family eats a normally balanced diet, you need not supplement the child's diet with large amounts of additional vitamins at this point. Do be sure that a balanced diet and adequate sources of iron are offered. Between

295

nine and eighteen months of age, iron deficiency may develop if the child's diet consists mainly of dairy products. Meats, cereals, some fruits, and green vegetables are good sources of iron at this time.

At this age, your child may also begin to show strong preferences for certain foods (especially highly sweetened foods) and strong dislikes for others. Since this period can herald the beginning of a lifetime of poor dietary habits, don't be blackmailed into catering to your child's food preferences. Offer what the rest of the family would normally eat and be assured that your child will consume an adequate amount if he is hungry enough. You may have to exercise some control by withholding desserts or other favorites until some of the other courses are eaten. This may result in tears and tantrums, but it is worth the price if good dietary habits are encouraged at an early age. Above all, be sure that other members of the family are consistent in how the child is fed and that they provide the child with good examples of sensible eating habits.

WILLIAM J. CASHORE, M.D.
Providence, Rhode Island

We do not have fluoridated water. Through what age should my child continue to take a fluoride supplement?

Most dentists will agree that the secondary teeth are well formed by age eight. They therefore recommend a fluoride supplement from infancy up to at least age six. An older child can also get fluoride through local treatments.

A. E. REARDON, M.D., F.A.A.P.
Duluth, Minnesota

Are vitamins missing from formula that my newborn will need?

The companies that produce formulas have done an excellent job of determining the amount of vitamins that babies need and of putting these vitamins into formula. Vitamins are often given as supplements for babies on infant formula. This is because many years ago there were no added vitamins in commercial milks and the vitamin C in milk was destroyed by heating. The commercial formulas available today are adequately treated with vitamins. Vitamin C is added after the processing, so that it is not lost in the heating of the formula. There are perfectly adequate amounts of vitamins in all of the commercially available formulas and no supplements are needed. In areas of the country where there is no fluoride in the water, it may be necessary to add fluoride.

RICHARD A. GUTHRIE, M.D.
Wichita, Kansas.

I am breast-feeding my newborn. Does she need a vitamin supplement?

Although the amounts of vitamin D and iron are relatively low in human milk, the healthy, full-term infant with a well-nourished, healthy mother does not develop deficiencies in early infancy. Vitamin D deficiency has been reported in later infancy in breast-fed infants in circumstances where exposure to sunlight was restricted. Therefore, vitamin supplements for the healthy, full-term, breast-fed infant are not necessary. However, a multivitamin preparation for infants, containing iron and 400 units of vitamin D, usually compounded with vitamins A and C, may provide a margin of safety for cases of unrecognized minimal deficiencies. At this level of supplementation, negative effects have not been recognized.

Premature infants and infants with health or nutritional problems frequently must have vitamin and mineral supplements, in addition to breast milk, in order to maintain proper growth and development. The infant's physician should make these specific recommendations.

MAUREEN EDWARDS, M.D.
Washington, D.C.

Baby Records

Baby's full name: _____

Date of birth: _____ year _____ month _____ day _____ time

Weight at birth: _____

Length at birth: _____

Place of birth: _____

Mother's name: _____

Father's name: _____

Grandparents: _____

_____

Brothers and sisters: _____

_____

Doctor attending birth: _____

Baby's pediatrician: _____

Baby's Growth

One Month

Weight:

Length:

paste
picture
here

Two Months

Weight:

Length:

paste
picture
here

Three Months

Weight:

Length:

paste
picture
here

Four Months

Weight:

Length:

paste
picture
here

Five Months

Weight:

Length:

paste
picture
here

Six Months

Weight:

Length:

paste
picture
here

Seven Months

Weight:

Length:

paste
picture
here

Eight Months

Weight:

Length:

paste
picture
here

Nine Months

Weight:

Length:

paste
picture
here

Ten Months

Weight:

Length:

paste
picture
here

Eleven Months

Weight:

Length:

paste
picture
here

Twelve Months

Weight:

Length:

paste
picture
here

Thirteen Months

Weight:

Length:

paste
picture
here

Fourteen Months

Weight:

Length:

paste
picture
here

Fifteen Months

Weight:

Length:

paste
picture
here

Sixteen Months

Weight:

Length:

paste
picture
here

Seventeen Months

Weight:

Length:

paste
picture
here

Eighteen Months

Weight:

Length:

paste
picture
here

Immunizations

Immunization	Date	Doctor

Illnesses,
Injuries,
Hospitalizations

Illness or Injury	Date	Doctor	Hospital

Family illnesses, allergies, and medical conditions:

Emergency Names and Numbers

Pediatrician: _____

Family Doctor: _____

Hospital: _____

Poison Control Center: _____

Ambulance: _____

Police: _____

Fire: _____

Baby's allergies or special medical conditions, if any:

_____

_____

_____

_____

_____

_____

Index